Youth Policy in a Changing World

D1607616

Marina Hahn-Bleibtreu
Marc Molgat (eds.)

Youth Policy
in a Changing World

From Theory to Practice

Barbara Budrich Publishers
Opladen • Berlin • Toronto 2012

A CIP catalogue record for this book is available from
Die Deutsche Bibliothek (The German Library)

© 2012 by Barbara Budrich Publishers, Opladen, Berlin & Toronto
www.barbara-budrich.net
   ISBN   **978-3-86649-459-6**
   eISBN   978-3-86649-508-1 (eBook)

Das Werk einschließlich aller seiner Teile ist urheberrechtlich geschützt. Jede Verwertung außerhalb der engen Grenzen des Urheberrechtsgesetzes ist ohne Zustimmung des Verlages unzulässig und strafbar. Das gilt insbesondere für Vervielfältigungen, Übersetzungen, Mikroverfilmungen und die Einspeicherung und Verarbeitung in elektronischen Systemen.

Die Deutsche Bibliothek – CIP-Einheitsaufnahme
Ein Titeldatensatz für die Publikation ist bei Der Deutschen Bibliothek erhältlich.

Verlag Barbara Budrich 🅑 Barbara Budrich Publishers
Stauffenbergstr. 7. D-51379 Leverkusen Opladen, Germany

86 Delma Drive. Toronto, ON M8W 4P6 Canada
www.barbara-budrich.net

Jacket illustration by disegno, Wuppertal, Germany – www.disenjo.de
Typesetting by R + S, Beate Glaubitz, Leverkusen, Germany
Editing: Alison Romer, Lancaster, Great Britain
Printed in Europe on acid-free paper by
paper&tinta, Warsaw

Table of contents

Introduction

Youth policy, youth research and young people – changing worlds, changing perspectives?[1]

By Marc Molgat, Marina Hahn-Bleibtreu and Eugénie Boudreau

Why do we need youth policies? How are or how can they be developed? What are the impacts of policy on young people? What can research bring to policy thinking, as well as to concrete policy and programme development for young people? These questions are all addressed in this volume by researchers from Latin America, Europe and North America. The attention is here on *youth policy*, whether the authors mean by this *bona fide* global youth policy frameworks or distinct and often patchwork policies affecting one area or another of young people's lives.

Of course, the contexts of each of the societies referred to in this volume are frequently distinct, as are the various categories or groups of young people described within these societies. After all, the experiences of a young migrant worker in China and the labour market integration of a young adult in Argentina seem not only separated by distance, but also by vastly differing social structures and conditions, values, opportunities and forms of support. So what can be said to unite the different perspectives, analyses and proposals brought forward in this publication? The first is a shared idea that young people today live in a rapidly changing world in which they should be considered as active citizens, capable of both participating in social institutions and of dealing with the limitations and resources that stem from them. This capacity is, however, more or less constrained by living conditions, socioeconomic status, market structures and state and community interventions in areas such as education, work and family life. The second unifying factor is a shared belief that public policy can and should be crafted to support young people as social actors, in their life experiences and their transitions to adulthood.

---

1   The editors thank the Austrian Federal Ministry of Economy, Family and Youth, for having funded the publication of this volume.

Following earlier developments and trends, and shifts in governmental orientations, the past two decades have been characterized by intense technological change and globalization processes. These have contributed to the restructuring of national industries and labour markets, the redefinition of public policy, and the heightened awareness that what is occurring elsewhere in the world can have profound impacts on one's daily life and local context. Although technology and globalization have produced marked improvements in the quality of life and living standards of large groups of the world population, such positive change has not been equally distributed. In some social groups already at the lower end of class or societal structures, and possessing less education and financial capital, there has been an increase in poverty and unemployment. In some countries, yet more important inequalities in wealth have been produced between those at the financial, economic and political centers and those at the margins, including large segments of youth populations. In this context, one could perhaps see young people as important 'victims' of globalization, as making up a large part of those who are forced to accept and adapt to worsening living conditions and opportunities. On the other hand, however, young people today can also be seen as striving against the negative effects of these trends, and as using technology and globalization to gain advantage, as witnessed, for example, through recent social movements for democratization in many Arab countries, and the 'Indignados' and 'Occupy' movements which denounce the concentration of capital and wealth.

In addition to their strong presence in social movements, young people also respond to modernization processes that are inherent to societies where there has been a shift away from industrial to 'knowledge societies', or to what is termed 'knowledge-based economies' by governments seeking to improve their economic competitiveness. This modernization process has exacerbated trends of individualization, i.e. the movement toward emancipation from tradition and from the social groups and places in which individuals were brought into the world (Giddens, 1994, 1991, 1990; Beck, 2000, 1992). Such 'disembedding' processes take place in social time and space, and allow individuals to exercise greater control over the orientation and timing of their own life course. For young people, these trends express themselves in the de-standardization of the transitions to adulthood which have perhaps been best analyzed by Walther (2006) in Europe, although similar trends exist in many other societies (Beaujot and Kerr, 2007, Bendit and Hahn-Beibtreu, 2008, Shanahan, 2000, Osgood, 2005). Transitions from school to work, from family of origin to own family and from financial dependence to independence are often no longer synchronous and do not follow linear trajectories. Instead many transitions are reversible and statuses co-exist within individual lives, leading Walther and his colleagues to characterize these reversible and fragmented transitions as "yo-yo transitions" (Walther *et al.*, 2002; Walther, 2006). For example, in many societies an increasing proportion of young people delay home-leaving or return to live with their parents, while at the same time maintaining full-time employment; others may return to postsecondary education or training after a certain period in the labour market. In many of these circumstances, young people continue to be at least partly autonomous but at the same time financially dependent on their families or on government assistance.

These changes highlight not only differences and diversity in the way young people make their way to adulthood, but also a certain relaxing of social norms about transitions for young women and men that are related to family life, education and work. But, just as important and maybe more so, they also reflect transformations related to globalization, economic restructuring, the greater 'flexibilization' of work and the fragmentation of the temporal horizons of life that create uncertainty for young people, block subjective aspirations and make planning for the future more difficult (Leccardi, 2006 and in this volume, chapter 13). In this sense, the structural and institutional aspects of social life matter greatly for young adults today and specifically for those who are most vulnerable (Molgat, 2011, 2007). As the modern world has become more unpredictable and risk-laden, individuals are not only free to make choices about their lives but are obligated to do so with less institutional or collective support (Beck, 2000; Giddens, 1991, 1994). This means that although some young people may choose to embark on yo-yo transitions, others experience them as an imposition for having failed "to enter a standard biography" (Walther, 2006); these 'others' are often those whose lives make them vulnerable to the very basic and 'old' structures of inequality (social background, education, gender, region, ethnicity, etc.) (Furlong and Cartmel, 2007). It is therefore important that public policies aimed at young people not only reflect de-standardized transitions to adulthood as being 'new' but also as presenting potentials for greater risk.

Youth policies thus need to be sensitive to the reasons why young people make particular transitions and why they may choose to engage or participate in certain activities, groups and institutions and not others. Understanding these reasons is critical in determining how young people should be supported through public policy. And research has a singularly important role to play in this respect. Increasingly, governments are thirsty for 'evidence-based policy', so it would seem natural for them to tap into what youth researchers are producing in terms of 'evidence'. However, this is not as simple as it sounds because the direct application of research to action is never linear. Research that pinpoints a new trend or sheds new light on a problem among young people does not necessarily 'solve' a given situation, although it can recommend changes or be used to establish policies and priorities. This is a classic problem of research in the social sciences, and reflects the different cultures of science, policy and practice (Settersten, 2003; Shonkoff, 2000). Within government, one is constantly reminded that research is but one voice within a larger political discourse in which various ideological, political and bureaucratic voices are also heard and enter into competition in the defining of policies and programmes (see Cicchelli in this volume, chapter 3).

It is in order to recognize and give legitimacy to these voices – and especially, one would hope, to those of young people and youth organizations – that the 'magic triangle of youth policy' has been promoted in certain world regions, and particularly in the European Union (Chisholm and Hoskins, 2005). This triangle ideally produces a 'trialogue' between government, youth researchers and non-government youth organizations and should be seen as a centerpiece of youth policy development. This ideal is of course difficult to achieve in practice because of misunderstandings and power differentials between the three sides of the triangle. There is also much room for discussion about the nature of the 'evidence' from research that actually enters the magic triangle, as well as how this evidence is then debated, appropriated and eventually sifted through the lens of policy makers and tied to policy statements and programmes.

This volume speaks to issues of youth policy using three distinct foci: development, effects, and perspectives. In the first part of the book, the contributors critically examine how processes, ideas and evidence contribute in different ways to structuring youth policy, and explain what challenges lie in the development of youth policy *per se*, as well as show how young people's experience poses challenges for policy. To initiate the reflection, Howard Williamson draws on the historical transformation of the concept of youth and youth policy to apprehend various youth policy frameworks and to consider the numerous elements that should be taken into consideration in creating sound youth policy. The second chapter, written by Marc Molgat and Susannah Taylor, addresses a central aspect of young people's lives in relation to policy: the process of transitions. On the basis of their analysis of the development of youth policies in Canada, they argue that these policies are often concentrated on the transition from school to work and oriented towards individualistic goals. They go on to suggest how researchers could attract more focus from policy makers on other transition strands and on the social structures that affect young people's lives.

Since youth policies are not developed in a vacuum, it is important to understand the circulation of knowledge between distinct spheres of discourse that influence policy-making, both within and outside the 'magic triangle'. It is to this task that Vincenzo Cicchelli turns in the third chapter, identifying what he terms *semantic coincidences* in media, scientific, policy and administrative discourses on youth 'autonomy' in France. In the following chapter, David M. Hansen draws from developmental psychology discourses to present a perspective on youth policy that is not widely present outside of the United States. Many youth policy researchers are indeed critical of the normative aspect of developmental psychology, which suggests that young people should follow a natural and homogeneous path to a 'normal', fully 'developed' and 'problem-free' integration into society.

The last chapter of this section is offered by Alejo Ramirez and presents his first-hand experience in the process of youth policy development, providing a glimpse into the various interactions between the international, regional, national and local levels of youth policies and programs. Understanding the various processes, ideas and evidence which contribute to youth policy-making, such as those presented in this section, provides ground for clearer comprehension of the effect of policies on youth.

The chapters in the second part of the volume focus specifically on this last point: the effects of policy. They demonstrate that policies bearing directly on young people contribute to structuring their orientations toward work and family life, as well as their transitions, over the long term. Further, various policy arrangements that do not necessarily target youth specifically may also have lasting impacts on the lives of young people.

In the first chapter, Johanna Wyn shows how neoliberal policies have had cross-cutting effects on a whole generation in Australia. Considering how these policies have transformed the social fabric of society, she stresses the importance of recognizing the long-term impacts that policies that are not directly targeting youth can nonetheless have on young people's lives. In the same vein, Syika Kovacheva analyses the changing expectations towards employees in the context of an increasingly global competitive market brought about by economic crises, neoliberal policies and globalization. She discusses the impact of these changing expectations on parenthood, and reflects on the youth and family policies that could support young people's transitions.

From another perspective, Helena Helve addresses *Transitions and shifts in work attitudes, values and future orientations of young Finns* in the context of welfare state oriented policies. One interesting effect that she points to is the institutionalization of a longer and more flexible period of 'youthhood' in a welfare state where young people are not solely encouraged to embark upon the labour market, but also to develop other aspects of their lives.

The two following chapters focus on the experiences of young immigrants. Sunaina Maira first questions the experience of young Muslims who have migrated to the United States of America after 9/11 and in the context of the War on Terror. She puts emphasis on the differentiated experiences of young people who belong to communities struggling with political, economic and social exclusion, and she stresses the importance of considering the genuine concerns of these youth in the policy-making process. Similarly, René Bendit examines different concepts of integration and modes of integration for migrant or ethnic minority youth in Europe. However, he more specifically studies the *indirect* and *direct* integration strategies which facilitate young migrants' integration into education and labour, and shows how they are only partially successful.

Further chapters examine policies in education, employment and migration aimed at more excluded and vulnerable sectors of society. In their chapter, Claudia Jacinto and Veronica Millenar study the impact of vocational training and internships in addressing the gap in educational and social capital for youth who come from low income backgrounds in Argentina. This is followed by a final chapter that tackles an important issue affecting many young adults in China, that of the treatment and social security of migrant workers. The author, Ngan-Pun Ngai, shows how policies concerning the residential status of migrants and their labour rights create discrimination, social discontent and inequality, before considering some integration strategies to alleviate these problems.

In the third part of the book, the contributors raise a number of issues that policies aimed at young people should consider, whether in terms of how 'youth' as a period of life should be understood today, or in reference to particular issues such as participation or labour market integration, where there may be misalignments or gaps with public policy.

Carmen Leccardi sets the stage in the first chapter of this section, where she presents a theoretical perspective on changes in how we conceptualize the world in terms of space and time. She suggests that these changes affect biographical time and planning, transitions to adulthood and young people's values. She notes the importance of policies and practices that take into consideration the present, at a time when young people's conception of the future is so uncertain and their perceptions of their own lives are constructed with increased agency.

In this context, a growing research interest in participation among youth exists, as exemplified in the next two chapters. Drawing on empirical data, Wolfgang Gaiser and Martina Gille demonstrate that participation among young people in Germany is not decreasing and that there is an increase in protest-oriented participation. Accordingly, they discuss youth policies that would allow young people to contribute to the shaping of their local and global environments. In the following chapter, Dina Krauskopf suggests that young people need to be considered as citizens who are different than the youth of previous generations, within a policy framework that encourages their participation in the social, political and economic life of their country.

Based on the Argentinian case, Ana Miranda then stresses the importance of analysing inequality of opportunities based on gender and socioeconomic background in the construction of transitions from school to work. She concludes that youth policy should favor the right to live out youth as a time to search, experiment, and gain education and training, irrespective of socioeconomic background. In the European context, Stefan Humpl and Eva Proinger present a different perspective and demonstrate how young people, as a sector of society, are more affected by increases in unemployment than the general population. They argue that the educational system is not currently meeting the demands of the labour market and that youth policies should support alternative educational opportunities for unemployed young people, while addressing integration and improving transitions.

Last but not least, Vânia Reis reflects on suicide among young people, an increasingly important phenomenon in Latin America and the Caribbean. She suggests going beyond the psychological and social dimensions of suicide to consider its ethical aspects (for example about life and the value of life), in order to incorporate them into prevention practices as well as into follow-ups with family and friends.

By building on the reflections, suggestions and ideas presented by all of the contributors to this volume, we hope that readers will gain insights into the processes of youth policy development, the cross-cutting impacts that these policies often have on youth, and the current transformations in young people's lives that require more research, public policy and actions in practice.

Bibliography

Beck, U. (2000) Living your own life in a runaway world: individualization, globalization, and politics, in Hutton, W. and Giddens, A. (eds) *Global Capitalism* (pp. 164-174), New York, New Press.

Beck, U. (1992) *Risk Society: Towards a New Modernity*, Thousand Oaks, Sage.

Beaujot, R. and Kerr, D. (2007) *Emerging Youth Transition Patterns in Canada,* Investing *in Youth: Evidence from Policy, Practice and Research,* Ottawa, Policy Research Initiative.

Bendit R. and Hahn-Beibtreu, M. (eds) (2008) *Youth Transitions: processes of social inclusion and patterns of vulnerability in a globalised world,* Opladen, Barbara Budrich Publishers.

Chisholm, L. and Hoskins, B. with Glahn, C. (2005) *Trading Up: Potential and Performance in Non-Formal Learning, Report from the Research Seminar on Non-formal Education in the Youth Sector and the Third Sector,* Strasbourg, Council of Europe.

Furlong, A. and Cartmel, F. (2007) *Young People and Social Change: New Perspectives,* Open University Press, Buckingham.

Giddens, A. (1994) Living in a Post-Traditional Society, in Beck, U., Giddens, A. and Lash, S. *Reflexive Modernization* (pp. 56-109), Cambridge, Polity Press.

Giddens, A. (1991) *Modernity and Self-Identity: Self and Society in the Late Modern Age*, Stanford, Stanford University Press.

Giddens, A. (1990) *The Consequences of Modernity*, Stanford, Stanford University Press.

Leccardi, C. (2006) Facing uncertainty, temporality and biographies in the New Century, in Leccardi, C. and Ruspini, E. (eds) *A New Youth? Young people, generations and family life* (pp. 15-40), Aldershot, Ashgate.

Molgat, M. (2011) Les insuffisances de la perspective de l'émergence de l'âge adulte pour comprendre la jeunesse. Quelques enseignements à partir de figures de jeunes en difficulté, Goyette, M., Pontbriand, A. and Bellot, C. (eds) *Les transitions à la vie adulte des jeunes en difficulté – Concepts, figures et pratiques* (pp. 33-55), Montreal, Presses du l'Université du Québec.

Molgat, M. (2007) Do transitions and social structures matter? How 'emerging adults' define themselves as adults, *Journal of Youth Studies, 10(5)*, pp. 495-516.

Osgood, W.D. *et al.* (2005) Six Paths to Adulthood, in Settersten Jr., R. A., Furstenberg Jr., F. F and Rumbaut, R. G. (eds) *On the Frontier of Adulthood: Theory, Research, and Public Policy* (pp. 320-355), Chicago, The University of Chicago Press.

Settersten Jr., R. A. (2003) Age structuring and the rhythm of the life course, in Mortimer, J. and Shanahan, M. J. (eds) *Handbook of the life course* (pp. 81-98), New York, Kluwer-Plenum.

Shanahan, M.J. (2000) Pathways to Adulthood in Changing Societies: Variability and Mechanisms in Life-Course Perspective, *Annual Review of Sociology, 26,* pp. 667-692.

Shonkoff, J. P. (2000) Science, policy and practice: three cultures in search of a shared mission, *Child Development, 71(1)*, pp. 181-187.

Walther, A. (2006) Regimes of youth transitions – Choice, flexibility and security in young people's experiences across different European contexts, *Young – Nordic Journal of Youth Research, 14(2)*, pp. 119-139.

Walther, A. et al. (eds) (2002) *Misleading trajectories – Integration policies for young people in Europe?,* Opladen, Leske + Budrich.

I   Youth Policy development: evidence, ideas and processes

1. Youth policy reviews of the Council of Europe and their impact on national youth policies

By Howard Williamson

A quarter of a century ago the generic, overarching and essentially meaningless term 'youth policy' was rarely used. Certainly at a European level the term had no currency. What there was in the way of 'youth policy' was fragmented and restricted to a range of programmes for 'youth' and training measures. There was, however, one publication anticipating the future prevalence of the concept, though *Youth Policy* (Blakely, 1990) was a rather pedestrian, if instructive, journey through the formal legislation, resolutions and provisions that affected young people within the orbit of the European Union.

At national level, in some countries at least, the idea of 'youth policy' was at least starting to be broached. I contributed to that debate in the United Kingdom, first in a critique of Willis' (1985) seminal report addressing local youth policy in the municipality of Wolverhampton in England (Smith and Williamson, 1985), and later through a variety of articles and conference presentations. Of most significance, arguably, were a paper published in *Youth and Policy* (Williamson, 1993) and a keynote summary, in the same year, of proceedings at a UK conference on 'Teenagers at Risk in Britain Today'. Speakers at that event had been selected for their national reputations in policy domains such as housing, health, criminal justice, mental health, equalities and poverty; I was listed on the conference programme as speaking about 'Youth Policy' (see Doyle, 1993).

Later I argued that all countries (and, indeed, relevant institutions) had a 'youth policy': by intent, default or neglect (Williamson, 2000). My point was that young people's lives were clearly influenced by purposeful, unintentional or neglectful actions (or non-actions) by state or quasi-state institutions. Furthermore, it was important to consider 'youth policy' through addressing the ways in which its different elements combined positively, clashed with each other, or sometimes simply passed each other by. Initially, through much of the 1990s, there was at least latent suspicion of this notion of 'youth policy', or stronger assertions that 'youth policy' was regulated by or restricted to only certain 'youth' activities. Indeed, there was one significant body of influence that maintained that 'youth policy' was largely the (developmental) world of education – even just 'non-formal education' – and that more regulatory intervention (such as criminal justice) or approaches dealing with the troubles of young people (such as mental health or family policy) had no place in the concept of 'youth policy'.

Tracking back, it becomes reasonably clear that, if there was such a thing as 'youth policy' prior to, for sake of argument, the mid-1970s, it was generally considered to relate largely, if not exclusively, to education – with perhaps vocational training and something called 'youth work' (see Coussée, 2008) sometimes added on. Most young people moved through their teenage years into adulthood, albeit under very different political regimes and in different economic circumstances, relatively smoothly. Paths were set, according to family and class background and perhaps educational achievement.

It was the economic crises of the 1970s and the political crises of the 1980s that transformed the nature of youth transitions, producing levels of uncertainty in young people that, at least prior to World War II, they had hitherto not experienced. Pathways to adulthood became riddled with confusion, anxiety and cul-de-sacs. There is, today, a massive literature on the changing shape and nature of youth transitions, generally commenting on the ways in which they have become prolonged, more complex, uncertain, reversible and fractured. Though greater opportunities may exist for many more young people (especially those with various forms of positive human, social and identity capital), the transition journey is also characterised by risk and vulnerability.

This has called, implicitly at least and often more explicitly, for more robust policy support and intervention in the broader areas of family life, health, learning and criminal justice (in preventative terms) as well as the more specific 'youth' areas of school exclusion or rejection, health risk behaviours (around substance misuse and sex), delinquency and anti-social behaviour, and other psycho-social disorders. This is the basis on which, despite many mantras about producing 'opportunity-focused' rather than 'problem-oriented' measures, the idea of, and indeed the need for a more transversal and intersectoral 'youth policy' has been advocated. It is now seen as imperative that policy development for young

people is based on an integrated package that proffers opportunity, protects, supports and sometimes regulates the young. In the UK, the last
strong political mantra (at least prior to the most recent General Election),
across youth policy domains was concerned with the 'triple-track' approach of prevention, support (which is often to be 'non-negotiable') and
enforcement. The new UK government favours the more amorphous
rhetoric of cohesion, contribution and 'fairness' under the banner of the
notion of the 'Big Society', though enforcement is also clearly waiting in
the wings. In both cases, however, it is very possible to detect any and all
of these threads across key political aspirations for young people, such as
lifelong learning, active citizenship, social inclusion, and personal and
community safety.

Today, of course, there are many versions of 'youth policy', at local,
regional, national and indeed trans-national levels. They establish different priorities, allocate different resources and have different infrastructures for delivery, but nearly always, at their heart, a core set of issues,
aspirations, objectives and measures of performance are present. This paper examines these issues concerning 'youth policy' within the context of
European developments in this arena, particularly the Council of Europe
international reviews of national youth policies that have been operating
since 1997.

Frameworks for youth policy

Few countries in fact have an evidently coherent framework of policy for
young people. This derives largely from two factors. First, there is usually a lack of consistency in the eternal challenge or problem of defining
'youth'. Second, ministerial portfolios are invariably, understandably,
stubborn in defending their particular domains of policy, in which young
people may often figure relatively marginally (though obviously in some
ministries, such as education, young people are very prominent). Nonetheless, an increasing number of administrations would proclaim some
linkages between various elements of policy affecting young people,
even if they might not necessarily claim that this presents a fully coherent
picture.

The two major European institutions, the Council of Europe (2008)
and the European Union (European Commission, 2009), also now have
reasonably robust youth policies, even though they have been years in the

making. Indeed, the first attempt at 'youth policy' in Europe, framed in the EU White Paper on Youth in 2001 (European Commission, 2002), revealed more about the divisions in the youth policy field than its coherence: a 'youth' white paper was not permitted to address key policy areas such as education or employment since these were the territory of policy-specific directorates within, or beyond the level of competence of the European Commission. It took a few more years, and the publication of the European Youth Pact (http://ec.europa.eu/youth/youth-policies/doc 1705_en.htm), before such major areas of young people's lives were incorporated into 'youth policy' thinking. The momentum has increased further in recent years with the EU Youth Strategy (European Commission 2009) and the development of 'Youth on the Move' (http://ec.europa. eu/education/news/news2540_en.htm).

There are, inevitably, many ways to construct youth policy. Though contemporary rhetoric prides itself on evidence-based foundations for the development of youth policy, there is – paradoxically – plenty of evidence that it sometimes remains formed and forged in what one observer referred to as an 'evidence-free zone'! Politicians and senior administrators are certainly adept at finding the research that can anchor their political whims and preferences, and ignoring that which does not. Such an approach at least slides towards greater rationality, but if political whim is tempered by some research data, then research data is itself tempered by stakeholder perspectives. In the youth field, this is most strongly asserted through youth organisations: at a European level the position taken by the European Youth Forum (regarding the European Commission) and the Advisory Council on Youth (regarding the Council of Europe). Indeed, these representative bodies of both national youth councils and pan-European youth organisations would say that they provide an experiential evidence base that complements rather than conflicts with a more conventional academic evidence base. This may often be so, but there have also been times in the policy-making process when the two sources of 'evidence' have been clearly at odds. Politicians and senior officials have had to take sides, sometimes weighing the analysis with some rigour, sometimes being rather more expedient.

The EU White Paper on Youth (European Commission, 2002) took pride in what it considered to be its pioneering approach to its composition. It consulted with and engaged young people directly, as well as youth organisations, youth researchers and member states. In that respect it started to forge what has come to be known as the 'magic triangle' of policy development in the youth field (see Milmeister and Williamson,

2006), one that involves youth policy, youth research and youth practice. Yet there remain huge questions about the balance that has been struck (and, indeed, should be struck) between these 'pillars', especially around issues of whose voice is being represented and what is their democratic mandate. Even the democratic mandate may (or should) not be considered sacrosanct: there is a reasonable argument that some groups of young people lose out in the democratic process that guides the formation of local, national and international youth organisations. These are often the more excluded and disadvantaged (in the quaint Euro-speak of the European Commission: 'young people with fewer opportunities'!) and there could be a case for the purposeful targeting of these groups on particular issues (such as substance misuse, or disability, or exclusion from the labour market) when policy aspirations are closely connected to addressing those issues.

That is in fact one example of the challenges and tensions within the youth policy-making process that has emerged from the work of the Council of Europe. The Youth Directorate of the Council of Europe embarked on a programme and process of what it called 'international reviews of national youth policies' in 1997. The purpose, which has stood the test of time, was threefold: to review constructively but critically the youth policy of one country from the perspective of a team of international 'experts'; to bring an understanding of youth policy in that country to all the member states of the Council of Europe (now numbering 50); and to construct a framework for thinking about the structure, dimensions and elements of the kinds of 'youth policy' that prevail in the wider Europe. That this latter objective is being achieved through the detailed and grounded exploration of national youth policies makes it somewhat different from approaches to youth policy formulation and development that derive from academic (or experiential) evidence or political imperative.

By 2011, eighteen countries had participated in this review process[1]. That they were from all corners of the wider Europe, and therefore at very different stages of development, capacity and effectiveness, has enriched the thinking about youth policy. It may be easy for some western European countries with long histories of democracy, strong traditions in making provision for 'youth', and established professional infrastructures

---

1   Finland, Netherlands, Sweden, Spain, Romania, Estonia, Luxembourg; Lithuania, Malta, Norway, Slovenia, Cyprus, Armenia, Hungary, Latvia, Moldova, Albania and Belgium. Ukraine is participating in a review in 2012.

(such as social work, psychology or counselling) to advance particular models of youth policy. But these established components of a youth policy making process often mean very little in countries that only relatively recently emerged from state socialism where a very different form of youth policy prevailed. Yet there may also be strengths in having no such traditions, which can sometimes stifle and constrain innovation rather than build constructively on established practice. Starting from an almost literal 'blank sheet of paper', with the requisite political commitment and reasonable resources, can produce a dynamism in youth policy formulation and development that is denied those countries with more entrenched traditions. Though it has not been subject to a Council of Europe review, the case of Serbia – the bedrock of Denstad's (2008) *Youth Policy Manual* – seems to testify to that[2].

During the Council of Europe review procedure, countries have been required to produce a national report on their youth policy, to which the subsequent international report (the outcome of the review) is intended to be complementary. Thus there are 'pairs' of formal documentation that have emerged from each review and serve as a basis for cross-national, European thinking about youth policy. Such an analysis was conducted after seven reviews, and again after the next seven (see Williamson, 2002, 2008). There may soon be a case for a third. The purpose of these synthesis reports was to extract and extrapolate both common and more distinctive aspects of youth policy within and across the respective countries. Though numerous concrete examples are provided, the conclusions to this process have been emphatically a *framework* and not a prescription for youth policy across Europe.

---

2   Though some foundations were laid through the work of youth organizations in Serbia in the early 2000s, the momentum was established later in the 2000s by a charismatic and dynamic Minister of Youth and Sports. She put together an impressive team of officials within the Ministry, supported an inclusive process of consultation that involved youth NGOs and representative youth bodies, and ultimately produced a clear youth policy framework with eight distinctive thematic objectives. It still, of course, remains to be seen whether this laudable framework and the objectives within it will succeed in realizing its aspirations through effective implementation.

The Council of Europe international review process

The review process has evolved over time. Initially there were no terms of reference nor clearly delineated procedures. Indeed, the first review (of Finland, see Williamson 1999) drew words from a poem by the then Finnish Minister of Culture, Claes Andersson, to capture the feelings of the review team:

> There is a road no one has taken before you
> Maybe it's yours
> If you find it, it will be
> It doesn't exist but comes into being when you walk it
> When you turn around, it's gone
> No one knows how you got here, least of all yourself

For this reason, that first international report, beyond commenting substantively on youth policy in Finland, also aimed to provide "some signposts for the conduct of future international reviews of youth policy, in terms of working methods, substantive frameworks and processes of reflection and analysis" (Williamson, 1997, p. 11). The composition of international review teams has remained, largely, the same: a nomination from each of the statutory bodies of the Youth Directorate of the Council of Europe (governmental and youth organisations, the former designated as the chair), a member of the secretariat from the Youth Directorate, and three researchers or experts, one of whom is the rapporteur. The working methods have also remained reasonably constant, with two visits to the host country, the first focusing on the central administration and 'top down' delivery of youth policy, the second paying more attention to the 'bottom up' experience of youth policy on the part of young people and at the local level. Two things have, however, evolved and changed. The process of reflection and analysis is now more robust, through building in time for the international team to consider what it has learned and to identify gaps that need filling before the conclusion to the review. And there have been changes to the substantive coverage of the review: first, there was something of an 'open book', then some emphasis was given to priorities identified by the host country (established during a preliminary visit) as well as a continuing 'open book' from the international side, and, currently, a more concentrated focus on both sides, with each identifying up to three core issues that command priority debate within the international report. The review process culminates in both a national hearing, to discuss the findings of the international team, held in the host country, and then, after any necessary revisions, an international hearing where the findings are presented to the Joint Council of the Youth Directorate – the inter-governmental steering group on youth co-operation in Europe (CDEJ) and the Advisory Council for Youth, representing the membership of the Council of Europe. Following approval from the Joint Council, the international report enters the public domain. Each review takes about a year, though its preparation can take at least six months more.

Some lessons

Each review, to date, throws up at least one new issue, dilemma or connundrum for youth policy reflection and development. Though it might be rather invidious to name the country that has produced the issue, it is definitely instructive to run through some of the disparate themes that have been thrown into relief during particular reviews. I have no intention of providing eighteen illustrations, but I will offer the following examples.

First, there are the relations between youth research and youth policy making. Long before proclamations of the 'magic triangle' (between youth research, policy and practice), the international reviews raised questions about those relationships – when they existed more in the breach than in the observance. Even when there is thriving youth research in a country, its professional and political connections to youth policy debate may be somewhat tenuous. Professionally, the substantive focus of youth research may be in quite a different place from the prevailing policy focus. Politically, consideration needs to be given to the platforms or doors for constructive dialogue between research knowledge and youth policy direction.

Second, there are always debates as to when 'childhood' ends, 'youth' begins and ends, and 'adulthood' begins. Beyond the UN definition of childhood, as 0-18, there are myriad conceptualisations that demand attention for their consistency, coherence and usefulness. The international youth policy reviews raised this issue long before current discussions about the relationships between childhood, youth and family policy that is commanding political attention in many constituent countries of the Council of Europe.

Third, questions for youth policy in relation to migration and minorities only slowly reared their heads. Where there are significant minority ethnic groups, sometimes – in some areas – even constituting a majority, there can be huge youth policy challenges around educational, labour market, linguistic and political participation. Youth policy is clearly embedded in wider national political arrangements and intentions, yet equally a key foundation for any work undertaken by the Council of Europe is the promotion of its founding principles: human rights, democracy and the rule of law. International youth policy reviews sometimes have to take a stand.

Fourth, it became apparent during the early reviews of countries from central and eastern Europe that the differential capacities of civil society and the state (and the relationships between them) meant that similar aspirations for youth policy could be (perhaps should be, and sometimes had to be) delivered by different means. Indeed, the weaknesses of municipal administration vis a vis the energy and commitment of relatively newly-formed youth NGOs, during the 1990s, meant that the only chance of some youth policy elements, such as participation or volunteering, being effective was through civil society. As that balance altered, however, different mechanisms for delivery had to be considered.

Fifth, the role of faith organisations and religion in the shaping or obstruction of youth policy aspirations only gradually emerged. Once recognised, however, it became clear that religious organisations can enable or oppose different aspects of youth policy at the same time. A similar point applies to the military. Though largely invisible in early youth policy reviews, military service became increasingly prominent, either through debates about the place of military service (or its alternatives) within youth policy, or recent or imminent abolition in some countries, and in particular in countries that have recent or current circumstances of conflict.

Sixth, a more recent emergent theme has been around questions of demography, economy and achievement. Young people who are able or are motivated are moving, more and more, towards the bright lights of their own capitals and beyond, to western Europe. This is an increasingly important item for youth policy in some countries, though sometimes only by neglect. 'Nothing can be done' can be one position. Elsewhere, youth policy is seeking to bring these young people 'home' or discourage their departure in the first place.

The framework

It is these, and many other lessons, that have contributed to an increasingly sophisticated framework to assist both the understanding, making and development of national youth policy.

The overarching framework derived from this grounded inquiry incorporates six elements, though a seventh concerning evaluation and performance measurement might be added. The first addresses conceptual approaches and definitions, both of 'youth' and 'youth policy'. These can be interminable challenges but, politically, decisions have to be made: what is the (age) range of 'youth' and how broadly (or narrowly) should 'youth policy' be defined? The second element relates to infrastructure questions: what are the laws, resolutions and budgetary allocations made that are directed at young people and youth policy? Formal statutes can both help and hinder the evolution of youth policy but, clearly, in some countries, they are essential if resources are to flow in the direction of young people and the issues they are facing. Thirdly, there is the question of delivery mechanisms: across formal structures of governance from central to local administrations, through youth or youth-focused NGOs, and through youth organisations, are there systems that can transport effectively to the right groups of young people the youth policy ideas that are formed and forged in the centre? If there are not, then even the most progressive and creative plans simply stagnate (as the late Children's Commissioner for Wales put it magnificently in 2005, policy can be "all flagships and no fleet" – it all sounds good, but nothing happens!).

The fourth element for consideration is the range of domains that may lie within the purview of 'youth policy'. I have noted the possibility of divisions of opinion between developmental (educative), regulatory (justice) and supportive (family) policy as legitimate components of youth policy. There is, nevertheless, now broad agreement that core domains of youth policy are education (formal and non-formal), training, employment, health, housing and justice. Yet, in some contexts, as noted above, the shaping of youth policy is significantly influenced by faith and military organisations. It is therefore important to take account of all those domains that bear directly or indirectly on young people's lives: where sex education is obstructed by the Catholic Church, or military service is compulsory, the role of religion and the armed forces can be critical in the making (or unmaking) of youth policy. Similarly, the fifth element is those cross-cutting issues that, at particular times, shape the overarching political and professional aspirations for youth policy: nation-building, social inclusion, economic competiveness and entrepreneurship, mobility and internationalism, demographic balance, democratic renewal. These 'umbrella' priorities (or strategic themes and objectives) can significantly influence the content of policy for young people across a number of different policy domains.

Finally, youth policy can only maintain a direction and dynamic if it is anchored by three distinct but connected themes: knowledge and research, the dissemination of good practice, and the professional training of youth practitioners. While policy makers in some countries struggle with an overload of often conflicting research data and 'youth knowledge', others suffer from an absence of useful knowledge, making policy in something of a vacuum between political directive and ideas from elsewhere. Likewise, practitioners can operate in well-meaning vacuums if they cannot benefit from an exchange of experiential views with colleagues from elsewhere, across local, regional and national boundaries. Platforms for knowledge exchange and transfer are thin on the ground in some places. Finally, the bridge between youth knowledge and youth practice that helps to deliver the aspirations of policy is the effective practitioner. Whether paid or voluntary, effectiveness is contingent on practice borne less of good intentions and more of reflective understanding of how a positive impact can be made in the contexts and with the 'clientele' at which policy is directed. This demands training strategies, with corresponding qualification and accreditation structures that equip practitioners with the requisite knowledge, skills and competencies.

Three reflective considerations

Over the years in which I have been engaged in youth policy research, development and implementation (as an academic, policy adviser and youth worker), I have distilled much of my thinking into three sets of ideas.

Avoiding paralysis – practice inside the triangle

The key point here is that the 'youth practitioner' has to navigate between these often competing pressures and priorities. Sometimes, of course, they will be broadly compatible but, more often, they will have to be addressed as creative tensions. The youth practitioner who is 'sucked' into any corner of the triangle risks becoming paralysed: instrumentalised by the state, unable to make realistic concessions to idealistic positions, or serving the expressed wants (rather than more reflected needs) of young people.

Checklisting youth policy – the five Cs

Coverage
Co-ordination
Capacity
Competence
Cost

This list endeavours to capture the key questions that should inform the planning, development and implementation of youth policy. In terms of coverage, what is the geographical reach, are all social groups being targeted, what is the range of issues being addressed (and are any being manifestly neglected)? What is the nature of co-ordination between the different bodies – at national, regional and local level, both horizontally and vertically – responsible for youth policy? How strong are the systems for delivery? Are the right people – both professionals and volunteers – in the right places and positions? And what is the resource base, both human and financial, available for 'making things happen'?

Maintaining the dynamic of youth policy

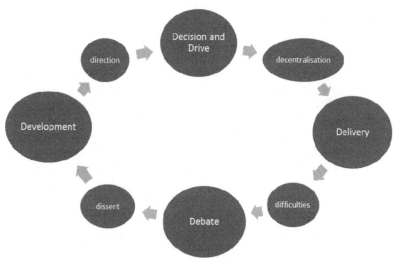

This flow chart attempts to represent a 'dynamic' that characterises the evolution (or stagnation) of youth policy. Policy ideas can commence at different stages of the cycle but, if all stages are not acted upon or made available, then there is a risk that creative and positive development will be obstructed. In other words, things can also stall at any stage in the process. Critically, there is a need for political championship of youth policy ideas at the top of the cycle, but equally professionals need the opportunity and space to deliberate on implementation challenges that invariably arise. However, for politicians to have the confidence to take new ideas forward, they need to be presented with a coherent development plan, not with division within the field.

Does anybody listen?

One expert member of a recent review, new to the field and the process, asked if the reviews only covered small, former Communist countries. I told him not, but implicit to his question was whether there was some form of 'new colonialism' going on, with western European youth policy ideas being 'imposed' on these countries. This is far from the point.

The international review process is one of 'critical complicity', in which the international team, drawn from at least six different countries, brings to bear a 'stranger's eye' on what is going on in the host country. It is there to be critical, but constructively so. Ultimately, it is committed to serving and supporting positive and opportunity-focused youth policy development in the host country, even if it also seeks to draw lessons for the wider international youth policy community.

There has always been an intention within the international review process to have a follow-up, perhaps after one year. This has been only partially and often poorly implemented. It is therefore quite impossible to say, formally, if international reviews have had an impact on the direction of the national youth policies they have reviewed. Indeed, even less formally, it would be extremely unwise to make any grand claims for any sweeping impact. And it would be certainly possible to identify one or two countries where the impact of an international youth policy review has been either non-existent or rather ephemeral. It would also be possible to suggest one or two countries where participation in the international youth policy review process has been more symbolic than substantive. A suddenly changed political landscape can usurp all that has gone before. Even with sustained political commitment, national resources can undermine purposeful youth policy development.

Yet, in support of the reviews, and as their co-ordinator over the past few years, I am also conscious that the review process, as well as its final product (the report and the national and international hearings) do generate questions and ideas that become lodged in a country's youth policy consciousness and debate. The international review team is able to raise both uncomfortable and unexpected questions and perspectives that, for various reasons, could not be, or would be unlikely to be, raised internally. It can, furthermore, introduce new ideas – both around the big themes of youth policy and around detail within existing areas of youth policy. This produces the cross-fertilisation of youth policy thinking in Europe. It may be some time before some items come to the surface and it may be impossible to attribute them to the international policy reviews, but the contribution will still have been made. I am thinking here of, for example, the following themes, drawn almost randomly from the reviews to date:

- Vocational training programmes within compulsory military service
- Confidentiality thresholds within 'youth friendly' sexual health clinics

- Personal officer schemes in custodial establishments for young offenders
- Youth information and advice
- Youth participation structures
- Mechanisms for supporting youth enterprise and entrepreneurship
- Building intergenerational activity

The general point is that these are absolutely familiar to those who know about them, but a complete surprise to those who do not. National youth policy, if it is to serve the needs of the diversity of young people moving along the complex pathways of transition in modern Europe, needs at least to take account of this mosaic of possibility. If some of it is rejected, that is the prerogative of the democratic politics of the country concerned, even if it may be against young people's interests, but at least the ideas have been thought about.

Conclusion

These observations on the issue of 'youth policy' are drawn largely from Council of Europe country reviews that incorporated some scrutiny of local experiences and municipal plans in the context of national frameworks and political aspirations. There are some exemplary forms of youth policy but these do not reside in particular countries and are instead distributed across many countries. Some may have a weak general youth policy but exceptional policy and practice in specific fields such as youth information, youth participation, health promotion or youth crime prevention. Claims about the quality of youth policy need to be interrogated closely. As Evans (1998) has noted, youth policy has to be considered at three points: when it is *espoused* (formulated), when it is *enacted*, and when it is *experienced*. Ultimately, it is not necessarily even the experience of youth policy that is important. It is how such policy makes a constructive impact, and produces positive outcomes on the life-chances of young people, especially those who are more disadvantaged, for whom public policy can and should make a difference to the growing inequalities and 'youth divide' (Jones, 2002) amongst young people in contemporary Europe.

Bibliography

Blakely, G. (1990) *Youth Policy*, London, Routledge.

Council of Europe (2008) *Agenda 2020*, Strasbourg, Council of Europe.

Coussée, F. (2008) *A Century of Youth Work Policy*, Gent, Academia Press.

Denstad, F. (2008) *Youth Policy Manual*, Strasbourg, Council of Europe Publishing.

Doyle, C. (1993) *Teenagers at Risk in Britain Today: an agenda for action*, Brighton, Trust for the Study of Adolescence.

European Commission (2002) *A New Impetus for European Youth: White Paper*, Brussels, European Commission.

Evans, K. (1998) Shaping Futures; learning for competence and citizenship, Aldershot, Ashgate.

European Commission (2009) *Investing and Empowering*, Brussels, European Commission.

Jones, G. (2002) *The Youth Divide: diverging paths to adulthood*, York, Joseph Rowntree Foundation.

Milmeister, M. and Williamson, H. (eds) (2006) *Dialogues and Networks: organising exchanges between youth field actors*, Luxembourg, Editions Phi.

Smith, D. and Williamson, H. (1985) Future... What future?, *Youth in Society*, November.

Williamson, H. (1993) Youth Policy in the United Kingdom and the Marginalisation of Young People, *Youth and Policy, 40*, pp. 33-48.

Williamson, H. (1999) *Youth Policy in Finland*, Strasbourg, Council of Europe Publishing.

Williamson, H. (2000) Youth work and government policies towards young people: the research, policy and practice forum, in Machacek, L. and Chisholm, L. (eds) *Comparative Youth Research and Policy, Contributions to the debate from ISA RC34* (pp. 22-33), Bratislava, Slovak Academy of Sciences.

2. Transitions to adulthood and Canadian youth policy initiatives: some lessons for transitions research

By Marc Molgat and Susannah Taylor

Is the concept of 'transition' still relevant for the development of youth policy? Although this question may seem surprising to many researchers investigating the transitions of young people from school to the labour market, it is perhaps less so for scholars who have an interest in young people facing vulnerability and who often enter into dialogue with policy and decision-makers in the public policy sphere. In these contexts, one is often confronted with the question of which groups of young people are the most 'at-risk' of either entering a specific problem situation (such as homelessness or dropping out of school) or, once there, of adopting more problematic behaviours and not being able extricate themselves from them (by developing substance abuse or criminal behaviours, for example). Although legitimate, these concerns often have the consequence of further stigmatizing young people who are already vulnerable, by qualifying them as 'at-risk' and by individualizing both their problems and the interventions intended to help them become less at-risk. This approach is quite common in liberal welfare states such as Canada's, where individualism and autonomy are held in high esteem, and where approaches to supporting young people are increasingly targeted at those who may be thought of as 'residual youth', i.e. those who are deemed unable to make it on their own. However, by concentrating on the identification of these sub-groups of young people, policy makers run the risk of isolating these young people's lives from the larger transition patterns to adulthood, thereby focussing policies and programs on their specific individual behaviours without linking them to larger contexts.

Over the past ten years, however, some initiatives in youth policy making in Canada seem to have taken a more global approach to young people. At the provincial government level, three Canadian provinces have either developed specific youth policy frameworks or policies *per*

se, or are in the process of doing so. Our objective in this chapter is to determine in what form the concept of transitions appears in these policy
initiatives and what this can tell us about the actual or potential role of
transitions research in youth policy development. The chapter begins
with a presentation of the context in which youth policy is being developed in Canada, before discussing the concept of transitions and the way
we have chosen to operationalize it for the analysis. The chapter then focuses on some key youth policy documents published by the governments
of Alberta, Québec and Ontario, before concluding with some suggestions for maintaining the legitimacy of transitions research in the youth
policy-making arena.

Youth policy development – the Canadian context

In Canada, the recent interest in developing global youth policies, as opposed to sector specific policies that affect young people, is driven by a
number of factors including economic and demographic trends, efforts
aimed at 'society building', a prevention agenda in the fields of health
and youth justice, and finally the growing acceptance that transitions to
adulthood are no longer standardized.

The economic and demographic context of Canadian society today
closely mirrors what is occurring in other industrialized societies. There
has been a transformation of the labour market toward a new post-
industrial economic order in which the manufacturing industry has lost
much of its sway to the profit of the production of 'knowledge goods'
and 'personal services'. This creates a demand for more highly educated
and trained employees (Beaujot and Kerr, 2007) while at the same time
causing more difficulties for young people in their search for stable and
permanent employment. Paradoxically, because of Canadian demographic trends, there will soon be more people leaving the job market
than entering it (Beaujot, McQuillan and Ravanera, 2007). The large size
of the baby boom cohorts, born after World War II and up to the early
1960s, and the dwindling fertility rates thereafter, have led to worries
about the sustainability of pension schemes and, among provincial governments in Canada, concern is being voiced about the imminent risks of
labour market shortages related to trades in particular (Emploi-Québec,
2011; Conference Board of Canada, 2007). Recently, both the Ontario
and Québec governments have initiated media campaigns to make voca-

tional/technological education more attractive both in high school and at the postsecondary level.

The second factor, what we refer to as 'society building', refers to a number of issues that are related to supporting or promoting various societal arrangements. The first of these issues is related to democratic institutions. Trends of declining youth interest and participation in the formal political process, as witnessed by the falling rates of young people voting in elections at all levels of government (Blais and Loewen, 2011), have created a sense of urgency to instill in young people the desire to participate in the democratic process. The second issue is tied to the need to ensure social cohesion in the context of high immigration rates and the multicultural policies that have been so dear to successive Canadian governments. Although most young adults from immigrant backgrounds, whether they or their parents were born in Canada, succeed very well at school and fare relatively well in the labour market (Boyd, 2009), some young people from immigrant backgrounds and from specific ethnic minority groups do not share the same success. This is the case, for example, of young Black men from Caribbean descent, as well as young adults whose parents or themselves have immigrated to Canada from Arabic countries (Molgat, 2008). The same can be said of First Nations youth in Canada, whose levels of schooling and employment are the lowest among all Canadian young people (Beaujot and Kerr, 2007). Finally, the province of Québec stands out for its long term interest in being recognized as a French-speaking nation within Canada, which has historically been rooted, in part, in a discourse on the necessity of 'occupying its territory'. As we shall explain further on in this chapter, the desire to maintain populations and the socioeconomic vitality of regions outside larger urban centres is tied to government interest in the geographical mobility patterns of young adults in Québec.

The third factor driving the development of youth policies in Canada relates to what can be termed a 'prevention agenda', which has become a salient feature of government discourse and interventions. The notion of prevention is often linked to health issues among young people, most notably the increasing rates of obesity and mental distress. In Canada, the rate of young adults aged 20 to 29 who are considered overweight or obese has been rising and was at 42.7% in 2007-2009 (Public Health Agency of Canada, 2011). In the area of mental health, the number of young people who suffer from various psychological ailments seems high (*Ibid.*, Desmarais *et al.*, 2001), although it is not clear to what extent these are related to increased societal pressures on young people or to heightened awareness and diagnosis of various types of mental illness. The prevention discourse has today been extended to a wide array of social problems among young people (Parazelli and Dessureault, 2010), for example those related to juvenile delinquency, violence and homelessness, to name but a few.

Finally, policy makers are now aware that young people's transitions to adulthood no longer follow clear standardized routes. Thirty to forty years ago, young people in societies such as the United States, Canada, France and the United Kingdom generally made fairly rapid and synchronized transitions to adulthood. The tendency was for young people to leave home and get married, and to have a job and their own family within a few years of leaving high school. This followed a historical trend of lowering ages of home leaving and marriage, and was tied to strong economic growth in the decades following the 2nd World War, to opportunities for young people, as well as to a strong normative discourse – at least in Canada and the US – favouring the integration of youth into the social structure through employment and family life. Changes to this pattern have been noted and researched in Canada in recent years. They show that young people are pursuing postsecondary education in ever greater numbers and are taking longer to enter the labour market in full time jobs (Molgat, 2011). Also, Canada ranks second among the countries of the Organisation for Economic Co-operation and Development (OECD) in terms of the postsecondary education levels of 25 to 34 year olds (OECD, 2011), yet the wages of young adults have been decreasing, particularly among males (Chung, 2006), and precariousness often marks the first years of employment even among those with higher levels of education. Largely due to these situations, the proportion of young adults living at home continues to rise: the latest census data indicates that more than 60% of 20 to 24 year olds and over a quarter of those aged 25 to 29 live with their parents (Statistics Canada, 2007). Finally, young adults are also putting off family formation; a clear majority of young people do not become parents before the end of their twenties (Clark, 2007). In all of these situations, except for the entry into parenthood, young adults may "reverse" their transitions (Charbonneau, 2006), for example by leaving the labour market and going back to school, or by returning home to live with their parents as do approximately 30% of those who leave home for the first time (Mitchell, 2006).

Conceptualizing transitions for youth policy analysis

In general then, young people in Canada, as in other Western societies, are seen to be postponing transitions or even to be reversing them, which has led researchers to explore the consequences of these different trajectories on the experiences of youth and to coin expressions such as "boundless youth" (Galland, 2007) and "yo-yo transitions" (Biggart and Walther, 2006), and to raise the question of the appearance of a "New Youth" (Leccardi and Ruspini, 2006). In all of these analyses, the themes of uncertainty about the future and individualization of risk loom large. In essence, they indicate that the socioeconomic conditions in which young people live today make it difficult for them to plan their futures (see Leccardi, in this volume) and force many of them to rely on their own resources and their family's support to ensure their transitions or to act as safety nets when transitions lead to difficulties or need to be 're-versed' (Settersten, 2005; Jones, 2009; Molgat and Vultur, 2009). The possibility for young adults of relying on institutional forms of support has waned, especially in liberal welfare states such as Canada's, despite the fact that young people clearly depend on social structures such as school, and the labour and housing markets, to make transitions to adulthood. Over the past few decades, these structures have been producing more risk for young people, as tuition fees and housing costs have been constantly rising above inflation, access to full time stable employment has been declining, and wages have been diminishing. In parallel, access to unemployment and welfare benefits has been restricted; governments have been generally reticent to offer support for young working parents (through daycare, for example) and have been loath to regulate the housing market – let alone invest in social housing – in order to provide affordable housing.

By highlighting these structural dimensions of the passage to adulthood, we wish to emphasize their importance in considering the transitions of young people in a life-course perspective (Elder *et al.*, 2004), and consequently their importance in approaching policy. Our analysis of the youth policy initiatives in the provinces of Alberta, Ontario and Québec is specifically aimed at determining to what extent they take into account the transitions of young people, including the way in which young people are situated in their socioeconomic contexts through their interactions with social structures and institutions.

In our view, current research on young adulthood points to four main contemporary trajectories or transition strands: 1) the professional strand;

2) the financial strand; 3) the relational strand; and 4) the identity strand (Molgat and Taylor, forthcoming). Each of these transition strands should be viewed as interrelated but not as linear or synchronous, i.e. occurring at the same time and speeds within individual biographies. For example, as we have just indicated, many young people in Canada take a longer time to complete their schooling because they move back and forth between work and school; others will delay their exit from the family home, or even return to live with their parents, even if they are employed; yet others will suffer setbacks in romantic relationships and couple life. Through these flexible transitions that make up individual biographies, the route to perceiving oneself as a full adult, or as a member of certain communities, or as 'competent' in different life areas such as work or parenthood is often sinuous. Nevertheless, in the four trajectories we have identified, transitions to adulthood do generally and eventually occur, with varying degrees of success and satisfaction in the eyes of young people themselves. We define these succinctly in the following paragraphs.

The contemporary *professional transition strand* is concerned with both education and employment and is often discussed as the transition from school to work. What was traditionally a more succinct school to work transition has become increasingly de-standardized (Molgat, 2007; Tremblay, 2003). In general, youth are staying in school longer and as a result, entry into the labour force has been postponed (Beaujot and Kerr, 2007; Franke, 2010). Precarious and low-paid youth employment also contributes to this de-standardization (Molgat, 2007; Tremblay, 2003). Attending high school and having some employment are characteristic of adolescence. Becoming an adult is marked by a change in the nature of one's education and employment. The markers of this change generally include the completion of high school and often further education, the presence of a link between an individual's training or studies and his or her employment, and having full time, stable and permanent employment that provides a working wage.

In terms of the *financial strand*, research has recently pointed to the significance of financial independence in how young people define what it means to be an adult. This factor has been highlighted by Jeffrey Arnett's research on young Americans (2004), and has also appeared in research undertaken with Canadian youth (Molgat, 2007). In referring to financial independence, young people speak of their ability to handle credit and savings, to pay off their debts, to enter rental agreements and, finally, to purchase a home. From a financial perspective, young people tend to be seen as consumers who need to become more responsible, but the sphere of consumption also relates to the question of employment income which has been dwindling for young people in Canada and to the issue of consumer rights. The financial transition strand is composed of three main elements, those of financial literacy, financial independence and residential independence (Molgat and Taylor, forthcoming).

As we have seen, markers such as couple formation and becoming parents used to be clear relational indicators of having become an adult. This is no longer the case. During the contemporary transition to adulthood, *the relational strand* represents the process by which an individual develops and embraces autonomy and a sense of responsibility for others. Therefore, although marriage and parenthood can be markers of adulthood, they are no longer necessarily indicators of it as such. In general, youth are now leaving home, forming unions and becoming parents later in life (Molgat, 2011; Beaujot and Kerr, 2007). During this time, young people learn to assume responsibility towards themselves, towards others (in interdependence) and towards institutions (those holding relevance in their lives). In this way, it is possible to understand how in the current context of prolonged education pathways and an uncertain labour market, an individual may become an adult by means of an achieved sense of responsibility and autonomy in the relational sphere, despite still being in part financially dependent on his or her parents (Gaudet, 2001). The markers of this strand include becoming fully autonomous, eventually forming a couple and becoming a parent, and the presence of peers and a social network.

Finally, in the *identity transition strand*, one can consider that young people move from exploring ascribed and other identities in adolescence to the construction of their own identities. In late modern societies, identity is no longer considered by researchers to be strongly ascribed by social background; it is also at least partly self-achieved. During the transition to adulthood, young people may rely on identity capital (personal resources that are closely tied to self-esteem) and social capital in the form of relationships that help build self-esteem, starting from one's own family to peer-groups and wider social networks and groups, to construct positive identities, as opposed to simply adopting those that are mass marketed (Côté, 2000). Young people develop different identities in different areas of life (school, work, family life, etc.) according to self-assessment and assessment by others as being "competent" (Jones, 2009). Although these identities may change positively as young people acquire more experiences, it is important to consider that if positive change is to occur, young people need to invest time and energy in the different areas of competence. This investment depends on whether young people have a feeling of personal efficacy and whether they have access to resources (material, emotional, social, cultural) that enable them to choose different identities, tactics, and strategies in building their identities (*Ibid.*). It is important to note that the multicultural, linguistic, and Aboriginal contexts of Canadian society play an important role in identity construction. Research in Canada on the ethnic and language identity construction of young people highlights the emergence of a 'multicultural generation' of young people who constantly negotiate their many identities by referring to culture, environment, and sense of community, at local, national, and global levels (Plaza, 2006; Sykes, 2008; Lock-Kunz and Sykes, 2007). Recent research on the identity of young people from official language communities in Canada paints a similar portrait, pointing to how young people from French-language communities construct hybrid identities or develop identity ambivalence in order to integrate several worlds at once in the course of their daily lives (Dallaire and Denis, 2005; Pilote, 2007; Pilote and Magnan, 2008). Among Aboriginal youth the trend is similar, although families and communities play both a potentially disruptive and supportive role, depending on how they have been able to cope with and overcome the effects of colonization, mistreatment by government, and endemic poverty and social problems (Kroes, 2008). In sum, the identity strand is marked by the mobilisation of identity and social capital to develop 'competent' identities in the various realms of one's life as well as the development of identities related to language, ethnicity, culture and gender.

Youth policy initiatives in Alberta, Québec and Ontario

We refer in this section to youth policy initiatives and not to youth policy *per se* because only the provinces of Alberta and Québec have adopted formal youth policies or policy frameworks, while Ontario has been recently moving towards the development of a youth policy framework. Furthermore, Québec is the only province to have devised comprehensive strategic action plans linked to its official youth policy. The analysis in the following pages does not attempt to systematically compare these policy initiatives; instead, it endeavours to identify which transition strands are taken into consideration and how they are integrated within a policy approach. It is important to note that we have deliberately chosen not to analyze a youth policy framework that was developed by a Canadian government think tank in 2008-09 (Franke, 2010), for the simple reason that this framework has not been officially adopted by any federal government departments as a guide to developing or implementing policy addressed to young people.

1   The *Youth in Transition Policy Framework* and 'guidelines for support' in Alberta

The government of Alberta adopted in 2001 its *Youth in Transition Policy Framework* (YTPF), which was aimed at providing "the direction and parameters for youth policy program development for youth in transition, aged 13 to 24" (Government of Alberta, 2001). The policy framework is set out succinctly in a five page document, and establishes a vision of youth, guiding principles, as well as policy directions, goals and outcomes. The document provides a very general perspective of youth in transition, by identifying it as the move through adolescence and the progress into young adulthood. The vision of youth as being composed of a majority of "healthy, happy, active, involved and independent" individuals who are "successfully managing" this transition with the support of family and friends, while they are at school or at work, underscores the residualist approach of the policy framework. No specific transition strands are identified, only specific "challenges" related to a) the increased need for parental support in general; b) the unique needs of Aboriginal and immigrant youth; c) the greater difficulties faced by young people who have a history of abuse, family breakdown, child welfare involvement, addictions, conflict with the law, physical or mental health concerns or developmental disabilities; and d) the problems of transition to adult services for those with special needs and disabilities.

Presumably then, it is only to young people who face these specific challenges that policies and programs should be addressed. Others are considered to be doing just fine; and when difficulties do arise for them, their families and communities can be called upon for support. The policy directions, in terms of goals and strategic outcomes, not only support this view but emphasize the construction of individual capacities. Programs, services, and resources should "recognize and support families" as the key to the stability of youth in transition, should be "targeted effectively" for youth in transition and should be delivered by communities. Consistent with its definition of transition and its vision of youth, the YTPF then defines strategic outcomes that are not to be measured according to the attainment of "success" in various transition strands (for example, from school to work), but rather by whether or not young people have acquired the "knowledge, skills, attitudes and abilities" to live happy and productive lives, are involved in and can access services that meet their needs, and are safe, supported and connected to caring peers and adults.

It is difficult to identify whether (and how) the YTPF has been used successfully in devising policies and programs. The main government department targeted by the framework, the Ministry of Human Services, administers employment and immigration programs, child and youth programs including child welfare, as well as programs for the homeless. In various policy documents on all of these issues, no mention is made of the YTPF. However, a document on transitions, aimed at child and youth practitioners, was published in 2006 by the government's Children and Youth Initiative. Titled *Guidelines for Supporting Successful Transitions for Children and Youth* (Government of Alberta, 2006), it was designed as a practical tool for giving 'research-based advice' to practitioners, but also parents, teachers, peers and mentors, on how to support children and youth during different transitions. The document provides advice for planning successful transitions in early childhood, transitioning into school, into Junior High School, into High School and finally into "adulthood", the latter being characterized as a period where young people experience "heightened independence" while still requiring support.

Although the document is specifically aimed at practitioners – presumably always engaged in individual intervention settings – it is nonetheless surprising that none of the transitions identified focus on the social structures such as schools or the labour market, in which transitions are occurring, let alone on how these could be problematic for young people. Consequently, the advice is grounded in an individualized and psychological approach to intervention, where no concern is given to how practitioners may think about the need for change in some of these contexts. For the transition to adulthood, the "tips" provided are based on the need for individual adjustment to context. The advice is centered on the importance of establishing goals, pursuing education and/or training, developing a personal "portfolio" (including a resume), developing versatility and skills for emerging labour market demands, having a good knowledge of services and opportunities, and creating opportunities for youth to become involved in their community. A separate section of the document then describes tips for enhancing the "social transitioning" of all children and youth. The emphasis here is on building developmental abilities linked to self-esteem and social skills through relationships with others and mirrors to a certain extent the identity transition we identified earlier. Although these guidelines are important for young people, they seem to be out of step with an analysis of transitions that focuses as much on systems, institutions and structures as on how individuals navigate the pathways set up by these same structures.

2   Québec's Youth Policy and Youth Action Strategy: from coherence to 'bricolage'?

In 2001, the province of Québec adopted an official youth policy that sets out a framework for the actions of government and its partners. The policy consists of a fifty-six page document outlining the background to the youth policy, four key policy directions and twenty strategic goals, as well as principles for the implementation of the policy (Government of Québec, 2001). Adopted in the wake of the government-led Québec Youth Summit held the previous year, the policy lays the groundwork for three successive action plans, the latest of which spans 2009 to 2014. Our analysis will focus on the policy itself as well as on this latest action plan.

The Québec youth policy is focused on the notion of 'active citizenship' which, according to the document, is the opposite of exclusion, and "refers to the full, complete participation of citizens in the life of a society and their commitment to it, but also their capability to do so" (Government of Québec, 2001: 17). In this sense, citizenship is viewed not only through the lens of individual rights and obligations, but also by considering the socioeconomic and cultural conditions that encourage full participation. It is in this perspective that the policy seeks to promote a more "mutually supportive, inclusive and equitable society" (*Ibid.*). This general point of view aligns well with life course and transitions theory which places emphasis not only on individual's lives but also on context. Although it is not possible to tie all of the orientations and strategic goals to a transitions framework and the particular strands we set out earlier in the chapter, many refer directly to the transition from school to work, and a few to the transition to parenthood.

The first and third policy orientations, *Engaging society in a culture of generational renewal and Facilitating access to the job market and improving the quality of working life*, take into account both the structures of school and labour market, and the support that young people need individually to gain access to and succeed in these environments. For example, by identifying education and training as a "collective priority", the policy states that universal access to quality secondary and post-secondary education must be ensured, regardless of where people live or their financial status, and that barriers to education must be removed through financial assistance and a greater diversity of training programs. Further consideration is given to the need to provide appropriate guidance counselling services and individual support during the transitions from one level of education to the next. In the area of access to employment and retention, the policy states, for example, that the government, in conjunction with its partners, should aim to increase job stability and support for young people entering the labour market, to make business and unions more aware of the need to integrate young people in the workplace, and to offer employment skills and abilities upgrading programs. Support programs for building knowledge and personal capacities linked to job-search needs are also identified as essential components of government or community-based interventions. In terms of the transition to parenthood, emphasis is placed in the second policy orientation, Ensuring young people achieve their full potential, on the need to support young families, both financially and in terms of day care, through economic and tax policies and access to government funded daycare programs; at the same time, young parents who are 'at risk', and in particular teenage and single parents, are identified as specific targets for prevention, support and guidance "in order for them to exercise their role [as parents] fully" (p. 32).

The Québec youth policy also identifies 'Developing a sense of belonging' as one of its four key policy directions, by stating that a sense of belonging to family, association, group, municipality, region or nation, is crucial to participation in society because it favours interconnectedness between members of society and tighter social bonds (p. 43). The notion of sense of belonging can be tied to the identity transition strand we described earlier. The social questions and intervention goals that are tied to this policy direction deal with how individuals can be brought to feel that they belong 'somewhere' with a view to contributing to society. The policy goals thus relate to: 1) encouraging young people to put down roots in different regions of the province despite their geographical mobility during their transitions to postsecondary education, to work, and to family formation; 2) promoting their participation in communities; 3) fostering their sensitivity to cultural pluralism while recognizing the specificity and importance of the French language and culture in Québec; and 4) promoting their openness to international realities. The only of these goals to integrate the notion of transitions is that of ensuring that the mobility of young people contributes to the socioeconomic development of the various regions in Québec, in that it recognizes that a sense of belonging to a particular region may develop differently at various points during the transition to adulthood.

Many of the other topics covered in the Youth Policy fall outside mainstream research on transitions to adulthood, which is concentrated on the passage from school to work. These include fostering access to culture and creativity, supporting recreation, sports and volunteer work, encouraging young people to become aware of the need for and to partake in sustainable development, and including young people in circles of influence and decision-making at all levels of public, private and community organizations. These topics raise the question of how transitions research might address them.

Approximately ten years after the creation of this policy, the government adopted its third *Youth Action Strategy* (2009-2014), subtitled *Investing in Youth – Empowering Québec's Future*. Although we cannot in the context of this chapter provide a detailed analysis of the strategy, it is quite clear that the transitions perspective of the Youth Policy has not been a strong guide for its development. The strategy outlines six major challenges, the first of which – the *Education and Employment Challenge* – is the only one to refer specifically to the transitions of young people by defining the transition to independence simply as a "desire shared by all young Québeckers" (Government of Québec, 2009). No other definition, further argument or data is provided to support this view of transitions. In order to respond to the 'education and employment challenge', the strategic action plan does not address changes that could be made to the school system or to the labour market, contrary to the outlook of the Youth Policy that focussed both on individuals and socioeconomic conditions. It rather addresses how young people – and specifically those who are most at risk of dropping out of school or having employment problems – can be guided, counselled or supported to adapt to these structures and to succeed in their transition to the labour market. Furthermore, the specific actions put forward by the strategy are often not connected to one another, nor are they always clearly relevant for the major challenge they are supposed to respond to. This is particularly true for the *Regional Challenge*, where specific measures range from supporting young people as they return to and stay in outlying regions, to helping young people in the Child Welfare system with their social integration and transition to independence, to promoting civic engagement among young people. As is the case in this specific 'challenge', when transitions are referred to in other parts of the Youth Action Strategy, it is most often to deal with the educational and labour market difficulties of specific groups, such as Aboriginal youth and young immigrants. In general, the latest Youth Action Strategy gives a strong impression of policy 'bricolage' where existing programs have been forcefully fitted into a strategic action plan and where the most worrisome social problems among youth – such as dropping out of school, obesity, violence and drug addiction to name but a few – have been given the most attention.

3   Building the psychological welfare state in Ontario?

There is currently no official youth policy framework in the province of Ontario, although there has been a drive towards its development, spurred on initially by research and a public awareness campaign supported by the United Way, a non profit charity organization whose main activities are to privately raise funds that are distributed to a wide range of community organizations. Under the auspices of the United Way in Toronto, a document reviewing youth policies in Canada, Europe and a few other countries was published in 2008 (Jeffrey, 2008), and was closely followed by a public opinion campaign aimed at convincing the provincial government of the need to devise a comprehensive youth policy that could guide government action in any area that touched upon young people's lives. This campaign coincided in 2008 with the publication of an exhaustive government report on the roots of youth violence. The report, titled *The Review of the Roots of Youth Violence*, was commissioned by the Prime Minister after a series of violent incidents involving young people and the seemingly inexplicable murder of a secondary level student within the walls of his own high school raised a great deal of media attention and public concern.

The recommendations of the report aim to set up an agenda for a new approach to youth violence by dealing with its root causes, namely poverty, discrimination and racism. To this end, the report defines four 'pillars' to guide an action strategy: 1) a repaired social context which "will bring together strategies to address the level, the concentrations and the circumstances of poverty, along with tightly related issues including racism, housing, education, mental health, family and community support, transportation and the justice system" (p. 18), in order to provide greater opportunities to disadvantaged young people; 2) a comprehensive youth policy framework, building on the province's early childhood development framework and founded on the developmental stages of youth, with the purpose of guiding and providing coherence to "policy and program decisions of all orders of government, the community and agencies" (p. 24); 3) a neighbourhood capacity and empowerment focus that establishes or enhances, in areas that are most in need, local centres where opportunities, services and community cohesion can be offered and fostered for young people; and 4) an integrated governance structure to allow the government to plan and deliver an approach to the range of issues affecting violence among youth.

In its general outlook on the causes of violence among youth, this report aligns well with a transitions perspective in which context must be taken into consideration to understand the transitions of young people toward adulthood. However, identifying the proposed youth policy framework as separate from contextual elements may yet lead to a very individualistic and psychologically normative outlook on the passage from adolescence to adulthood. In fact, the Ontario ministry of Children and Youth Services is currently devising its 'comprehensive' youth policy framework by attempting to define in developmental terms what should be considered as 'normal' behaviour during adolescence and youth. In the spirit of the *Roots of Youth Violence* report, such a developmental perspective can be conceived as a rampart against treating young offenders in a patchwork and piecemeal approach and considering them as 'adults' who have behaviour problems related to violence, drugs, crime, etc. Although this is part of a well-intentioned strategy to avoid the treatment of young offenders as adults in the criminal justice system, and as a way of fostering intervention from a youth work perspective, it is cause for concern that developmental psychology be the only foundation of the youth policy framework. Because the goal of such a policy is to have evidence-based information widely disseminated among various government departments, agencies and community organizations that deal with youth, and especially 'problem youth' in more disadvantaged communities, it may be difficult to make the necessary links, within programs and interventions, between young people's actions and behaviours and the social context in which they live. In effect, the intervention goals deriving from such a framework would, in our opinion, almost inevitably be constructed around encouraging and supporting young people to individually attain the developmental stages of adolescence and what is now termed "emerging adulthood" (Arnett, 2004), as opposed to seeking out how society may more accurately reflect and support all of the transitions that the young need to make on the road to adulthood. In this sense, the current path of the Ontario youth policy framework seems set to converge with the more individualistic outlook of the Alberta youth policy and the most recent Québec Youth Action Strategy.

Conclusion

This analysis of policy initiatives in Canada shows that certain transition strands are taken into consideration (school to work; some aspects of relational transitions, i.e. entry into parenthood and early years of parenthood; some aspects of identity development) while others are not (transition to financial independence including financial literacy, financial and residential independence; other aspects of the transition strands). In addition, it shows that some aspects of youth policy initiatives fall outside typical youth transitions research, such as health, access to culture, recreation and sports, volunteer work, participation in decision-making and politics, to name but a few. In general, it is possible to conclude that these recent policy initiatives have led to the adoption of a residualist approach to youth despite the pretence of these policies being global and comprehensive. Their focus is more often on the most worrisome social issues, that can be corrected either by limited government intervention, especially if it touches the economy and the labour market, or by intervention focussed on making youth less 'at-risk' by supporting them through the development of individual capacities and skills, in order to foster their better adaptation, integration, and contribution to society. In this context, the structural dimensions affecting young people's lives are generally downplayed or simply not addressed, despite the fact that they play an important role in the transitions to adulthood, as research makes abundantly clear.

In this light, a few considerations with regards to how transitions research could be made more relevant for youth policy initiatives can be suggested. We propose three but are aware that many more could be identified. First, it would seem important to broaden the scope of transitions research by emphasizing not only the passage from school to work but also the other transition strands, and how they are interwoven and interconnected. Related to this point, it may also be useful to consider other dimensions of young people's experiences in a transitions perspective, such as political participation or engagement with various cultural practices. Second, it is essential that researchers critically appraise existing policies and proposed 'comprehensive' models and frameworks for understanding youth and youth policy. Finally, although researchers are often reticent to do so, it may be useful to actively engage with policy makers either by making them more aware of our own research findings or by contributing directly to government analyses that lead to policy development, implementation, and evaluation. In this last form of contribution however, researchers need to avoid becoming too disillusioned by the fact that policy and program development is a complex and messy business, where much more than scientific knowledge enters the policy making arena.

Bibliography

Arnett, J. J. (2004) *Emerging Adulthood: The Winding Road from the Late Teens Through the Twenties*, New York, Oxford University Press.

Beaujot, R. and Kerr, D. (2007) *Emerging Youth Transition Patterns in Canada: Opportunities and Risks*, Ottawa, Policy Research Initiative.

Beaujot, R., McQuillan, K. and Ravanera, Z. (2007) Population Change in Canada to 2017 and Beyond: The Challenges of Policy Adaptation, *Horizons*, 9(4), pp. 3-12.

Biggart, A. and Walther, A. (2006) Coping With Yo-Yo Transitions: Young Adults' Struggle for Support, between Family and State in a Comparative Perspective, in Leccardi, C. and Ruspini, E. (eds) *A New Youth? Young People, Generations and Family Life* (pp. 41-62), Aldershot, Ashgate.

Blais, A. and Loewen, P. (2011) Youth Electoral Engagement in Canada, Government of Canada, Elections Canada http://www.elections.ca/res/rec/part/youeng/youth_electoral_engagement_e.pdf (accessed December 22, 2011).

Boyd, M. (2009) Social Origins and the Educational and Occupational Achievements of the 1.5 and Second Generations, *Canadian Review of Sociology*, 45(1), pp. 339-369.

Charbonneau, J. (2006) Réversibilités et parcours scolaires au Québec [Reversibility and Educational Pathways in Québec], *Cahiers internationaux de sociologie*, 120, January-June, pp. 111-132.

Chung, L. (2006) Education and earnings, *Perspectives on Labour and Income*, 18(3), catalogue no. 75-001-XPE, Statistics Canada, http://www.statcan.gc.ca/pub/75-001-x/10606/9230-eng.pdf (accessed December 22, 2011).

Clark, W. (2007) Delayed Transitions of Young Adults, *Canadian Social Trends*, 84, (catalogue no. 11-008-XPE), Statistics Canada, http://www.statcan.gc.ca/pub/11-008-x/2007004/pdf/10311-eng.pdf (accessed December 22, 2011).

Conference Board of Canada (2007) *Ontario's looming labour shortage challenges*, Ottawa, Conference Board of Canada.

Côté, J. (2000) *Arrested Adulthood: The Changing Nature of Identity and Maturity in the Late-Modern Age*, New York, New York University Press.

Dallaire, C. and Denis, C. (2005) Asymmetrical Hybridities: Youths at Francophone Games in Canada, *Canadian Journal of Sociology*, 30(2), pp. 143-167.

Desmarais, D. and collaborators. (2000) *Détresse psychologique et insertion sociale des jeunes adultes. Un portrait complexe, une responsabilité collective [Psychological Distress and Social Integration of Young Adults. A Complex Portrait, a Collective Responsibility]*, Sainte-Foy (Canada), Les Publications du Québec.

Elder Jr., G. H., Kirkpatrick Johnson, M. and Crosnoe, R. (2004) The Emergence and Development of Life Course Theory, in Mortimer, J. T. and Shanahan, M. J. (eds.) *Handbook of the Life Course* (pp. 3-19), New York, Springer.

Emploi-Québec (2011) *Le marché du travail au Québec.* Perspectives à long terme 2011-2020 [The labour market in Québec. Long term perspectives 2011-2020]. Emploi Québec, Government of Québec, http://www.cetech.gouv.qc.ca/publications/pdf/WEB_Perspectives_a_long_terme_2011_2020.pdf (accessed December 22, 2011).

Franke, S. (2010) *Current Realities and Emerging Issues Facing Youth in Canada: An Analytical Framework for Public Policy Research*, Development and Evaluation, Ottawa, Policy Research Initiative.

Galland, O. (2007) *Boundless Youth: Studies in the Transition to Adulthood*, Oxford, The Bardwell Press.

Gaudet, S. (2001) La responsabilité dans les débuts de l'âge adulte [Responsibility at the Beginning of Adult Life], *Lien social et Politiques*, 46, pp. 71-83.

Government of Alberta (2006) *Guidelines for Supporting Successful Transitions for Children and Youth*, http://www.child.alberta.ca/home/documents/youthprograms/Guidelines_for_Supporting_Successful_Transitions_for_Children_and_Youth.pdf (accessed December 22, 2011).

Government of Alberta (2001) *Youth in Transition Policy Framework*, http://www.assembly.ab.ca/lao/library/egovdocs/alchs/2001/157610.pdf (accessed December 22, 2011).

Government of Ontario (2008) *The Review of the Roots of Youth Violence*, http://www.children.gov.on.ca/htdocs/English/documents/topics/youthandthelaw/rootsofyouthviolence-summary.pdf (accessed December 22, 2011).

Government of Québec (2001) *Québec Youth Policy – Bringing Youth into Québec's Mainstream*, http://www.jeunes.gouv.qc.ca/documentation/publications/documents/Sommaire-anglais.pdf (accessed December 22, 2011).

Government of Québec (2009) *Youth Action Strategy 2009-2014. Investing in Youth – Empowering Québec's Future*, http://www.jeunes.gouv.qc.ca/documentation/publications/documents/strategie-action-jeunesse-2009-2014_en.pdf (accessed December 22, 2011).

Jeffrey, K. (2008) *Youth Policy: What Works and What Doesn't? A Review of Youth Policy Models From Canada and Other Jurisdictions*, Toronto, United Way.

Jones, G. (2009) *Youth*, Cambridge, Polity Press.

Kroes, G. (2008) *Aboriginal Youth in Canada: Emerging Issues, Research Priorities, and Policy Implications. Report of the Roundtable on Aboriginal Youth*, Ottawa, Policy Research Initiative.

Leccardi, C. and Ruspini, E. (eds) (2006) *A New Youth? Young People, Generations and Family Life*, Aldershot, Ashgate.

Lock Kunz, J. and Syke, S. (2007) *From Mosaic to Harmony: Multicultural Canada in the 21st Century. Results of Regional Roundtables*, Ottawa, Policy Research Initiative.

Mitchell, B. (2006) *The Boomerang Age: Transitions to Adulthood in Families*, Vancouver, University of British Columbia Press.

Molgat, M. (2011) Les insuffisances de la perspective de l'émergence de l'âge adulte pour comprendre la jeunesse. Quelques enseignements à partir de figures de jeunes en difficulté» [The Insufficiencies of the Emerging Adulthood Perspective for Understanding Youth. Teachings From Figures of Disadvantaged Young People], in Goyette, M., Pontbriand, A. and Bellot, C. (eds) *Les transitions à la vie adulte des jeunes en difficulté [The Transitions to Adulthood of Disadvantaged Young People]* (pp. 33-55), Montréal, Presses de l'Université du Québec.

Molgat, M. (2008) Youth, Mobility and Work in Canada: Internal Migration, Immigration and Public Policy Implication, in Bendit, R. and Hahn, M. (eds) *Youth Transitions: Processes of Social Inclusion and Patterns of Vulnerability in a Globalised World* (pp. 115-131), Opladen, Barbara Budrich.

Molgat, M. (2007) Do Transitions and Social Structures Matter? How Emerging Adults Define Themselves as Adults, *Journal of Youth Studies*, 10(5), pp. 495-516.

Molgat, M. and Taylor, S. (forthcoming) *The Transitions of At-risk Youth from Adolescence to Adulthood.*

Molgat, M. and Vultur, M. (2009) L'insertion professionnelle des jeunes québécois diplômés et non diplômés de l'école secondaire. Quel rôle joue la famille? [The Professional Integration of Young Québeckers with and without High School Diplomas. What Role Does the Family Play?], *Recherches sociographiques*, 50(1), pp. 1-66.

Organisation for Economic Co-operation and Development (OECD) (2011) *Educational Attainment by Gender and Average Years Spent in Formal Education*, http://www.oecd.org/dataoecd/56/9/37863998.pdf (accessed December 22, 2011).

Parazelli, M. and Dessureault, S. (2010) Prévention précoce, nouvelle gestion publique et figures d'autorité [Early Prevention, New Public Management and Authority Figures], *Les politiques sociales*, 1-2, pp. 13-26.

Pilote, A. (2007) Suivre la trace ou faire son chemin? L'identité culturelle des jeunes en milieu francophone hors Québec [Following Tracks or Making Their Own Way? The Cultural Identity of Youth in Francophone Communities Outside Québec], *International Journal of Canadian Studies*, 36, pp. 229-251.

Pilote, A. and Magnan M.-O. (2008) L'école de la minorité francophone au Canada: L'institution à l'épreuve des acteurs [Francophone Minority Schools in Canada: Institutions Resisting Actors], in Thériault, J.-Y., Gilbert, A. and Cardinal, L. (eds) *L'espace francophone en milieu minoritaire au Canada: Nouveaux enjeux, nouvelles mobilisations* (pp. 275-317), Montreal, Fides.

Plaza, D. (2006) The Construction of a Segmented Hybrid Identity Among One-and-a-Half-Generation and Second-Generation Indo-Caribbean and African Caribbean Canadians, *Identity: An International Journal of Theory and Research*, 6(3), pp. 207-229.

Public Health Agency of Canada (2011) *The Chief Public Health Officers Report on the State of Public Health in Canada 2011 – Youth and Young Adults – Life in* Transition, Government of Canada, http://www.phac-aspc.gc.ca/cphorsphc-respcacsp/2011/pdf/cpho-resp-2011-eng.pdf (accessed December 22, 2011).

Settersten Jr., R. A. (2005) Social Policy and the Transition to Adulthood: Toward Stronger Institutions and Individual Capacities, in Settersten Jr., R. A., Furstenberg Jr., F. F. and Rumbaut, R. (eds) *On the frontier of adulthood: Theory, research and public policy* (pp. 534-560), Chicago, University of Chicago Press.

Statistics Canada (2007) 2006 Census: *Family portrait – Continuity and change in Canadian families and households in 2006 – Findings*, catalogue No 97-553-XWE2006001, Statistics Canada, http://www12.statcan.ca/census-recensement/2006/as-sa/97-553/pdf/97-553-XIE2006001.pdf (accessed December 22, 2011).

Sykes, S. (2008) *Life on the Reef in the Canadian Ocean: The 'New' Second Generation in Canada, Discussion Paper*, Ottawa, Policy Research Initiative.

Tremblay, D.-G. (2003) Juggling youth unemployment and employment precariousness in Canada and Quebec: from a social to a more liberal approach to employment policies, in Roulleau-Berger, L. (ed) *Youth and Work in the Post-Industrial City of North America and Europe* (pp. 175-189), Brill, Leiden-Boston.

3. Public debates and sociological research based on the semantic of autonomy: The case of French young people

By Vincenzo Cicchelli

Autonomy is the situation where young people have the necessary support, resources and opportunities to chose to live independently, to run their own lives
and to have full social and political participation in all sectors of everyday life,
and be able to take independent decisions.

Policy Paper on Youth Autonomy, Adopted by the Council of Members, 23-24
April 2004, Brussels.

One of the departure points in examining adolescence and youth should
be, in my view, to consider them as a sociological object as well as an object of political-administrative intervention. The spread of social and human sciences knowledge throughout contemporary society has affected
the craft of the sociologist in two ways. On the one hand, research objects
are now, more than ever, framed by public opinion, social debates and
political decisions while on the other, social scientists themselves, *via*
their expertise, have contributed to the injection of sociological ideas into
the universe of social phenomena (Giddens, 1991).

This state of affairs does not only concern the areas of adolescence
and youth, and is not completely new either, having first appeared at the
outset of sociological reflection on these two life stages: for example,
from the 1920s onwards in the United States, where early empirical research on young gang members (Thrasher, 1927; Zorbaugh, 1929), *jack
rollers* (Shaw, 1930), and *flappers* (Thomas, 1923) was carried out in the
specific urban context of Chicago. For the first time, the way the social
sciences, public opinion and public authorities looked at youth issues
converged significantly, especially since local authority bodies and phil-
anthropic foundations funded such research.

Broader knowledge circulation

More than eighty years later, sociological studies, research commissions, administrative data, and public policies continue to shape these two life stages and to attribute content and representations to them (Wyn and White, 1997).

I have already shown that there is some credence to this view by setting out the timeline for how French sociology found an incentive to look at certain issues and to focus on specific age groups (Cicchelli and Pugeault, 2006). I did not in any way assume a causal link between political debate, administrative needs and the specific content of sociological research. Such a position would have ignored the relative autonomy of sociological works. The sociological craft is indeed based on: a) long research periods; b) obtaining results that do not necessarily reflect an administrative decision; c) preference to critical views; d) independence of sociologists from decision-makers; e) the weak impact of action-research on career paths. It is, on the contrary, more truthful to claim that political debate and scientific research *converge* on the necessity and urgency of solving specific problems and focusing on some specific populations.

Thus, despite pursuing divergent objectives (*decision* versus *knowledge*), political debate and sociological research have in fact created three age categories in France: *young people*, *young adults* and, lastly, *adolescents*. While in the 1970s and 1980s, the question of the professional and social insertion[1] of young people generated extensive research on transition from youth to adulthood, young adults attracted attention during the second half of the 1990s – when the issue of how families and the State should support students and unemployed young people came to the forefront. Following that period, a shift in the field of risks has led to attention being directed to a new category, the *adolescent at risk* (with related issues such as prevalence and prevention). Finally, the injunction to participate in associative life and in society in the broadest sense refers to teenagers, young adults and young people.

---

1   In French public debate, the expression 'social insertion' is often used for young people experiencing social exclusion, marginality, poverty, unemployment. The expression 'social integration' is more related to the questions of ethnicity.

A common semantic based on autonomy

The recourse to scientific expertise in order to support analyses and to provide a rationale for public policies, the spread of sociological and psychological knowledge, and the funding of research have given rise to a powerful interaction of reciprocal influences in discourses that I have called *semantic coincidences*.

I strongly support the idea that over the past twenty years a common semantic around youth has emerged and that autonomy is the key word (Cicchelli, 2011*a*). The definitions of autonomy used in political, sociological and administrative discourses are generally related to the urgency of specific social problems. However, the core of this common semantic refers to the *paradox* of autonomy and heteronomy. In a more uncertain world (Leccardi, 2005; Blossfeld and Mills, 2005), the lengthening of the period of youth can explain the increase in the social dependency of young people. Young people are socialized by school and supported by their family for a greater length of time than in the past. As children stay in school longer, they are dependent on their families for longer. Actually, a momentous body of social discourses in the last two decades has focused on the issue of the dependency of young people.

Autonomy is an unmistakable phenomenon of modern youth (young people are autonomous in several realms like fashion, tastes, music, peer group relationships, dating, etc., see Galland, 2010), but at the same time young people are more dependent than ever on their parents, school and public policies. In France, public policies are focused on encouraging the professional and social integration of young people, widening their full and equal participation in civil society, and expanding their international mobility.

Five ideal-types of autonomy

Unsurprisingly, autonomy has been defined for twenty years in several different ways in order to enhance young people's ability: a) to manage a transition to adulthood that has been complicated by changes in the labour market, namely by economic recessions (Morin, 2009), and by the inflation of qualifications and their associated devaluation; b) to ease their increasing dependence on their families, especially when they are students or unemployed; c) to develop their psycho-social maturity to enable them to protect themselves from all kinds of epidemiological and health risks; d) to commit to a personal and/or associative project that will have a positive impact on solidarity, the environment and so on; e) to acquire new capacities in order to choose the way in which they would like to live. In this case, 'autonomy' is the equivalent in French public debates of 'empowerment' in the Anglo-Saxon world. People are autonomous when they run their own lives.

In the following pages, we will look at each ideal type[2] of autonomy, obtained by combining public and political debates, sociological research and expertise.

a) In France, the lengthening of the period of youth is linked to difficulties concerning professional and social integration (Galland, 2007). The transition from childhood to adulthood is becoming increasingly complex. In this context, the pathways of young people are becoming more reversible than in the past. The crossings of thresholds are no longer definitive events and individuals can go back and forth between situations that used to be permanent states. Due to the increase in unemployment and the greater flexibility, as well as lack of clear links, between the educational environment and the labour market, young people can continue with their education whilst having a part-time internship or a flexible job. Whereas in the past, the steps towards adulthood were marked by normalised sequences and orders, today we are witnessing a multiplicity, reversibility and simultaneity of the situations of young adults (Loncle, 2010).

In this case, becoming autonomous means being able to escape from the increase in social dependency, to integrate into the labour market and to achieve a transition to adulthood in order to avoid "misleading trajectories" (EGRIS, 2001; Walther et al., 2002).

b) Since children stay in school longer, they are dependent longer on their families, and not just for reasons of economic hard times. From adolescence onwards, and while the individual still belongs to his/her family, familial socialization can be understood as a process of progressive integration of younger persons in which both parents and children unite in a complex partnership that requires a strong reciprocal support.

As long as children have not completed their studies and begun a meaningful first job (not just an 'odd job'), their parents consider that their

---

2   According to German sociologist Max Weber, an ideal type is a constructed ideal that is used to approximate reality by selecting and accentuating certain of its elements.

task of upbringing is not yet complete (Singly and Cicchelli, 2003). At the same time young people must also demonstrate that they are not waiting for the end of their schooling and the beginning of a 'real' installation in professional life before becoming autonomous. Even very young children must show some autonomy (Glevarec, 2010) – their parents must not repress the expression of their needs – while at the same time being objectively kept in a dependent situation for a long time. Each child must be 'born' socially, and must gradually earn his/her place within the generations. Parents and children negotiate to reach an agreement establishing the degree of each young person's autonomy.

How do adolescents and subsequently young adults still belong to their families while endeavouring to attain autonomy? Autonomy and heteronomy join forces and overlap in meaning; it is then up to each young adult to determine their modes of expression. The feeling of being autonomous is achieved in a number of ways that vary in content and in timing according to the individual; each person is autonomous in as much as he/she can claim to be heteronymous in one regard and autonomous in another (Cicchelli and Martin, 2004). Moreover, the dialectic between autonomy and heteronomy shapes all interactions between young people and adults.

The great debate in France since the discovery of an increasing dependence of young people centers around how they can cope with this new social and economic situation. Public intervention should therefore contribute to promoting a re-formulation of the social support system as well as intergenerational support, instead of simply waiting for the professional integration of young people. Becoming autonomous means getting some distance from overwhelming parental influence and strong economic dependency.

c) Historians of youth show that accounts of young people in the twentieth century have constantly teetered between fear and hope: the young were viewed as rebels as well as being depicted as passive subjects. They were alternatively held responsible for destroying the social bond with their wild violence, or anointed with messianic virtues (Passerini, 1996).

After having been considered for a long time as a danger – this representation has never totally disappeared, as the French riots of November 2005 have shown (Cicchelli et al., 2007) – youth has come to be seen as a demographic requiring protection. In recent years, the new moral panic about adolescents at risk has emerged in France. How are adolescents facing multiple risks (such as sexual abuse, drug and tobacco addictions, teenage pregnancies, violence, and sexually transmitted diseases)? In this specific case, an adolescent is considered autonomous if he/she is able to avoid these risks, which are associated with a lack of maturity and judgment. This is to be achieved through promoting an adolescent's assertiveness, self-confidence and self-esteem to enable them to protect themselves.

d) Youth has recently been considered as human capital that can be used as a long-term investment in facing the uncertainties of contemporary society. New forms of involvement in the public sphere were born after the decline of traditional social institutions in which young people had participated, such as political parties, trade unions, and popular education movements. These classic agencies of political socialization have lost much of their appeal among young people, and other institutions did not take their place. Above all, however, what seems to have declined is the way young people are connected with these agencies. A certain militant style, typical of French modernity, has been devalued (Ion, Franguiadakis and Viot, 2005), in favour of a more ephemeral and elective participation in a collective mobilisation. The emerging movements in the fields of world justice, ecology, human rights, meeting events like the World Youth Days, the defence of great causes, the persistence or protest participation – petitions, strikes, street manifestations – (Muxel, 2001) thus demonstrates that the occupation of public space is a feature of political socialization of French young people. "A true socialization to social protest and to the concrete expression of one's disappointment" really exists (Bréchon, 2001, p. 68). Young people develop a less conformist, more critical, perhaps more instrumental attitude toward the political sphere. Their involvements are certainly more pragmatic.

The semantic associated with participation is based upon four key words: autonomy, project, engagement, and responsibility. On these grounds, several institutional programs have been developed in which personal autonomy means the capacity to initiate active citizenship and social participation. Only if autonomous can a young person become a member of the social body (Cicchelli, 2009).

e) Autonomy can finally mean the capacity of young people to be self-reflective, to deliberate, to judge, to choose among alternatives in the face of circumstance and to act upon different possible courses of action. Autonomous people are supposed to make meaningful decisions in their lives.

This last definition of autonomy seems to be very well suited to the increase of youth mobility throughout Europe (and beyond). An analysis of the European Union's various formal encouragements to the mobility of young people shows that the EU's intent is to increase human and social capital among European population groups (Barrington-Leach *et al.*, 2007). Mobility, which is essential to knowledge based societies, is thus naturally integrated into this *empowerment* project. A study conducted by interviews on the mobilities of Erasmus students in Europe (Cicchelli, 2012) shows that stays in foreign countries are seen by most of these students as an opportunity to discover a society whose cultural codes are not well known to them. From their perspective, familiarity with their own society's culture has become insufficient to understand the global society in which they live. An education in which openness is a virtue, is in their eyes founded on enlarging their circle of relations through international encounters, on being able to orient themselves among the various types of European societies, and on being able to situate themselves on different geographical levels (sub-national, national and transnational). Some characteristics of these travels continue to strike the imagination, often thanks to the literary and cinematographic productions of juvenile journeys through which emerge the dialectics of *self-discovery* and *meeting others,* in a framework far from home (Cicchelli, 2010). The mobility of students is without doubt inherited from an ancient tendency for the elites to favour cosmopolitanism. Its novelty resides in the fact that, for the first time, these mobilities are favoured by European institutions (Cicchelli, 2011*b*).

The ambivalence of autonomy

As we have seen, the same word, autonomy, is used in public debates as well as in scientific research to refer to different situations in young lives. The condition that ensures that such discourses of autonomy will be formulated and that they will lead to public policies that support young people is the dual dimension of autonomy: in all meanings of the word 'autonomy' shown above, young people are supposed to become independent (as a result of public and administrative intervention), although most of the support frameworks are based on the assumption that they are already a little autonomous. The autonomy of young people is therefore an ambivalent virtue: it is conceived both as starting point and as status, simultaneously as an initial condition and as a program.

The use of this word in political discourse unveils the anxieties of adults over the vulnerability of young people. What is important to retain is a sense of duty among adults to protect and educate the younger generations. Basically, what is at stake is the development of a series of *capabilities* in young people in the realms of ethical judgments, school success and social interaction.

In the context of longer studies, the prolonging of dependence is not simply a formality, either for parents or for young people. This explains the approach adopted by parents in defining the limits of their care and the manner in which it is to be provided; the manner in which this is done will be conditioned by the ability or otherwise of the young adult to behave as a *responsible* person. In other words, when parenting continues, parents oversee results at school and management of the money they give to their children. Parents ask their children for proof of maturity.

The prolonging of assistance is much less positively regarded when it is made necessary by the professional insecurity of the young adult, particularly in the case of those with few educational qualifications who have repeatedly tried to integrate into the labour market. The problem of *prolonging assistance*, which in the eyes of the individual concerned risks breeding *the need for aid*, is more complicated than when the young adult is studying for a degree or diploma. For families in this position, the development of an individual socially integrated with respect to professional and family status entails greater difficulties. Unemployed young adults living in the family home appear to have as close a relationship with their parents as students. However, in cases where financial resources are provided essentially by the parents, effective dialogue between the two generations is below average (Galland, 1997). More than 50% of unemployed young adults who have always lived with their parents admit that cohabitation has its problems, whereas the proportion of employed persons and students living in similar conditions is far less significant (Villeneuve-Gokalp, 2000)[3].

How does one go about ensuring that the *assistance* provided is not transformed into *permanent support*? Encouraging young people to show their sense of personal responsibility and checking that duties are really carried out is one of the tools to ensure the first without falling into the trap of the second, as is asking for proof of maturity while maintaining subtle and efficient oversight and supervisory measures during such periods.

---

3   On the notion of intergenerational ambivalence when young people abandon their studies and during the process of school-to-work transition, see Molgat (2007).

Moreover these considerations allow us to shed light on two central questions related to the autonomy of young people in contemporary societies: what kinds of merits are the adults measuring? What abilities are adults trying to develop among young people? We are witnessing the emergence of a conception of young people in terms of *capabilities*. Seeing young people in this way implies supporting their autonomy, calling on their sense of responsibility, betting on their ability to set up projects and carry them out – whether or not those capacities are already acquired or in the process of being acquired.

This chapter has started with the largely shared assumption that the circulation of knowledge between different kinds of spheres of discourses (media, scientific, policy and administrative discourses) is a major feature of knowledge-based societies. I have intended to address both adolescence and youth as an object of knowledge as well as an object of policy intervention. After providing a short history of the ways in which political discourses have converged with scientific research and constructed age categories, I have suggested an analysis of the five semantic coincidences that one can find when the question of youth autonomy is assessed in contemporary France. Finally, students, young unemployed people, 'at risk' adolescents and young adults are supported by all kinds of agencies, institutions and organizations in France. Entry to adulthood is nowadays accomplished through a process of distinction or individualisation of biographical pathways framed by institutions and authorities of supervision or mediation. Young people have never been so singular *and* at the same time socially dependent, supervised and monitored by adults (Cicchelli, forthcoming).

Bibliography

Barrington-Leach, L. et al. (2007) *Investing in youth: an empowerment strategy*, Bureau of European Policy Advisers (BEPA), http://ec.europa.eu/dgs/policy_ advisers/publications/docs/Investing_in_Youth_25_April_fin.pdf (accessed June 14 2012).

Blossfeld, H.-P. and Mills, M. (2005) Globalization, uncertainty and the early life course: A theoretical framework, in Blossfeld H.-P., Klijzing E., Mills M. and Kurz K. (eds) *Globalization, Uncertainty and Youth in Society* (pp. 1-24), London and New York, Routledge.

Bréchon, P. (2001) Moins politisés, mais plus protestataires, in Galland, O. and Roudet, B. (eds) *Les valeurs des jeunes. Tendances en France depuis 20 ans*, Paris, Injep/L'Harmattan.

Cicchelli, V. (2001) La construction de l'autonomie. Parents et jeunes adultes face aux études, Paris, Presses Universitaires de France (PUF).

68 Vincenzo Cicchelli

Cicchelli, V. (2009) The Contemporary Engagement of Young People in France: Normative Injunctions, Institutional Programs, and the Multiplying Forms of Grouping, *Italian Journal of Sociology of Education*, 2, pp. 104-126.

Cicchelli, V. (2010) Les legs du voyage de formation à la *Bildung* cosmopolite, *Le Télémaque. Philosophie, Education, Société*, 38, pp. 57-70.

Cicchelli, V. (2011a) Société des savoirs et production sociologique: l'exemple de la jeunesse Histoire@Politique. *Politique, culture, société, Revue électronique du Centre d'Histoire de Science Po*, 14 http://www.histoire-politique.fr/index.php?numero=14&rub=dossier&item=133 (accessed 17 june 2012).

Cicchelli, V. (2011b) The Cosmopolitan 'Bildung' of Erasmus students' going abroad, in Hébert Y. and Abdi A. (eds) *Critical Perspectives on International Education*, Rotterdam/Taipei, Sense Publishers.

Cicchelli, V. (forthcoming) *L'autonomie de la jeunesse étudiante: questions politiques, questions sociales*, Paris, La Documentation Française.

Cicchelli, V. (2012) *L'esprit cosmopolite*. Voyages de formation des jeunes en Europe, Paris, Presses de SciencesPo.

Cicchelli, V. and Martin, C. (2004) Young Adults in France: Becoming Adult in the Context of Increased Autonomy and Dependency, *Journal of Comparative Family Studies, 35(4)*, pp. 615-626.

Cicchelli, V. and Pugeault-Cicchelli, C. (2006) Les recherches sociologiques sur la jeunesse en France et leurs liens avec les préoccupations politico-administratives, *Papers. Revista de Sociologia, 79*, pp. 101-120.

Cicchelli, V., Galland, O., de Maillard, J. and Misset, S. (2007) Les jeunes émeutiers de novembre 2005. Retour sur le terrain, *Le Débat, 145*, pp. 165-181.

European Group for Integrated Social Research (EGRIS) (2001) Misleading Trajectories: Transition Dilemmas of Young Adults in Europe, *Journal of Youth Studies, 4(1)*, pp. 01-118.

Galland, O. (1997) Chômage et relations entre générations, *Économie et Statistique, 304-305, 4/5*, pp. 179-190.

Galland, O. (2007) *Boundless Youth: Studies in the Transition to Adulthood*, Oxford, The Bardwell Press.

Galland, O. (2010) Introduction: une nouvelle classe d'âge?, *Ethnologie française, 1*, pp. 5-10.

Giddens, A. (1991) *The Consequences of Modernity*, Cambridge, Polity Press.

Glevarec, H. (2010) *La culture de la chambre. Préadolescence et culture contemporaine dans l'espace familial*, Paris, Ministère de la Culture et de la communication.

Ion, J., Franguiadakis, S. and Viot P. (2005) *Militer aujourd'hui*, Paris, Autrement.

Leccardi, C. (2005) Facing uncertainty: Temporality and biographies in the new century, *Young – Journal of Youth Research, 13(2)*, pp. 123-146.

Loncle, P. (2010) *Politiques de jeunesse. Les défis majeurs de l'intégration*, Rennes, Presses universitaires de Rennes (PUR).

Molgat, M. (2007) Capital social et ambivalence intergénérationnelle: le soutien parental aux jeunes qui ont quitté les études secondaires sans diplôme, *Enfances, Familles, Générations, 7*, http://id.erudit.org/iderudit/017791ar (June 17 2012).

Morin, E. (2009) *La peur du déclassement*, Paris, Le Seuil.

Muxel, A. (2001) *L'expérience politique des jeunes*, Paris, Presses de Sciences-Po.

Pasquier, D. (2005) Cultures lycéennes. La tyrannie de la majorité, Paris, Autrement.

Passerini, L. (1996) La jeunesse comme métaphore du changement social. Deux débats sur les jeunes: l'Italie fasciste, l'Amérique des années cinquante, in Levi, G. and Schmitt, J.-C., (eds), *Histoire des jeunes en Occident* (pp. 339-408), Paris, Le Seuil.

Shaw, C. R. (1930) *The Jack-Roller: A Delinquent Boy's Own Story*, Chicago, The University of Chicago Press.

Singly, F. de and Cicchelli, V. (2003) Contemporary Families: Social Reproduction and Personal Fulfillment, in Kertzer, D. and Barbagli, M. (eds) *Family Life in the Twentieth Century* (pp. 311-349), London, Yale University Press.

Thomas, W. I. (1923) *The Unadjusted Girl*, Boston, Little-Brown & Co.

Thrasher, F.M. (1927) *The Gang*, Chicago, University of Chicago Press.

Van de Velde, C. (2008) *Devenir adulte. Sociologie comparée de la jeunesse en Europe*, Paris, Presses Universitaires de France (PUF).

Villeneuve-Gokalp, C. (2000) Les jeunes partent toujours au même âge de chez leurs parents, *Economie et Statistique, 337-338*, p. 61-80.

Walther, A. et al. (eds) (2002) Misleading Trajectories – Integration Policies for Young People in Europe?, Opladen, Leske + Budrich.

Wyn, J. and White, R. (1997) *Rethinking Youth*, Thousand Oaks, Sage.

Zorbaugh, H. W. (1929) *The Gold Coast and the Slum*, Chicago, University of Chicago Press.

4. A 'Bottom-up' Approach to Youth Development and Policy in the United States

By David M. Hansen

Since the turn of the 21st century, there have been concerted efforts in the United States – mainly from grass-roots and non-profit agencies – to make explicit society's obligations and roles in supporting youths' preparation for and full participation in society. These efforts are partly in response to a long-standing approach to youth policy that is based on the belief that 'problem-free' youth equals 'fully prepared' youth (Pittman, Irby, and Ferber, 2000), which may partially account for the United States minimalist approach to youth policy; that is, create policy when there is a problem to alleviate. To accomplish the objective of this chapter – to outline why we need youth policy in the United States (minimal or not) that is firmly rooted in youth-apithology[1] and youth-practice – it is first necessary to situate youth policy making and participation within the broader socio-cultural and historical context of the United States. That said, I am not a policy-maker, but a researcher focused on youth-apithology rather than on youth pathology; I view youth-policy through a normative human development lens. Most policy made in the United States that could be construed as youth-policy, however, does not emanate from an apithological understanding of youth, which is not surprising given few policy-makers have formal training in disciplines related to youth. At the core of the issues discussed here is how evidence in the form of theory, research, and practice on normative, healthy youth development can inform policy makers and policy making in the United States. Before discussing how relevant findings from research on youth development and practice can inform policy makers, it is important to

---

1   My research team and I have recently begun to use the term 'apithology' and its derivatives to refer to youth development that connotes healthful psychological, social, civic, etc. growth. This is an attempt to avoid the stigma often associated with the disciplines of 'positive' development/psychology or youth development proper, which struggle for scientific legitimacy.

situate the discussion within the peculiar approach to issues of equity, participation, and youth policy in the United States.

A 'Bottom-up' Approach to Youth Policy in the United States

Some of the struggle the United States faces in meeting its obligation to fully prepare its youth for participation in adult collective society originates in a long-standing philosophy, rooted in the formation of the nation, about *who* bears responsibility for the preparation of youth for adult life and *what* it means to be fully prepared. From a historical perspective, the individual and the family have borne much of the responsibility; there persists a cultural view that if an individual is unprepared for adult life, the individual and the family are to blame (Mintz, 2004). Colloquial phrases such as "a land of opportunities" and "pull yourself up by your own bootstraps" belie the belief that it is up to the individual to leverage existing opportunities and forge their own success, which makes failing to 'succeed' primarily an individual failure. The responsibilities of government, policy, and institutions to help prepare youth have been downplayed relative to individuals and family, although formal education has become one notable exception. In the relative absence of youth-policy, and, amid a persistent individualist philosophy, individuals and non-governmental organizations have come to assume major responsibility for supporting youths' full participation in society. The United States, then, has a 'bottom-up' approach to youth participation: it relies on grass-roots initiatives and non-governmental entities, especially non-profit organizations, to address issues of equity and participation, which may explain the minimal existence of non-education related youth policy.

With this bottom-up approach as the background for issues of equity, participation, and youth policy, I highlight two sources of research evidence that can, and, in my opinion, *should* inform youth policy. In a final section I suggest implications for policy in the United States. In order to maintain precision in communication, the term 'youth' is used to refer to individuals between the ages of 18 and approximately 25[2], while the term

---

2 This age range roughly corresponds to the years spent in college-for those who are college bound-and before entering the labor market full-time. Although some attempt to treat this period as a distinct developmental stage (e.g., "emerging adulthood), which implies a biological component, its definition is more malleable than previous periods. Thus I prefer to separate adolescence in the manner specified.

'adolescent' is in reference to individuals between the ages of ~12 and 18 (corresponding to mandatory middle school and high school years of education in the United States).

Adolescent Development in Organized Activities

Organized activities for adolescents, including community-based programs (e.g., YMCA/YWCA) and extracurricular activities, have been consistently identified as settings that support adolescents' learning in general, and learning of adult-like competencies in particular (Eccles, Barber, Stone, and Hunt, 2003; Eccles and Templeton, 2002; Mahoney, Larson, Eccles, and Lord, 2005; National Research Council and Institute of Medicine, 2002). Adolescents appear, for example, to learn strategic planning skills for influencing institutions (Larson and Hansen, 2005), critical civic 'praxis' (Ginwright and Cammarota, 2007), and initiative and personal agency (Larson, Hansen, and Walker, 2005). The importance of these skills and competencies for adult life, for example, has increased as 'high performance' global economies demand individuals who can innovate and solve complex problems while working with a wider range of diverse groups (Larson and Hansen, 2005; SCANS, 1991). Such learning is not however a universal characteristic of participation in any organized activities. Instead, the type of organized activity and its aims (e.g., civic activism) affect what is learned (Hansen, Larson, and Dworkin, 2003; Larson, Hansen, and Moneta, 2006; Hansen, Crawford, and Jessop, 2011). Programs that aim to involve adolescents in social change, for instance, create opportunities to engage in complex, critical thinking and strategic planning around civic issues, whereas other programs that aim to provide a place to participate in sports or arts create a different set of learning opportunities.

Emerging research suggests that organized activities support adolescents' process of addressing numerous developmental tasks (Halpern, 2005; Heath, 1998; Hansen and Moore, 2011; Larson, 2000). One example of a developmental task of adolescence is learning to engage with challenge. Emerging theory suggests that learning to engage with challenge – the linking of intrinsic motivation (e.g., enjoyment) with challenges of working on a goal or project – represents progress toward becoming an agentic adult, and that organized activities support its development (Csikszentmihalyi, 1990; Hansen and Moore, 2011; Larson,

2000; Larson, Hansen, and Walker, 2005). Engaging with challenge goes beyond transitory states of motivation or interest that occur when engaging in an enjoyable activity (e.g., entertainment). Rather it requires sustained motivation to achieve or work toward an objective over time when faced with obstacles or challenges that threaten to derail progress. Learning to engage with challenge emanates from within individuals as they gradually become motivated to meet or address the challenges or obstacles.

What conditions of organized activities support adolescents' addressing relevant developmental tasks? First, adolescent participation in organized activities in the United States is generally *voluntary* and *self-determined*. Research and theory indicate that self-determination is an important component for the exercise and development of agency skills (e.g., Larson and Rusk, in press; Ryan and Deci, 2000), such as learning to engage with challenge. Second, many organized activities provide distinct opportunities for adolescents' to have *authentic experiences* (Camino, 2000, 2005; Heath 1994, 1998; Larson and Walker, 2006; Larson and Hansen, 2005; Larson, Hansen, and Walker, 2005). Authentic experiences reflect operating within real-world and real-time conditions and constraints typically faced by adults: accomplishing goals or objectives when there are multiple actors with competing objectives, ill-defined problems or tasks, institutional and human systems with inherent paradoxes and modes of operation that are seemingly irrational, actions that cause unintended consequences, etc. (Heath, 1998; Larson and Angus, 2011; Larson and Hansen, 2005; Okagaki and Sternberg, 1990). In contrast to authentic experiences, formal education, where adolescents spend a large portion of their day, is characterized by well-defined tasks and problems with clear-cut solutions and means to solve them; in many ways the educational setting is the antithesis of real-world, authentic experiences. Third, recent research further indicates that the conditions of organized activities support the development of agency skills. According to Self-Determination Theory (SDT), humans have a basic need for autonomy – to initiate and engage in behaviors that will lead to a desired goal (Deci and Ryan, 2000). Autonomy supportive climates foster a sense of autonomy by providing opportunities for an individual to make choices and self-determine goals and objectives. In a study evaluating the over-time associations between the conditions of one type of organized activity and adolescent development, those activities characterized by higher autonomy support fostered an increase in adolescents' engagement with challenge over one year (Hansen and Moore, 2011). Autonomy supportive conditions have also been linked in qualitative research to adolescents' development of *new modes of thinking*, such as strategic planning skills (Larson and Hansen, 2005). From a developmental perspective, then, the developmental process in organized activities – voluntary participation → supportive conditions → engaging with challenge and new modes of thinking – supports the development of adolescents' agency-related skills. I suggest, as have others, that these skills are fundamental to adult life, including full participation in society (Halpern, 2005; Hansen, Crawford, and Jessop, 2011; Heath, 1998; Larson, 2000).

The discussion thus far has avoided mention of the broader context of participation, e.g., ethnicity, race, socioeconomic status, poverty, institutional discrimination, etc. (Bronfrenbrenner, 1979; Evans and English, 2002; Halpern, 2005; Kraus, Piff, and Keltner, 2011; Lerner, 2004; McLoyd, 1998; Sherrod, 2008). Instead, I have focused on the potential of the organized activity setting to support adolescent and youth participation. In this section, I will situate adolescent development within this broader context. "Growing up poor, in a devalued group, and in a devalued and neglected neighborhood profoundly affects adolescents' ability to address the tasks of that age period" (Halpern, 2005, p. 13). We know, for example, that growing up in a low-income, urban community places additional stressors on individuals (Attar, Guerra, and Tolan, 1994; Brooks-Gunn, Klebanov, and Liaw, 1995; Brown, Cowen, Hightower, and Lotyczewski, 1986; Dubow, Tisak, Causey, Hryshko, and Reid, 1991; Rutter, 1981; Wachs, 1992), and these conditions have been associated with cognitive and socio-emotional developmental delays (Evans and English, 2002; Kraus, Piff, and Keltner, 2011; McLoyd, 1998). The damaging effects of exposure to persistent socioeconomic disadvantage also extend to adolescent and youth participation in society. For example, living in high poverty, urban communities can lead to skepticism and a lower perception of personal agency among adolescents (Halpern, 2005), which translates into less civic involvement over time (Jankowski 1992, 2002; Sherrod, 2003). What role, then, do organized activities play in the lives of disadvantaged adolescents?

Qualitative research on development among disadvantaged adolescents participating in organized activities suggests these programs can provide opportunities for adolescents to engage in activities that support their development in general (e.g., socioemotional development) *and* their preparation for participation in society in particular (Camino, 2000; Ginwright and Cammarota, 2007; Larson and Hansen, 2005; Zeldin, 2004). For example, a study of urban adolescents and young adults involvement in the governance structure of organized activity programs found that the participants increased a sense of agency, developed their civic identity, and increased their connection to other adults in the community (social capital: Zeldin, 2004). Participation in such activities can also support the development of different civic competencies among disadvantaged adolescents, such as community-level change strategies (Camino, 2000; Hansen, Crawford, and Jessop, 2011; Hansen and Larson, 2005). As a whole, then, organized activities in the United States are one setting in adolescents' lives that can be supportive of their development in general, and, more specifically, of their preparation and participation in society. From a developmental viewpoint, the organized activity setting in the United States provides adolescents an initial entrée into the realm of participation and citizenship.

Neuropsychological Foundations of Adolescent Participation

The emerging research from social sciences provides suggestive evidence that the conditions of organized activities support adolescents' agency-related skill development. From a social or psychological perspective, then, adolescents' involvement in organized activities in the United States provides opportunities to learn important skills for participation in society. But research from the field of neuroscience also indicates that adolescence may be a 'critical' or 'optimal' period during which foundations for agency-related skills can be learned. Thus, although inclusion of neuroscience research findings in a chapter on equity, participation, and youth policy may seem odd to some, the remarkable advances in understanding adolescent brain development provides additional and strong imperatives for how society prepares its adolescents and youth for full participation.

Research findings from cognitive and neuroscience fields suggests that adolescents are *neuro-developmentally primed* to integrate complex, higher-order, behavioral, cognitive, and emotional/motivational functioning across cortical and subcortical regions. The physiological process of reorganization includes a substantial increase (overproduction) of neurons unparalleled since early childhood (especially in the prefrontal cortex), a corresponding pruning or elimination of neurons that are unused or underutilized because their synaptic connections do not result in new functionally adaptive behavior or thinking, and the myelination of new axonal pathways between regions, especially between the prefrontal cortex and other regions

(Giedd, 2008; Keating, 2000; Spear, 2000). Although structural and functional changes in the brain may continue into the 30s (Griedd, 2008), the massive overproduction and pruning process occurs before age 16 (Spear, 2000). The end-result of this major brain remodeling is an individual who is capable of more adult-like skills, competencies, and disposition.

Of particular importance in this remodeling process is the role that the prefrontal cortex plays. The prefrontal cortex (PFC), which is implicated in the types of higher-order, complex thinking skills, becomes functionally integrated with all other brain regions (e.g., motivation/emotion) and assumes greater control over cognition and behavior (Giedd, 2009; Goldberg, 2009; Keating, 2000; Kuhn and Franklin, 2006; Luna *et al.*, 2001; Mascolo, Fischer, and Neimeyer, 1999; Spear, 2000). What this means practically is that an individual can, for the first time in her life, draw on all of the brains resources – learning, emotion, motivation, logic – to solve problems, set and achieve goals, create personal and social purpose and give meaning to learning, etc. (This integration may partly explain why adolescents often ask teachers "why do I need to know this?" or "how is this relevant for me?"). We have suggested elsewhere that these changes help explain why adolescents become increasingly concerned that their learning is purposeful and meaningful (Hansen, Crawford, and Jessop, 2011).

What is often overlooked or downplayed in neuroscience research is the role that experience plays in 'sculpting' the remodeling and ultimately the functional utility of the resultant skills, competencies, and dispositions. There is ample evidence, however, that experience, rather than simple biological or neurological maturation, affects if and how abilities and competencies are formed, e.g., experience affects the brain's "functional wiring diagram" (Damasio, 2010; Keating, 2004; Markham and Greenbough, 2004; Spear, 2000). But just as importantly, it is not just any experience that will support the ultimate functional utility of these skills, competencies, and dispositions. I propose that only experiences that elicit and require complex thinking and behavior indicative higher-order skills (e.g., agency-related skills) will support the development of qualitatively more complex, adaptive skills, competencies, and dispositions, and therefore of the types that will support full participation and citizenship. Stated differently, not all experiences have the same potential to shape the functional 'wiring diagram' in the remodeling process.

Implications for Youth Policy in the United States

In this last section I will focus on the practical implications of the research findings reviewed here, and, where appropriate, make suggestions
for policy within the United States context. In general, there is fairly
widespread opinion in the United States that in order for today's adolescents and youth to thrive as adults in the 21st century they will need a
complex set of skills, competencies, and dispositions. It is also becoming
clearer that rich developmental experience is important, if not essential,
for adolescents to develop these real-world skills, competencies, and dispositions, especially those that support engaged citizenship. While non-
educational youth policy is minimal in the United States, the emergent research findings strongly suggest a need for policy to support adolescent
and youth development beyond the traditional boundaries of formal education. Relying on the traditional teaching methods of education alone, I
propose, will limit adolescents' development of important 21st century
agency-related competencies: at worst it could stunt such development.
For adolescents, the organized activity setting is one of the few settings in
their lives that has the potential to support development of important
skills and offers them initial entrée into adult-like participation and citizenship. Although it is currently one of the few settings where adolescents have opportunities to develop these 21st century skills, it does not
have to be the only setting. So, how can stakeholders use this information
to shape youth policy and support adolescents and youths development?

The research on adolescent development in organized activities *and*
on adolescent brain development strongly suggests the United States
needs to re-think how it 'educates' its youth. Traditional, formal education, while efficient in educating masses, is currently unable to meet the
neuro-developmental needs of the adolescent. What this implies, then, is
that adolescents and youth are not only capable of contributing to and
participating in society (i.e., they have the requisite neuro-developmental
capacities) but that key experiences reflecting the level of thinking skills
for full participation in society will ultimately support sustained and
qualitatively better participation over time. This real neuro-developmental need propels adolescents towards authentic experiences: those
that mimic the daily conditions and constraints faced by adults as they
make meaning in their lives and occupations. Learning within a context
of authentic experiences, I suggest, can lead to qualitatively deeper learning that will support adolescents' readiness to become fully integrated
into adult life.

One promising approach to learning involves creating 'adult-youth' (meaning adult-adolescent) partnerships through which both adults and youth address common goals and work side-by-side to meet the common objectives (Hansen, Crawford, and Jessop, 2011). In such a partnership, there is relative equality in the relationship; each person contributes skill and experience, although one person may have more extensive experience in a particular domain. Research on adult-youth partnerships suggests they promote the development of critical civic praxis among adolescents and adults (Camino, 2000; Ginwright and Cammarota, 2007; Larson and Hansen, 2005; Zeldin, 2004); such partnerships have also been promoted for 'youth' (e.g 18-25) and adults. There is also much to be gleaned from the rich history of apprenticeship systems in Europe and elsewhere. From a neuro-developmental readiness perspective, high quality apprentice training offers the authenticity of experience that supports learning, i.e., there is a tangible purpose and objective for learning. But they also offer adolescents and youth access to adults and their skills, competencies, and dispositions, which is important if complex, higher-order thinking is to emerge. One recent educational experiment – Studio Schools in England (Studio Schools Trust, 2011) – attempts to fully integrate learning within the real-world context by clearly defining employability skills, connecting learning to real, tangible work that occurs alongside adults on the job. Although it is too early to judge the effectiveness of Studio Schools based on research, the concept fits well with the research findings presented here.

In sum, mounting research evidence provides a convincing case for adolescents (and youth) to learn certain skills, competencies, and dispositions that will sustain their full participation in contemporary society. The research findings from different disciplines further indicate the types of experiences that will support these skills. What remains is for the full array of stakeholders, e.g., youth workers, policy-makers, and educators, to create innovative solutions for supporting the learning for which adolescents and youth are capable and ready. Given the complexity of the learning that needs to occur, no single 'one size fits all' solution will work.

Bibliography

Attar, B., Guerra, N. and Tolan, P. (1994) Neighborhood disadvantage, stressful life events, and adjustment in urban elementary-school children, *Journal of Clinical Child Psychology, 23,* pp. 391-400.

Brooks-Gunn, J., Klebanov, P. and Liaw, E. (1995) The learning, physical, and emotional environment of the home in the context of poverty: The Infant Health and Development Program, *Children and Youth Services Review, 17,* pp. 231-250.

Bronfenbrenner, U. (1979) *The ecology of human development,* Cambridge MA, Harvard University Press.

Brown, L., Cowen, E., Hightower, A. D. and Lotyczewski, B. (1986) Demographic differences among children in judging and experiencing specific stressful life events, *Journal of Special Education, 20,* pp. 339-346.

Camino, L. (2005, February) Youth-led community building: Promising practices from two communities using community-based service-learning, *Journal of Extension, 43*(1). http://www.joe.org/joe/2005february/a2.php.

Camino, L. A. (2000) Youth-adult partnerships: Entering new territory in community work and research, *Applied Developmental Science, 4,* pp.11-20.

Csikszentmihalyi, M. (1990) *Flow: The psychology of optimal experience,* New York, Harper-Collins.

Csikszentmihalyi, M. and Larson, R. (1984) *Being adolescent,* New York, Basic Books.

Damasio, A. (2010) *Self comes to mind: Constructing the conscious mind,* New York, Pantheon Books.

Deci, E. L. and Ryan, R. M. (2000) The 'what' and 'why' of goal pursuits: Human needs and the self-determination of behavior, *Psychological Inquiry, 11,* pp. 227-268.

Dubow, E., Tisak, J., Causey, D., Hryshko, A. and Reid, G. (1991) A two-year longitudinal study of stressful life events, social support, and social problem-solving skills: Contributions to children's behavioral and academic adjustment, *Child Development, 62,* pp. 583-599.

Eccles, J. S. and Templeton, J. (2002) Extracurricular and other after-school activities for youth, in Secada, W. S. (ed) *Review of Educational Research, 26* (pp. 113-180), Washington DC, American Educational Research Association Press.

Eccles, J., Barber, B., Stone, M. and Hunt, J. (2003) Extracurricular activities and adolescent development, *Journal of Social Issues, 59,* pp. 865-889.

Evans, G. W. and English, K. (2002) The environment of poverty: Multiple stressor exposure, psychophysiological stress, and socioemotional adjustment, *Child Development, 73,* pp. 1238-1248.

Giedd, J. N. (2008) The teen brain: Insights from neuroimaging, *Journal of Adolescent Health, 42,* pp. 335-343.

Ginwright, S. and Cammarota, J. (2007) Youth Activism in the Urban Community: Learning Critical Civic Praxis within Community Organizations, *International Journal of Qualitative Studies in Education (QSE), 20(6),* pp. 693-710.

Goldberg, E. (2009) *The New Executive Brain: Frontal Lobes in a Complex World,* Oxford, Oxford University Press.

Halpern, R. (2005) Instrumental relationships: A potential relational model for inner-city youth programs, *Journal of Community Psychology, 33(1),* pp. 11-20.

Hansen, D. M., Crawford, M. J. and Jessop, N. (2011) Volunteerism, community involvement, and civic engagement, in Creasy, G. and. Jarvis, P. (eds) *Adolescent development and school achievement in urban communities,* New York, Taylor & Francis.

Hansen, D. M., Larson, R. W. and Dworkin, J. B. (2003) What adolescents learn in organized youth activities: A survey of self-reported developmental experiences, *Journal of Research on Adolescence, 13,* pp. 25-55.

Hansen, D, M. and Moore, E. W. G. (under review, submitted August, 2011) The impact of program climate and engagement with challenge on rural adolescents' strategic planning skills, *Journal of Research on Adolescence*.

Heath, S. B. (1994) The project of learning from the inner-city youth perspective, in Villarruel, F. A. and Lerner, R. M. (eds) *Promoting community-based programs for socialization and learning*: New Directions for Child Development, 63 (pp. 25-34), San Francisco, Jossey-Bass.

Heath, S. B. (1998) Working through language, in Hoyle, S. M. and Adger, C. T. (eds) *Kids talk: Strategic language use in later childhood* (pp. 217-240), New York, Oxford University Press.

Jankowski, M. (1992) Ethnic Identity and Political Consciousness in Different Social Orders, *New Directions for Child Development, 56*, pp. 79-93.

Jankowski, M. (2002) Minority Youth and Civic Engagement: The impact of Group Relations, *Applied Developmental Science, 6(4)*, pp. 237-245.

Keating, D. (2004) Cognitive and brain development, in Lerner, R. and Steinberg, L. (eds) *Handbook of adolescent psychology* (pp. 45-84), Hoboken, Wiley & Sons.

Kraus, M. W., Piff, P. K. and Keltner, D. (2011) Social class as culture: The convergence of resources and rank in the social realm, *Current Directions in Psychological Science, 20*, pp. 246-250.

Kuhn, D. and Franklin, S. (2006) The Second Decade: What develops (and how), in Kuhn, D. and Siegler, R. S. (eds), *Cognition, perception, and language* (volume 2 of Damon, W. and Lerner, R. M. (eds) *Handbook of Child Psychology*, (6th ed.)), Hoboken, N.J., Wiley and Sons, pp. 953-993.

Larson, R. (2000) Toward a psychology of positive youth development, *American Psychologist, 55*, pp. 170-183.

Larson, R. W. and Angus, R. M. (2011) Adolescents' development of skills for agency in youth programs: Learning to think strategically, *Child Development, 82*, pp. 277-294.

Larson, R. and Hansen, D. (2005) The development of strategic thinking: Learning to impact human systems in a youth activism program, *Human Development, 48*, pp. 327-349.

Larson, R., Hansen, D. and Moneta, G. (2006) Differing profiles of developmental experiences in across types of organized youth activities, *Developmental Psychology, 42(5)*, pp. 849-863.

Larson, R., Hansen, D. and Walker, K. (2005) Everybody's gotta give: Adolescents' development of initiative and teamwork within a youth program, in. Mahoney, J., Larson, R., and Eccles, J. (eds) *Organized activities as contexts of development: Extracurricular activities, after-school and community programs* (pp. 159-184), Hillsdale, Lawrence Erlbaum Associates.

Larson. R. and Richards, M. (eds) (1989) The changing life space of early adolescence, *Journal of Youth and Adolescence, 18(6)*, pp. 501-626.

Larson, R. W. and Rusk, N. (in press) Intrinsic Motivation and Positive Development, in Lerner, R. M., Lerner, V. J. and Benson, J. B. (eds) *Advances in Child Development and Behavior: Positive Youth Development*, Oxford, Elsevier.

Larson, R. and Walker, K. (2006) Learning about the 'real world' in an urban arts program, *Journal of Adolescent Research, 21*, pp. 244-268.

Lerner, R. M. (2004) Liberty: Thriving and civic engagement among America's youth, Thousand Oaks, Sage.

Luna, B., Thulborn, K. R., Munoz, D. P., Merriam, E. P., Garver, K. E., Minshew, N. J. and. Sweeney, J. A. (2001) Maturation of widely distributed brain function subserves cognitive development, *Neuroimage, 13*, pp. 786-793.

Mascolo, M.F., Fisher, K.W. and Neimeyer, R. (1999) The dynamic codevelopment of intentionality, self, and social relations, in Brandstädter, J. and Lerner, R. M. (eds) *Action and self-development: Theory and research through the life span* (pp. 133-166), Thousand Oaks, Sage.

Mahoney, J. L., Larson, R. W., Eccles, J. S. and Lord, H. (2005) Organized activities as developmental contexts for children and adolescents, in Mahoney, J. L., Larson, R. W. and Eccles, J. S. (eds) *Organized activities as contexts of development: Extracurricular activities, after-school and community programs* (pp. 3-22), Mahwah, Lawrence Erlbaum Associates.

McLoyd, V. C. (1998) Socioeconomic disadvantage and child development, *American Psychologist, 53*, pp. 185-204.

Markham, J. and Greenough, W. (2004) Experience-driven brain plasticity: Beyond the synapse, *Neuron Glia Biol., 1*(4), pp. 351-363.

Mintz, S. (2004) *Huck's raft,* Cambridge MS, Bellnap Press of Harvard University Press.

National Research Council and Institute of Medicine (2002) *Community programs to promote youth development,* Washington DC, National Academy Press.

Okagaki, L. and Sternberg, R.J. (1990) Teaching thinking skills: We're getting the context wrong, *Developmental Perspectives on Teaching and Learning Thinking Skills, 21,* pp. 63-78.

Pittman, K., Irby, M. and Ferber, T. (2000) Unfinished business: Further reflections on a decade of promoting youth development, in Public/Private Ventures (ed) *Youth development: Issues, challenges, and directions* (pp. 17-64), Philadelphia, Public/Private Ventures.

Ryan, R. M. and Deci, E. L. (2000) Self-determination theory and the facilitation of intrinsic motivation, social development, and well-being, *American Psychologist, 55,* pp. 68-78.

Rutter, M. (1981) Protective factors in children's responses to stress and disadvantage, in Kent, M. and Rolf, J. (eds) *Prevention of Psychopathology,* 3 (pp. 49-74), Hanover NH, University Press of New England.

Secretary's Commission on Achieving Necessary Skills (1991) *What work requires of schools: A SCANS report for America 2000,* Washington DC, U.S. Department of Labor.

Sherrod, L. R. (2003) Promoting the development of citizenship in diverse youth, *PS: Political Science and Politics,* April, pp. 287-292.

Sherrod, L. R. (2008) Youth's perceptions of citizenship, in Ruck, M. and Horn, S. (eds) Young people's perspectives on the rights of the child, *Journal of Social Issues, 64*, pp. 771-790.

Spear, L. P. (2000) The adolescent brain and age-related behavioral manifestation, *Neuroscience and Biobehavioral Reviews, 24*, pp. 417-463.

Studio Schools Trust (2011) Studio schools brochure: Introduction to the model, http://studioschoolstrust.org/studio-schools/what-studio-school-0 (accessed December 12 2011).

Wachs, T. D. (1992) *The nature of nurture,* Los Angeles, Sage.

5. The Ibero-American Youth Co-operation and Integration Plan 2009-2015: strategic opportunities and challenges[1]

By Alejo Ramírez

In October 2008 in San Salvador, the Heads of State and Government of the twenty-two Member States of the Ibero-American Conference signed the *Declaration of the 18th Ibero-American Summit (Declaración de San Salvador)*, on the theme of youth and development. On this occasion they stressed "the importance, for the present and future of the societies in the region, of meeting the needs of youth, both as a protagonist and beneficiary of development and of public policy designed to guarantee the highest levels of fairness, social justice, solidarity, engagement and inclusion" (SEGIB, 2008a: 1).

The *San Salvador Agreement on Youth and Development*, which was also adopted by the Conference, states in point 1 that: "We approve the Ibero-American Youth Co-operation and Integration Plan 2009-2015, presented by the Ibero-American Youth Organization as a reference point for the future actions of our Governments on matters of youth policy, which will enable, among other things, proper coordination between the institutions, agencies and international organizations which are involved in this field. At the same time, we stress the importance of including continuous revision of the Plan and of adapting it to the national objectives of the member states..." (SEGIB, 2008b: 1).

The San Salvador Declaration embodied three years of efforts, which started when the Organización Iberoamericana de Juventud [Iberico-American organization for youth] (OIJ) undertook, during the 15th Ibero-American Summit in Salamanca "... to draw up a Youth Cooperation and

---

1 Editors' note: this chapter presents the point of view of the Organización Iberoamericana de Juventud and makes use of references differently from the traditional academic style. Therefore, at times, arguments from the perspective of the OIJ are made without references.

Integration Plan to protect and promote the rights of young people and to foster integration between new generations of Ibero-Americans" (SEGIB, 2005: 5).

For their part, at the Extraordinary Meeting of Ministers and others responsible for Youth on April 3, 2008 in San Salvador, those present agreed to "give the OIJ responsibility for carrying out the procedures necessary for the drawing up of the Strategy for the Implementation of the Ibero-American Youth Cooperation and Integration Plan, which would ensure that concrete measures be taken in favour of young Ibero-Americans" (SEGIB, 2009: 76).

Also in 2008, alongside agreements on the Plan, the *Ibero-American Convention on Youth Rights* (OIJ, 2005) came into force, constituting an instrument of international law that examines the need of young people in the region for this commitment and for judicial bases which will recognize, guarantee and protect their rights. In the Convention, the signatory States commit to enacting this instrument with the aim of recognizing young people as possessing rights, as strategic participants in development and as people who are capable of exercising rights and freedoms in a responsible manner. When the Convention came into force it formed a judicial reference for the implementation of the Ibero-American Plan for Cooperation and Integration of Youth (OIJ, 2008a) and a means of guidance, as the Plan seeks to find a way of making the rights of Ibero-American youth more concrete.

In the political sphere, the activation of the Plan by the OIJ is supported by the Declarations of the 15th and 18th Ibero-American Summits, as well as in the implementation mandate granted by the Meeting of Ministers and others responsible for Youth. Implementation is also guided by the principles and rights described in the Convention.

A framework of international cooperation

From the start of the formulation and design process, the Plan has been based on a series of principles and fields of activity that emanate from international agreements on youth and development. The Plan was conceived to enact and be guided by the principles of participation, coordination, intercultural awareness, anti-discrimination and solidarity, and gender equality. Its areas of activity were related to institutions, youth participation, education, health, employment and culture and these were integrated to give momentum to the Ibero-American agenda while harmonizing it with its own agenda of international cooperation. To this end, the principles of the Plan took their inspiration from documents such as the Declaration of the 39th General Assembly of the United Nations, which designated 1985 as the International Year of Youth (with the slogan *Participation, Development, Peace*). Ideas were also taken from the United Nations Convention on the Elimination of all forms of Discrimination against Women, the Convention on the Rights of Childhood and Adolescence, the United Nations Convention on the Rights of Persons with Disabilities, the International Convention on the Elimination of all forms of Racial Discrimination and the International Convention on the Protection of the Rights of Migrant Workers.

In the areas of institutional activity, the Plan took into account the World Programme of Action for Youth (WPAY), which was developed by the United Nations in 1995, and where attention focussed on institutional performance in the areas of education, health, employment, culture and the full participation of young people and their organizations in society. In the same way, following the Declaration of the World Conference of Youth Ministers in Lisbon, 1998, the importance of promoting youth at an institutional level and of encouraging public policy in this area was included. In this Declaration, an appeal was made to guarantee that processes of formulating, applying and monitoring national youth policies have a high level of political commitment and adequate resources (UNESCO, 1998).

Similarly, the implementation of the Plan was influenced by an appeal formulated in the 2005 *World Youth Report* (WPAY, 2005), in which governments were urged to address the problems of youth in a more sensitive and effective way, as well as to increase opportunities for the social participation of youth and to consider their demands as part of the solution rather than the problem.

The Plan also has a direct connection to the United Nations Millennium Development Goals (MDGs). First, the timeline for the process of the Plan corresponds to the first stage of the Millennium Declaration (2009-2015); secondly, within the Implementation Strategy there is a series of strategic objectives directly related to the MDGs. Finally, in order to achieve better coherence of cooperation between various actors and with the OIJ, the Plan has its basis in the Paris Declaration on Aid Effectiveness and the Accra Agenda for Action (OECD, 2005/2008). In this sense, the Plan rests on solid and basic principles in seeking to incorporate the work of other partners in international cooperation who are working in the area of youth.

The importance of youth in the region

The social, economic, political and cultural importance of youth in Ibero-America lies in the demographic magnitude that it represents. The youth population in Ibero-America makes up 37% of the total population, which in absolute figures is about 135 million young people (CEPAL, 2004). One of the most important demographic aspects is the transition of the population that is taking place in many countries in the region, with a growing concentration of the population in the productive age groups, particularly the 15-24 age group. This phenomenon is known as a population bulge or 'demographic bonus,' produced by falling birth and death rates, which offers a great opportunity for governments to reap the benefits of having a growing proportion of young people of working age in relation to the dependent population.

This youth sector of the population is the largest that has ever been recorded and, because of falling fertility rates, even though the population will continue to increase over the next 20 years, the maximum growth point of the youth population has been reached and will not be repeated in the foreseeable future of Ibero-America. As has been said in the discussions of specialists in this area, there is a historic opportunity for the countries of the region to take advantage of this demographic bonus, by making an investment in young people's human capital, especially in health and education.

The bulge in the youth population thus represents a challenge but also an opportunity (ONU, 2008; OIJ, 2009 and 2008b). If the countries of Ibero-America make a commitment to create opportunities in the present to ensure a future of greater well-being, increases in expenditure in secondary and tertiary education will be unavoidable, given that youth account for the greatest proportion of people in these levels of education. Likewise, countries will have to extend the reach of public health programmes in a targeted way to deal with morbidity and mortality among youth, whether in the fight against HIV/AIDS or in the prevention and cure of addictions, as well as in the reduction of deaths from external causes related to violence or traffic accidents. Similarly, they will have to generate policies which favour job creation, with a view to confronting the need to create places for young people in the labour market.

However, the demographic bonus is a temporary stage which will begin to disappear as demography advances and the dependent population increases. Ibero-America as a whole is in its second phase of demographic transition, characterised by a slowing in the growth rate of the youth sector of the population and a decrease in the proportion of young people within the total population. Some countries such as Spain, Portugal or Cuba are already in a third phase of demographic transition, marked by a decrease in the number of young people and negative rates of growth in this section of the population (CEPAL, 2004).

In any case, it is clear that if there is insufficient investment in human capital and if economic growth does not reach a level that will allow for the social inclusion of youth, the demographic dividend may turn into the very opposite, that is, into a social deficit that prevents millions of young people from putting into practice their right to development and, consequently, that puts at risk the social and political stability of the States.

It is equally important to note that youth in today's society fulfils an undeniable role in transmitting and reproducing social and cultural conditions. Attitudes and skills that are developed when one is young set the course for adult life. So those who suffer poverty and exclusion generally create homes where living conditions are precarious, in which children face malnutrition, unemployment, underemployment, the risk of becoming addicted to substances or of dying a violent death. In the area of health, the eating habits of childhood and adolescence, independently of income level, will determine adult health. For example, a person who is obese at a young age will in general suffer diabetes or heart problems when they are older, with a consequent impact on the cost to the public health services. Also, a person who does not learn to create collaborative networks when they are young will find it difficult to take part in activities in their community when they are older, and will not appreciate the value of democracy. The youth sector of the population is therefore a fundamental link in the renewal of the social pact and governance.

Through the various implementation stages of the Plan, we have emphasised how important it is that the governments of the Ibero-American countries put forward appropriate strategies to take advantage of the youth population bulge and increase public investment in a sustained manner.

Inescapable situations for Ibero-American youth

Young people in the Ibero-American countries find themselves immersed in a series of contradictions and paradoxes which are pre-existing in countries with medium and high levels of income. Identifying these unavoidable situations enables us to better understand the complexity of the challenges faced when drawing up public policies for youth. Within the framework of cooperation driving the Plan, identifying these situations with governments and youth organizations helps to give context and relevance to the decisions that may be taken.

The generation that heard the announcement of the first International Year of Youth in 1995, and that witnessed the approval of the World Programme of Action for Youth in 1995, has today been completely replaced by a new generation. Regardless of this, the trio of aims proposed halfway through the 1980s – development, peace and participation – as well as the themes included in the World Programme of Action for Youth (WPAY), are in many ways still valid for the current generation of young people. But we must underline changes in the economic, social, environmental and cultural factors which particularly affect young people in the twenty-first century. They are:

a. Continuing poverty, linked to structural economic conditions and cultural patterns of exclusion which cause wealth and inequality to be concentrated, both at the national level and between countries and regions. It is important to note that poverty is not merely a statistical measure which counts those living on one or two dollars a day, it is a burden that fills the lives of millions of people in the region with suffering. The phenomenon of poverty among the young is a serious obstacle to achieving the Millennium Development Goals, because if the situation of young people is called into question by this severely limiting factor, it consequently puts all development at risk. In other words, continuing poverty among the young means that success is not guaranteed for any development project. Overcoming poverty in a region characterized by the largest equality gaps in the world presents an ethical challenge of enormous proportions.

b. Youth is the main protagonist of the changes that are occurring at a global level. Globalization is introducing hitherto unknown cultural norms, whether through consumerism and communications or because of the way global events occur simultaneously. There is no doubt that globalization is a phenomenon from which can create huge benefits for the whole of humanity, such as increasing world trade, enabling easier communication and understanding between cultures, increasing solidarity between peoples or sharing the values that build a world of greater wellbeing and security. However, it is also undeniable that the benefits of this phenomenon are not necessarily directed at people and communities. On the contrary, its greatest benefits are reaped by transnational companies and financial and stock market capital, as well as by illegal activities. It is a fact that the deregulation of international capital and goods markets has not been sufficient to generate global benefits. One of the most cruel paradoxes confronting the young today comes from the fact that they can expect to become better at adapting to change, but also to face a greater risk of social exclusion. Young people seem to be more capable of dealing with change and they have become the first generation to share a continually changing world culture within a framework of greater respect for cultural diversity. However, they are also the generation under the greatest pressure and in which the tension emanating from the current dynamic can be seen, as no other generation has faced a similar situation, characterized by accelerated change and the need to adapt in order to survive.

c. The increase in the use of information and communication technology is having a decisive impact on the socialization of young people, via the Internet and the mobile phone, tools which allow them to access 'the knowledge society' and which bring them a wealth of information that had never previously been available on this scale. Moreover, it promotes entrepreneurship through innovation and makes it easier to reach global markets. One aspect worthy of note is the effect on the meaning of objective reality when it is influenced by virtual reality. The current generation experiences the world through screens and digitalized information. There is a wide consensus on the radical importance of these technological tools in the new division of labour and training of staff. However, there is still a digital divide between countries, as well as between those who are and are not poor. We find ourselves here facing a paradox involving youth: more information, but a lack of participation. The current generation of youth has greater access to information and knowledge through the Internet and mass media, but, on the other hand, it has less access to decision-making powers which are largely in the hands of the adult and older adult generations, because of the lengthening of the average lifespan. The world is run, in the main, by adults, despite the fact that young people are heavily involved in contemporary events. For example, young people make up the largest proportion of social network users on the Internet and they consume much more information from mass media than do adults. However, they participate less in formal decision-making groups, especially at State and local community levels.

d. It is important to note the paradox that exists in young people's health: better health and less medical attention. Young people are in good health because of their very youth, but in most countries in the region their particular patterns of morbidity and mortality have not been recognized by public policies. There is a specific morbidity-mortality profile for youth, owing to the higher incidence of traffic accidents, physical violence, abuse of harmful drugs both legal and illegal, sexually transmitted diseases including HIV/AIDS, teenage pregnancy (Ibero-America has one of the highest incidences in the world after Sub-Saharan Africa), malnutrition, obesity, mental illness (schizophrenia, depression, bulimia, anorexia) and suicidal tendencies. Consequently, young people are living a paradox between apparently good health and the risks to it, because of the scarcity of targeted and integrated health strategies, both preventive and at first response and hospital levels. In a similar way many countries are still unaware that investment in good health habits in adolescence and youth will result in less pressure on the health services when the current generation of young people reaches adulthood. Measures to promote young people's health should be seen as early intervention.

e. The increasing participation of young people – as both victims and perpetrators – in armed conflicts, organized delinquency and violence is an alarming phenomenon. This situation must be addressed not only with punitive measures, although these are essential, but above all with actions and policies which will lead people to live peacefully on a daily basis, by giving them opportunities to develop fully as human beings. Justice and security should appear on the agenda of all actions and policies for youth, accompanied by the key factors in development: education, health, employment, environment and participation. While on this subject, it is appropriate to mention the importance of avoiding 'criminalizing' youth. On the contrary, we must trust young people, because their contribution, which is essential, will depend on this. With that in mind we have to allow them to make mistakes and to understand those mistakes in order to prevent them and correct them, but without destroying the individual human being. Nowadays thousands of young people are locked up in detention centres which, far from rehabilitating them in order to reintegrate them into society, are centres of degrading and humiliating imprisonment. It would be advisable for countries where violence and criminality have become embedded to find a fair approach for young people who are in conflict with the law and to promote a culture of peace based on holistic development.

f. Migration has become a global phenomenon. One third of the world's migrants are young people in search of work and inclusion in a different place. Migration has many contradictory aspects. It can have positive effects both for those who emigrate and for the receiving societies, as they receive human capital with skills and commitment. At the same time there are negative effects, depending on the migrant's situation and the circumstances of the movement, as well as on the labour situation and the subsequent use made of money which is sent back. Evidence shows that in the long term migrants' place of origin is severely affected, because the exodus of its youth takes away its potential for growth. In any case, one of the great paradoxes of globalization is that goods travel more easily from one country to another, whereas people are faced with risks and limitations. The world is in urgent need of an international agreement on migration which would regulate its benefits and disadvantages. Ibero-America could/should establish guidelines for such an agreement.

g. The end of the last decade was marked by a worldwide financial and economic crisis. It has become an ongoing crisis, despite some indications of recovery, such as the revival in world trade and the partial flow of bank credit. However, the global economy is not yet showing sufficient recovery to generate enough jobs to replace those that were lost and to open new sources of work, especially for the young people who are seeking to get into the labour market each year. We must also note that world-wide inflation in the price of food, for those who are living in poverty, makes it much harder for them to get out of this situation. Similarly, we must not forget the increase in the tax burden or in external debt for taxpayers – including the young – who are beginning to pay through their taxes for the misuse of funds caused by the lack of regulation in the international financial system. In any case, it is clear that investment in young people cannot wait for the economy to recover. On the contrary, investing in all aspects of their development should be seen as a policy to reactivate economic growth.

h. Climate change is a consequence of the concentration in the atmosphere of the emission of gases from the greenhouse effect, mainly derived from the generalized use of fossil fuels as a source of energy. This is a fact that demands binding changes and measures of unprecedented scope to mitigate climate change throughout the world. We must understand that a planet with an average temperature two degrees higher will be an environment we are not used to, even without considering the increase in the sea level and the effect that will have on coastal regions. The recovery in economic growth must be accompanied by the use of renewable energy and the introduction of practices that will help to reduce emissions, such as the very simple measure of disconnecting cell-phones once the battery has re-charged. Young people's awareness of the problem and the measures they take will be a deciding factor in this issue.

Within this same area, the use and conservation of natural resources, closely linked to climate change and the recovery of economic growth, is a problem which entails a radical transformation in the way humanity manages natural resources. Since the 1992 Rio summit on sustainable development it has been clear that the use and conservation of natural resources is a legacy from one generation to the next. This primarily puts the responsibility for decisions concerning such matters as water management, the conservation of ecosystems, and the exploitation of marine resources and waste management on the current adult generation. Every action and policy will impact on the future life of children and young people. We are talking about strategies to ensure the continuity of the species, an unparalleled situation in the history of the human race. It would therefore be very appropriate to include the view of young people in each decision, as these resources are also theirs and it should be considered their right to conserve and use them.

i. Democracy has been consolidated in the great majority of the countries of Ibero-America, with the exception of Honduras, as the preferred political system, as it enables the majority to elect governments and authorized representatives to take decisions, while at the same time respecting the rights of minorities. But democracy is also a product of history which can be improved upon and its permanency is not guaranteed. It is also put at risk by religious fundamentalism, xenophobia, neo-nazism and extreme nationalism. Democracy also finds itself challenged when a government does not respect or promote human rights, or when the low level of real development makes citizens feel that there is no point in turning out to vote. In the least developed countries in the region it is particularly necessary to increase the quality of democracy by including citizen participation in policy design. In order to achieve this, public policy on youth requires the participation of organizations, collectives and individual young people who have suggestions and ideas for designing, managing and monitoring policy in order to improve its relevance. Democracy throughout the region will be enriched by effective means of participation that integrate the initiative of young people. It is of course also essential to encourage social capital among youth which will nurture democracy. This has to be linked to increasing networks of communication between young people and facilitating the links between these networks, communities and society as a whole.

Positioning the Plan

The preparation leading up to the Plan entailed a number of challenges related to implementation, one of which was the basic problem of how to position its nature and objectives among the signatory countries themselves. It is usual for governments to sign and enact agreements to cooperate; this forms part of their integration into the international community, but it is more complicated when it comes to having a clear idea of how to put into practice international policy decisions, for, as we know, details of implementation are not part of declarations and are delegated to executive bodies. To meet this challenge, the first task of the OIJ was to position and communicate a clear image of the characteristics, objectives and scope of the Plan.

It is also important to bear in mind that within the Ibero-American area there are no precedents of multilateral methods of cooperation in the field of youth. The closest reference is the United Nations WPAY, but it does not have strategic objectives nor does it have an integrated agenda of the various actions being carried out by agencies of the organisation who are working in this field. The Regional action programme for the development of youth in Latin America (PRADJAL), which was promoted by the OIJ in the 90s did not implement actions either, but had a diagnostic role. Consequently, the implementation of the Plan is a new idea for all the countries in the region.

In order to achieve a clear positioning of the Plan, taking into account the possible communication barriers which could cause problems in understanding it, an implementation meeting was arranged and held in Quito in December 2008, and was attended by 14 countries. At the meeting an operational idea of the Plan was presented, ideas to enhance its application were gathered and certain messages were emphasised which have been reiterated in all forums in which the OIJ takes part. They define the following scenario.

Strategic objectives and activities for each action item

Item	Strategic objective	Activities
Institutionality	• Increase the relevance of public youth policy (PPJ) in national development plans • Encourage official youth organizations (OOJ) to carry out their mandates • Achieve recognition for OOJs to give impetus to PPJ • Include in PPJ multiple approaches, that are inter-generational and that take into account both genders	• Strengthening of the OOJs • Promotion of the youth perspective in the development of legislation and in the positioning of PPJ in the social role of each State • Development of National Plans for Youth • Strengthening of the OIJ • Training of experts and civil servants in youth matters • Ibero-American System of Youth Information • Ibero-American forum on good practice in PPJ • Creation and consolidation of multi-sector, cross-sectional, bilateral and multilateral opportunities for coordination
Participation	• Increase the representation of youth associations, platforms and various youth sectors in the design, co-execution and co-evaluation of PPJ • Increase the representation and legitimacy of youth associations and platforms • Encourage the social participation of young people in various settings • Emphasize the distinct forms of informal youth participation	• Ibero-American youth platform • Creation of networks between young people and their organizations • Social pacts with businesses and the third sector in the development of specific spaces for the young • Support for programmes suggested and developed by young people • Inclusion of young people in the monitoring and control of activities of public authorities • Ibero-American network of youth information • Programme of Young Volunteers • Consultations and surveys of young people about their situation and environment • Promotion and support for youth associations • Support for the creation of pluralistic platforms in civil society and in the area of youth
Education	• Improve the quality of secondary and tertiary education • Increase access to secondary and tertiary level education • Decrease the education gap • Increase access to ICTs • Teach the use and conservation of natural resources and the conservation of the environment	• Ibero-American literacy and basic education plan • Mobility programme for teachers and students in secondary and tertiary education • System of grants to support the education of young people suffering from poverty and inequality • Programme to encourage young people at risk of low educational achievement (second chance programme) • Programme of education and training for integration in the labour market with emphasis on scientific innovation and ICTs • Strengthening of education programmes with respect to democratic values, citizenship and human rights

Item	Strategic objective	Activities
		• Inclusion of environmental education in the curricula at secondary and tertiary levels • Standardization of educational processes and qualifications • Recognition of informal education • Support for the development of facilities in rural locations and on the periphery of cities
Health	• Reduce the incidence of teenage pregnancy • Reduce the levels of STD infection • Reduce the number of deaths of young people from external causes • Guarantee access to public health services which are friendly and approachable	• Information on adequate nutrition and the prevention of illnesses linked to poor dietary habits • Encouragement of public programmes for the prevention and cure of all addictions • Promotion of actions to prevent and eradicate all forms of violence • Dissemination of information on situations and actions which entail risk • Development of sexual and reproductive health programmes, focussing on the prevention of STDs, HIV and unplanned pregnancies • Promotion of approachable health services for young people which will lower the specific morbidity/mortality rates of this group
Employment and enterprise	• Increase the proportion of young people in work • Improve working conditions for young people • Promote enterprise among young people • Promote equal opportunities at work	• Encouragement of decent employment together with the International labour organization's Regional plan for youth employment in Latin America • Technical and financial support for self-employment in accordance with particular potential and new sources of employment • Ensuring compliance with the employment rights of young migrants • Improvement of labour mobility for young people in Ibero-America • Eradication of exploitative work situations affecting young people • Strengthening of public employment information services • Encouragement of a culture of entrepreneurship from primary to tertiary education • Encouragement of programmes to help young people join the workforce • Encouragement of programmes to help young people with disabilities join the workforce
Culture and recreation	• Promote spaces for young people's cultural expression and to encourage all forms of young people's cultural expression • Nourish historical memory,	• Cultural exchanges with young people as protagonists • National strategy to promote young people's cultural expression in all areas • Commercial promotional strategy for all types of artistic and cultural expression by the young

Item	Strategic objective	Activities
	cultural roots and the preservation of cultural heritage • Encourage sport among the young • Promote recreational facilities for the young	• Incorporation of aesthetic education into the curricula, as a basis for ethical sensitivity • Inclusion of the cultural expression of young people with disabilities • Encouragement of historical memory, cultural roots and the preservation of cultural heritage • Support for programmes of collective reparation in cases of displacement and conflict • Promotion of sport among young people • Creation and joint management of recreational facilities for young people

Institutional reform of youth policy

The institutional landscape demands a reform of public administration, especially as institutional development in this area continues to be linked to a short term focus and political clients. Despite appeals which have been made to governments since 1985 [asking them to carry out institutional reform of greater depth, because of the challenges facing young people], the achievements made show that we have arrived at a point where it is necessary to extend them further. It is true that the existence of official youth organizations is largely guaranteed throughout the region, but it is also a fact that effectiveness and institutional training have still not become standard good practice, nor is there evidence of their having helped transform pre-existing situations. The OOJs (official youth organizations) have been assessed as having varying levels of technical and political skill, which means that there is clearly a pressing need to promote and maintain renewed focus on the administration of public policy in Ibero-America.

With this in mind, within the framework of the actions of the Plan and taking into account the current situation of each country, the OIJ proposes a set of 11 criteria to improve the administration of policy and to strengthen official youth organizations:

1) The defence and promotion of the rights of the youth population, with the understanding that in a democratic system, public institutions must set established rights within a constitutional framework, as a form of management centred on the well-being of young people and by means of extending their human, economic, social and cultural rights, as well as the fundamental freedoms which are the birthright of all human beings.

2) The incorporation of young citizens into governmental decision-making, as a substantive element in high-level public policy, guaranteeing, through mechanisms for consultation, dialogue or scrutiny, the contribution and participation of the beneficiaries of the implementation of principles underlying policy and the law.

3) The drawing up of public policy using a multi-faceted approach from the point of view of its subject, that is, taking a very wide view when investigating and understanding the reality experienced by young people in order to capture the complexity of social phenomena and avoid simplistic responses. For example, a young person will not describe himself or herself simply as an unemployed person, a student or a migrant. Within these identities he or she is the product of a multi-faceted social context. It is hoped that governmental decisions will be based on the interconnection of the events that make up a person's life. Since the young person is a person in a context influenced by many determining factors, he or she does not only exist among peers and therefore needs solutions which will integrate him or her into the whole of society.

4) An inter-sectoral approach which can be seen in the ability of public institutions – ministries of education, health, employment, environment, justice – and the different levels of government – national, regional, municipal – to respond to the multi-faceted way in which the experiences and circumstances of the lives of the various sections of the youth population present themselves. An inter-sectoral approach means that public institutions are organized internally in such a way that they can respond to these multiple aspects by harmonizing with national, regional and local development objectives.

5) Placing particular importance on establishing training programmes for civil servants and experts specialized in the administration of public policy for youth, at both local and national levels. The training of career civil servants and the increasing awareness of youth in the public sector are crucial factors in ensuring that processes which require structural change and a long period of implementation are long-lasting.

6) The use of scientific evidence and the results of applied investigation, the devising of diagnostic studies in order to keep criteria up-to-date and the creation of a national youth observatory. The intention here is that knowledge will help to ensure that decisions are taken which favour the improvement of social conditions for young people.

7) The establishing of partnerships with social actors involved in the holistic development of young people, such as families, churches, the private sector, trade unions, social organizations and, in particular, youth associations and networks.

8) The design and implementation of country specific plans to encourage public policy at national, regional and/or local levels, in which strategic objectives, goals and expected outcomes will be established.

9) Shared monitoring of results and effects, by means of information and collaboration networks in which the various sectors of government, agencies of international cooperation, organizations in civil society and the private sector will participate, in compliance with the model proposed by the Accra Action Plan.

10) The inclusion of cooperation in development by aligning national objectives within international agreements (MDG, WPAY, World Youth Conference, Ibero-American Conference). In many cases cooperation is still seen as an 'obligation' or as a condition of resources. The aim of the OIJ is that countries should assume the role of partners in the achievement of the results sought for in international agreements.

11) Reform of the regulatory framework which guarantees in law the institutionality, participation, inter-institutional coordination and, ideally, a percentage of social expenditure destined specifically for all aspects of the development of young people.

Challenges

Implementing the Plan has been an institutional learning process for the OIJ and for the countries involved, on a subject which had not previously been considered as rigorously as it demands to be: international cooperation organized on the basis of globally-agreed principles. One could say that the Plan did not begin in an easy year. Indeed, 2009 was beset by all kinds of problems, but that is the reality of the Ibero-American context and when confronted by it the OIJ has been able to adapt and achieve certain successes in a coherent and, as we can see, relevant way. Of course, the most valuable evaluation comes from those who have benefited from the work of the organization, especially official youth organizations.

But the work that has been begun is indeed only a beginning, an initial effort that still requires greater depth and permanence. The process has borne fruit in terms of collaboration agreements, but this is not strictly speaking so creditable; its real significance lies in keeping expectations high, consolidating the gains that have been made and taking on new challenges in the countries presently involved and in new ones.

To sum up, the main challenge consists in maintaining the initial effort and continuing until obvious changes are produced in the six action items of the Plan. In order to do this it is essential to have the backing of financial agencies. In the OIJ we are aware that the reality young people experience has hardly changed, but we also want to make clear that in many cases there has been an unprecedented event in the lives of young people: they are taking part in public consultations in arenas where no-one had ever previously asked their opinion.

We have every faith that the agencies backing the Plan share this view of keeping up the impetus and consolidating efforts, especially because the reality experienced by young people in Ibero-America is far from encouraging. On the contrary there is an obvious risk of social instability in the region if investment in all aspects of development for young people is not increased, and unless social conditions can be created which will make the right to development a reality. The Plan is only one energizing factor among the many efforts which are necessary to improve, rapidly and in a sustained way, the whole range of actions which are urgent and necessary. The OIJ is committed to undertaking the mission which has been entrusted to it with honesty and a sense of moral justice.

Bibliography

CEPAL (Comisión Económica para América Latina y el Caribe) (2004) *La Juventud en Iberoamérica. Tendencias y Urgencias,* Santiago de Chile, CEPAL – Nationes unidas.

OECD (Organization for economic cooperation and development) (2005/2009) *The Paris declaration on Aid Effectiveness* and the *Accra agenda for action,* Paris, http://www.oecd.org/dataoecd/11/41/34428351.pdf (accessed June 15, 2012).

OIJ (Organización Iberoamerciana de Juventud) (2009), Juventud y bono demográfico en Iberoamérica, Madrid, OIJ, http://www.oij.org/file_upload/publicationsItems/document/EJ1264092367.pdf (accessed June 15, 2012).

OIJ (Organización Iberoamerciana de Juventud) (2008a) Plan iberoamericano de co-operación e integración de la juventud [Ibero-American plan for cooperation and integration of youth], Madrid, OIJ http://www.agendajoven.org/attachments/049_Plan%20Iberoamericano%20de%20Cooperaci%C3%B3n%20e%20Integraci%C3%B3n%20de%20la%20Juventud%202009-2015.pdf (accessed June 15, 2012).

OIJ (Organización Iberoamerciana de Juventud) (2008b) *Nuevos desafíos con las y los jóvenes de Iberoamérica,* Madrid, OIJ, http://www.oij.org/file_upload/publicationsItems/document/EJ1206818403.pdf (accessed June 15, 2012).

OIJ (Organización Iberoamerciana de Juventud) (2005) *Convención Iberoamericana de Derechos de los Jóvenes,* Madrid, http://www.oij.org/file_upload/publicationsItems/document/20120607115106_98.pdf (accessed June 15, 2012).

SEGIB (Secretaría General Iberoamericana) (2009) Conferencia Iberoamericana de jefes de estado y de gobierno – Reuniones ministeriales dectoriales, Informe final 2008 [Ibero-American Conference of Heads of State and Government – Sectoral ministerial meetings, Final report 2008], Madrid, http://segib.org/documentos/esp/Informe%20final%20RMS%2008%20castellano.pdf (accessed June 15, 2012).

SEGIB (Secretaría General Iberoamericana) (2008a) *Declaración de San Salvador [Declaration of the 18th Ibero-American Summit],* San Salvador, http://segib.org/upload/Declaracion%20de%20San%20Salvador(1).pdf (accessed June 15, 2012).

SEGIB (Secretaría General Iberoamericana) (2008b) *Compromiso de San Salvador para la juventud y el desarollo [San Salvador Agreement on Youth and Development],* San Salvador, http://segib.org/upload/Compromiso%20de%20San%20Salvador(1).pdf (accessed June 15, 2012).

SEGIB (Secretaría General Iberoamericana) (2005) Declaración de Salamanca Declaration of the 15th Ibero-American Summit], Salamanca, http://segib.org/documentos/esp/Declaracion%20de%20Salamanca.pdf (accessed June 15, 2012).

UNESCO (1998) *Lisbon declaration on youth policies and programmes,* Paris, http://www.unesco.org/cpp/uk/declarations/lisbon.pdf (accessed June 15, 2012).

WPAY (United Nations World Programme of Action for Youth) (2005) *World youth report 2005 – Young people today, and in 2015,* New York, United Nations, http://www.un.org/esa/socdev/unyin/documents/wyr05book.pdf (accessed June 15, 2012).

II – Reflecting on the effects of policy

1. The long-term effects of youth policies in Australia

By Johanna Wyn

While the role of evidence in supporting youth policy development is generally acknowledged, there has been relatively little attention given to evidence about the effects of policies on young people's lives over the longer term. This includes a curious lack of attention to the ways in which policies enacted within one domain, such as labour relations for example, have ongoing effects across other policy domains such as health and education. The discussion draws on longitudinal research to reflect on the ways that youth policies impact on young people's lives over time, creating lasting effects in which intended and unintended consequences blend.

Youth policy is a complex area and its scope and implementation differs between countries. In Australia, responsibility for the development and implementation of policies for young people occurs at many sites. At the federal and state and territory levels of government Offices for Youth generally have responsibility for 'youth policy'. These policies tend to be focussed on young people's participation and civic engagement and tend to play a supporting role to other policy areas. However, the policies that arguably have the most significant impact on the lives of young people in Australia are enacted from the government departments that have jurisdiction over education, the labour market and industrial relations, health and justice, at both the federal and state or territory level. In other words, policies that are relevant to young people occur across many different policy areas. This means that youth policy is relatively invisible and the effects of government policies on young lives are not well-researched.

This chapter addresses this gap, focusing on the question of how government policies impact on young people's lives, drawing on Australian longitudinal research. Longitudinal research provides the benefit of hindsight, revealing how both intended and unintended consequences of policies are played out over time. Lives are complex and multifaceted and the impacts of policies, intended to impact on one area of life (such as education for example), may go well beyond their intended effects.

This discussion of the wider impact of policy interventions and the intersecting areas of influence across policy domains has had some exposure in the literature on inter-sectoral approaches to policy. The idea of cross-sectoral policy approaches acknowledges a) that lives are complex and b) that policy domains have intersecting goals and outcomes. Over the last 15 years the idea of integrating youth policies through various mechanisms that aim to prevent disadvantaged young people from falling through the spaces between services that are not 'joined up', has become a regular theme of youth policy (Tett et al., 2003). Inter-agency working is seen as a way of preventing marginalisation from school (Stead et al., 2004) and crime (Burnett and Appleton, 2004) and for improving health outcomes for young people (Robinson et al., 2005). In recent years, the Australian federal government has implemented a series of initiatives that bring different policy domains and government departments together to support inter-agency collaboration on the ground. For example, the Youth Partnerships initiative, a collaboration between the Australian federal and state governments, has focused on building multi-sector partnerships between schools and other local organisations to increase the proportion of young people who complete secondary education and to reduce social, individual and behavioural problems for young people (Department of Education and Early Childhood Development, 2011). While inter-sectoral approaches continue to be seen as a way forward in addressing entrenched disadvantage amongst young people, the broader and longer-term implications of policy effects that intersect has attracted very little attention. Inter-sectoral approaches tend to be enacted as short-term, pilot projects and focus on the point of delivery of services by professionals – not on the longer term effects of policies on young people's lives.

The starting point for this reflection on policy is the education and labour market policies that were initiated in Australia in the 1990s. These policies were implemented with the specific goal of increasing Australia's competitiveness and prosperity with the emergence of global markets. Drawing on the *Life Patterns* longitudinal data it is possible to analyse how these policies impacted on the lives of young people over a period of over 15 years. *Life Patterns* is an ongoing longitudinal research program tracking the lives of two generations of young Australians, corresponding to Generations X and Y (Cuervo and Wyn, 2011; Wyn et al., 2008). The research program includes a comparative analysis with

Andres' Canadian longitudinal study *Paths on Life's Way* (Andres and Wyn, 2010). Gen X, a term derived from the popular media and market research, is generally regarded as referring to people who were born between 1966 and 1976 and in 2011 were aged 35 – 45.

Policies for young people

Education, labour market and industrial relations policies enacted in Australia in the 1990s had a profound and immediate impact on young people, as they were intended to. What is less known is that they continue to have effects that resonate well into their adult lives. These policies were a significant factor in the creation of a distinctive generation, popularly identified as Generation X. Policies of the 1990s represented a dramatic shift from Keynesian approaches that had informed government policies in English-speaking countries, including the UK and Australia, during the 1950s through to the late 1970s (Mizen, 2004). Keynesian policies aimed to include young people in society through universal state provision, including the expansion of (free and secular) secondary education and welfare measures; a commitment to democratic participation; full employment through labour market policies and a system of negotiation with workers through unions. Policies were based on the assumption that Governments should have responsibility for social relations. Monetarist policies, emerging in the early 1980s, reflected the disengagement of the state from economic-social policy nexus to rely on market forces, placing responsibility for social integration onto individuals (*Ibid.*).

Monetarist policies were not identified as 'youth policies' as such, but through education and workforce policies they specifically targeted young people and they have played a powerful role in defining the experience and meaning of life for young people who left secondary school in the early 1990s (Wyn and Woodman, 2006). These policies were enacted in response to economic changes in the preceding decade (Wooden and Van den Heuvel, 1999; Andres and Wyn, 2010), backed by neoliberal ideologies that placed the emphasis on economic markets as drivers of change. During the 1980s, full-time jobs for the educationally unqualified began to disappear as economies shifted from a reliance on manufacturing and primary industry to new forms of economic activity. The policy documents of the day heralded the dawn of the 'knowledge economy' (OECD, 1996) and the opening up of 'new economies' based on new technologies, and value adding service occupations (OECD, 2001). The immediate impact on young people of this shift was high levels of youth unemployment, which peaked in Australia in the mid 1990s (Sweet, 1998).

A rapid increase in unemployment at that time created a new policy problem – 'youth transitions'. This was a particular problem in Australia, where there was a strong tradition to leave school as soon as possible and get a job, creating a form of cultural resistance to completing secondary education (Wyn, 2009). By the 1990s, young people who entered the labour market without a school completion or vocational education certificate risked unemployment or precarious employment in low-skill, low-paid jobs (Lamb and Mason, 2008; Dusseldorp Skills Forum, 2002). Education became the focus of new policies that saw education as a tool for building human capital, providing the skills and capabilities needed for Australia's transformation from an industrial to a post-industrial economy, and to enable Australian workers to be competitive in emerging global markets (Wyn, 2009).

Hence, a key policy solution to the 'youth transitions' problem was the introduction of a raft of initiatives aimed at encouraging young people to continue with their education past the compulsory years (which ended at age 15), and to complete secondary education (which usually occurred at age 17). In 2011, Australia's Learning or Earning policy compels young Australians to be in education, training or employment until the age of 20 years as a condition of receipt of income support (COAG, 2009).

A second and related response to the problem of youth unemployment, associated with the need to create a more highly educated pool of labour to meet the needs of the new economies, was the expansion of tertiary education, bringing in a new era of mass tertiary education (OECD, 2007). In Australia, this expansion began in the late 1980s, and in 1991, when the *Life Patterns* cohort was leaving secondary school, demand for tertiary education places outstripped supply (Andres and Wyn, 2010). By the mid 1990s it was normative for young people to enter tertiary education.

This expansion of tertiary education was funded by a mix of government grants (to universities) and personal investment by students and their families. Consistent with neoliberal philosophies, education was framed as a personal investment (while at the same time being a public good). Young people and their families met increasing educational costs in the form of tuition fees through their own resources, which meant that disadvantaged groups were discouraged from participating (James *et al.*, 1999). The government introduced a Higher Education Contribution Scheme (HECS) in 1988, which enabled students to borrow from the government to pay educational fees, and to pay back their debt to the government once they started earning.

A third policy initiative of the 1990s was the radical reworking of industrial relations and workplace laws and regulations to create a new form of labour market, within which employers gained unprecedented powers in the use of labour and workers experienced a worsening of their working conditions. The *Workplace Relations Act, 1996* had particular implications for young workers (Bailey *et al.*, 2007). Under this Act, minimum standards for workers (such as rates of pay, working hours and conditions) which had previously been awarded on an occupational basis, negotiated by unions, were now negotiated by individual employees with their employer (Todd, 2004). Under this regime, young workers were especially vulnerable to exploitation and to poorly-paid, casual and part-time work (Campbell, 2000).

The policies described above were enacted in response to global economic changes that impacted on many countries (OECD, 2007). The particular framing and content of policies in Australia however, was the result of political and ideological decisions informed by neoliberal discourses. It is perhaps ironic that one of the tenets of neoliberalism is that markets will determine the shape of society, because, as the story of Gen X reveals, neoliberal, market-based policies ultimately create social outcomes that only governments can fully address.

The following section describes some of the ways in which these policy approaches impacted on the lives of young Australians who left secondary school in 1991, describing unintended consequences, illustrating the short-sightedness of neoliberalism as a policy framework and providing food for thought about new approaches to integrated policy formation.

Gen X: their story

Analysing the life experiences, opportunities and constraints on young Australians and Canadians during the 1990s and 2000s, Andres and Wyn argue that Generation X was a generation of reluctant, accidental change makers (Andres and Wyn, 2010). Although Generation X made a clear break with the patterns of life established by the Baby Boomers (the previous generation), the young people who are characterised as Gen X did not set out to do this. In the late 1980s and early 1990s, their goals were for modest comfort, security in work and relationships and opportunities to better themselves (*Ibid.*). These goals would have placed them comfortably within the expectations held by the Baby Boomer generation, and did not foreshadow the significant, generation-creating shift that actually occurred in their lifetime.

The education, workplace and labour market reforms identified above had the immediate effects that they were designed to produce. For example, following the OECD policy advice that in order to ensure economic prosperity and be globally competitive, Australia needed to have a workforce with a higher level of educational credentials (OECD, 1996), educational participation rates were substantially improved. During the 1990s, Australia experienced an education revolution, dramatically lifting educational participation rates within one generation. This is illustrated in the *Life Patterns* research program by the fact that a majority of the participants were the first in their family to go to a university or other post-secondary school education provider (Wyn *et al.*, 2008). Only 47% of the fathers and 30% of the mothers of the *Life Patterns* cohort had some form of post-secondary education. By contrast, the vast majority of the *Life Patterns* cohort attended a post-secondary educational institution within one year of graduating from secondary school (Andres and Wyn, 2010).

Workplaces changed dramatically too. By the mid 1980s the Australian economy had already shifted from a reliance on primary industry and manufacturing to a more diversified economy, based on new economies in the service sector. However, following the Industrial Relations Act of 1996 the rules of the game changed (*Ibid.*), as stable full-time work and related benefits were "replaced with 'just in time' employment, short-term contracts and part-time positions" within which "young people were positioned as disposable and dispensable items in the economic management of workplaces", enabling the Australian economy to become globally competitive (Wyn and Woodman, 2006 pp. 505-506).

Education and labour market policies became the pillars of economic change in Australia in the 1990s, as they were designed to do. They also engineered significant unintended social changes, the effects of which continue to reverberate well into the 2000s. The following discussion analyses the interrelated and far-reaching effects of these policies on young people and on the social fabric of Australian society.

Achieving their goals

The *Life Patterns* longitudinal study found that 'achieving a balance in life' was a powerful and consistent preoccupation with young Australians, influencing their decisions and recurring over time (Wyn *et al.*, 2008; Cuervo and Wyn, 2011). It became a leitmotif, recurring through the post-school years when young people were juggling study and work, though to the years of becoming established in a job or career and well into their thirties. It became clear that one of the reasons for this recurring theme was the extraordinary difficulty, widespread across the cohort, of achieving a balance between the competing demands of study, work, relationships and leisure on their time. One insight into this challenge in their lives is provided by Woodman (2011), who has analysed the significance of temporality. Exploring the lives of young people from the second cohort of the *Life Patterns* study in the first years out of secondary school (aged 18-20), Woodman identifies a significant shift in patterns of time use when young people move from secondary school to post-secondary school. He found that young people's lives were physically and temporally regulated during the school years, because of the quarantining of the 'school hours', (generally from 8.30 am to 3.30 pm on week days). Young people across *all* school systems are organised in this way. The predictability and uniformity of this temporal regime made it possible for young people to schedule time with each other, to have regular leisure, to be with family and to engage in part-time work.

This pattern changes dramatically when young people leave secondary school. The most significant change is the intensification of individual time schedules and a decreased synchrony between individuals. Post-secondary educational institutions offer a wide range of delivery modes, making it possible to have individual 'choice' but at the same time making it difficult to have common time with friends or family. In the 1990s in Australia, new workplace arrangements involving more 'flexible' uses of labour and the destandardisation of working hours also ensured that individuals work patterns were variable and unpredictable. Individual young people struggled to manage their complex work and study schedules, feeling the pressure of finding regular, reliable times for social interaction and leisure.

Despite new patterns of family cross-generational inter-dependency, this generation of young people felt their lives fragment. The increased time spent in education and part-time, casual employment during their early to mid-twenties, combined with labour market instability and more stringent welfare provisions, increased the economic dependency of young people on their parents (Pusey, 2007; Schneider, 2000). However, in their own words, many felt lost and unsupported by the lack of predictability of time with individuals and groups that provide a sense of security and give advice. Their subjective experience of a thin and threatened social fabric is illustrated by the fact that by the age of 28, 15% of these young people felt that they were mentally 'unhealthy' and 13% felt physically 'unhealthy' (Andres and Wyn, 2010).

Historian Janet McCalman argues that the quality of the social fabric of a society is reflected in marriage and fertility rates. Relative poverty (or lack of financial independence), insecurity of employment and other factors, such as the increased costs of education (or housing) are barriers to the establishment of stable relationships, including family formation (McCalman, 2004). Drawing on a set of birth records of Melbourne's Royal Women's hospital between 1857 and 1900, McCalman found that poor men with uncertain job prospects were the least likely to form families. She found that chronic instability of life circumstances had a negative impact on health and the capacity to form stable families. She sees similarities with the circumstances of young Australians in the 1990s.

> The fragmented, short-term, constantly changing work experience of post-industrial youth is exacting a toll already in postponed marriage and childbearing, which for many will become foregone in the next decade (McCalman, 2004 quoted in Eckersley *et al.*, 2006).

They were a generation in search of work-life balance and as they strained to achieve the modest goals they had set for themselves, they struggled to manage the escalating demands on their time associated with education, work, leisure and relationships. In 1996, aged 23, 30% of the young Australian women in the *Life Patterns* research program expected that they would be married within five years. It took nearly three times as long (13 years) to reach a 30% marriage rate. Their experience is reflected in the sharp decline in rates of marriage and childbearing in Australia during the 1990s, leading to the introduction of a 'baby bonus' – a one-off payment to the mother of a child in order to bring about higher rates of fertility.

An even starker indicator of the impact of the neo-liberal education and labour market policies enacted in Australia in the 1990s is found in the comparison of Australian and Canadian young people by Andres and Wyn (2010). The comparison of the Australian *Life Patterns* longitudinal study with Andres' Canadian *Paths on Life's Way* longitudinal study found that, despite having identical hopes and dreams when they left secondary school, by age 30 the Australian women were only half as likely as their Canadian counterparts to be parents (Wyn and Andres, 2011).

In an extended comparative analysis of the impact of government policies of the 1990s on Canadians (British Columbia) and Australians (Victoria), Andres and Wyn point out that one of the crucial differences between the circumstances of young people in the two studies that may account for the dramatic divergence in their family lives is the nature of workplace and labour policies *(Ibid.)*.

In young people's own words, increases in working hours and insecure employment made it difficult to form stable long-term relationships and to consider starting a family. Indeed, the rate of childbearing dropped so low in 2001 that the Australian government introduced a new policy measure to counter the (unintended) effects of previous policies by offering a bonus payment of $3000 to each Australian woman who gave birth or adopted a child from July 1 2004. This initiative was associated with a modest increase in fertility (*Drago et al.*, 2009). (Andres and Wyn, 2010 p. 233).

Conclusion

The story of the *Life Patterns* cohort of young Australians, from the time they left secondary school in 1991 through to 2011 when they were in their mid to late thirties, is a story of individual struggle to achieve the modest life goals of job security and stable family life. Their lives were forged against the powerful currents of neoliberal policies, whose sole purpose was to engineer a new economic order for Australia. These policies have been relatively successful. Post-secondary education is now normative for Australians and older manufacturing industries have been replaced by globally competitive forms of economic activity, including the service sector.

While these developments and gains are widely recognised, there is less acknowledgement of the extent to which the costs for these changes have been borne by individuals. Even less is understood about the implications of neoliberal policies for the fabric of society – institutional processes that enable a quality of life. This chapter has focused on one indicator of this – personal relationships and family formation. The longitudinal data reveal the way in which education and industrial relations policies have shaped the possibilities for individual lives.

This perspective reveals that to characterise Generation X as the generation that pioneered an 'extended youth' is to oversimplify what was, for them, an enforced and often unwanted stalling of life trajectories. It would be more accurate to characterise the long period of struggle in the immediate post-school years and into their late twenties as a 'foreclosed adulthood'. At the individual level, economic insecurity and the fragmentation of social connections made it difficult for a significant proportion of Generation X to achieve their modest goals. While the expansion of education has opened up opportunities, it has also created new demands on young people's time and their finances. Combined with long periods of precarious work – a direct outcome of industrial relations policies of the 1990s – this has had the effect of weakening those intangible but very important social ties and connections that enable individuals to build their lives. Weakening opportunities for family formation can be seen as an unintended outcome of policies. Later policy interventions such as the baby bonus do not recognise that it is the quality of social life that acts as an enabler (or barrier) to family formation.

This chapter concludes that there is a strong new agenda for research on the longer-term implications of conditions on young people's lives. Hindsight can provide a valuable interpretation of changing youthful patterns of life, particularly when the evidence supports a more sophisticated analysis of the longer term implications for each generation.

Bibliography

Andres, L. and Wyn, J. (2010) *The Making of a Generation: The Children of the 1970s in Adulthood*, Toronto, University of Toronto Press.

Bailey, J., McDonald, P., Oliver, D. and Pini, B. (2007) Compound vulnerability? Young workers' employment concerns and the anticipated impact of the Workchoices Act, *Australian Bulletin of Labour, 33(1)*, pp. 60-88.

Burnett, R. and Appleton, C. (2004) Joined-up services to tackle youth crime: A case study in England, *British Journal of Criminology, 44(1)*, pp. 34-54.

Campbell, I. (2000) Spreading the Net: Age and Gender in the process of casualisation in Australia, *Journal of Australian Political Economy, 45*, pp. 65-100.

Council of Australian Governments (COAG) (2009) *National Partnership on Youth Attainment and Transitions, Communique, 5 February,* Canberra, Council of Australian Governments, http://www.coag.gov.au/coag_meeting_outcomes/2009-02-05/docs/20090205_communique.pdf

Cuervo, H. and Wyn, J. (2011) Rethinking youth transitions in Australia: A historical and multidimensional approach, Melbourne, Youth Research Centre.

Department of Education and Early Childhood Development (2011) *Youth Partnerships: coordinating services to help young people stay on track*, Melbourne,

DEECD. http://www.education.vic.gov.au/sensecyouth/youthpartnerships/ (accessed 18 August 2011).

Drago, R., Sawyer, K., Sheffler, K., Warren, D. and Wooden, M. (2009) Did Australia's baby bonus increase the fertility rate? *Melbourne Institute Working Paper Series, 1/09*, Melbourne.

Dusseldorp Skills Forum (2002) *How Young People are Faring*, Sydney, Dusseldorp Skills Forum.

Easen, P., Atkins, M. and Dyson, A. (2000) Inter-professional collaboration and conceptualisations of practice, *Children & Society, 14(5)*, pp. 355-367.

Eckersley, R., Wierenga, A. and Wyn, J. (2006) Flashpoints & Signposts: Pathways to success and wellbeing for Australia's young people, Melbourne, Youth Research Centre.

James, R., Wyn, J., Baldwin, G., Hepworth, C., McInnis, C. and Stephanou, A. (1999) Rural and isolated students and their higher education choices: A re-examination of student location, socioeconomic background and educational advantage and disadvantage, Canberra, Australian Government Printing Service.

Lamb, S. and Mason, K. (2008) How young people are faring, 2008, Report for the Foundation for Young Australians, Melbourne, Foundation for Young Australians.

McCalman, J. (2004) A Historian's View of Post-Industrial Youth, Paper prepared for Australia 21, in Eckersley, R., Wierenga, A. and Wyn, J. (2006) *Flashpoints & Signposts: Pathways to success and wellbeing for Australia's young people*, Melbourne, Youth Research Centre.

Mizen, P. (2004) *The Changing State of Youth*, New York, Palgrave.

Organisation for Economic Cooperation and Development (OECD) (1996) *Lifelong Learning for All*, Paris, OECD.

Organisation for Economic Cooperation and Development (OECD) (2007) *Higher Education and Regions: Globally competitive, locally engaged*, Paris, OECD.

Organisation for Economic Cooperation and Development (OECD) (2001) *Knowledge and skills for life: First results from PISA 2000*, Paris, OECD.

Pusey, M. (2007) The changing relationship between the generations...It could even be good news?, *Youth Studies Australia, 26(1)*, pp. 9-16.

Robinson, M. and Cottrell, D. (2005) Health Professionals in multi-disciplinary and multi-agency teams: changing professional practice, *Journal of Interprofessional Care, 19(6)*, pp. 547-560.

Schneider, J. (2000) The increasing financial dependency of young people on their parents, *Journal of Youth Studies, 3(1)*, pp. 5-20.

Stead, J., Lloyd, G. and Kendrick, A. (2004) Participation or practice innovation: tensions in inter-agency working to address disciplinary exclusion from school, *Children & Society, 18(1)*, pp. 42-52.

Sweet, R. (1998) Youth: The rhetoric and the reality of the 1990s, in *Dusseldorp Skills Forum, Australia's Youth: Reality and Risk*, Sydney, Dusseldorp Skills Forum.

Tett, L., Crowther, J. and O'Hara, P. (2003) Collaborative partnerships in community education, *Journal of Education Policy, 18(1)*, pp. 37-51.

Todd, S. (2004) *Improving work-life balance – What are other countries doing?* Canada, Human Resources and Skills Development.

Woodman, D. (2011) Young People and the Future: Multiple temporal orientations shaped in interaction with significant others, *Young – Nordic Journal of Youth Studies, 19(2)*, pp. 111-128.

Wyn, J. and Andres, L. (2011) Navigating complex lives: a longitudinal, comparative perspective on young people's trajectories, *Early intervention in Psychiatry, 33 (Supplement 1)*, pp. 1-5.

Wyn, J. (2009) *Touching the Future: Building skills for life and work*, Melbourne, Australian Council for Educational Research.

Wyn, J. and Woodman, D. (2006) Generation, Youth and Social Change in Australia, *Journal of Youth Studies, 9(5)*, pp. 495-514.

Wyn, J., Smith, G., Stokes, J., Tyler, D. and Woodman, D. (2008) *Generations and Social Change: Negotiating Adulthood in the 21st Century*, Melbourne, Australian Youth Research Centre.

2. Changes in youth transitions to parenthood in Bulgaria: Challenges to youth and family policies

By Siyka Kovacheva

The economic crisis that took place in Europe toward the end of the turbulent first decade of the 21st century hit young people disproportionately hard. Their educational prospects worsened significantly with the rise of tuition fees and cuts in university budgets in most European countries while youth unemployment rates grew much faster than those of the other age groups. How are these changes affecting family formation and parenthood, which is the other important passage to adulthood?

Young parenthood has come to the fore in public debates in Europe fueled by concerns with dropping birth rates and ageing populations. Global market competition spurs such anxieties by demanding higher activity rates, and a more qualified and more flexible workforce. In this context, can the young generation today meet those rising expectations and what kind of youth and family policies should be devised to assist them in making transitions to adulthood and successful social integration?

This paper searches for answers to the above questions in the context of the social transformation of Bulgaria. Over the past twenty years the country has experienced a radical liberalisation of its economy and has opened to the global market with its ups and downs, as well as its opportunities for entrepreneurship and unemployment which were stifled during the previous regime. Meanwhile, the economic shift was accompanied by a significant population decline due to a sharp drop in fertility and a rise in emigration abroad. All these changes have had a strong impact on youth transitions to work and family formation, and the prospects and modes of the new generation's social integration. The changes have also posed the current policy dilemma of how to support young people in work and parenthood in a way that leaves room for and promotes young people's agency.

Theoretical and methodological considerations

This paper employs the theoretical approach developed in the discussions within the framework of the UP2YOUTH project (Walther, Stauber and Pahl, 2009; du Bois-Reymond, 2009a). It builds upon the understanding that social change is not only influencing youth transitions but is also driven by young people responding to the changing world. Agency in this context is understood as the individual's ability to set goals, make choices, reflect upon one's actions and take charge of one's biography (Alheit, 2005; Walther *et al.*, 2006). It has to be underlined that agency is a relational concept and is expressed in one's relationships towards other people and to the societal institutions which provide resources and limits for individual actions.

The concept of agency is particularly relevant for the exploration of young people's lives in Europe in late modernity when youth transitions have become less standardized, more flexible, less associated with one another, and more reversible than in the past. Under such conditions of risks and uncertainties, young people are no longer following pre-destined transitions structured along class and gender lines but are facing more choices. Young people are often seen as active agents of their transitions, coping with biographical dilemmas, making sense of gender, and devising new models of working and parenting as well as new strategies for achieving a work-life balance (Chisholm and Kovacheva, 2002; Stauber, 2006).

These changes are a manifestation of the process of individualization which affects all young people in late modern societies. However, their individual biographical journeys are still shaped by the welfare, gender and family regimes, and the dominant religious and cultural norms of their own country, as well as by the structural inequalities within that country among different subgroups of youth. While there is evidence of individualization among young people in Europe, it is to a different extent and in different forms, depending on the distinct social situations in their countries and the diverse social resources that the young have at their disposal: family support, educational achievements, lifelong learning opportunities, social and cultural capital. Young people's choices for actions or non-actions are not borderless and are embedded in a structure of opportunities and constraints. The understanding that the growing importance of reflexivity and choices meet with the structural impacts of old, as well as new, predictors is conveyed in the concept of structural individualization (Furlong and Cartmel, 1997; Walther *et al.*, 2006). It entails the contextualisation of the study of young people's agency with regard to social inequalities.

Parenthood is a complex transition process which young people have to pass through and increasingly have to manage (Leccardi and Ruspini, 2006; du Bois-Reymond and Chisholm, 2006). At present it is intermingled with the transition from education to employment and from precarious to more stable jobs, (but also a possible return to school or precariousness), from the parental home to independent housing (or back to sharing with one's parents), through various forms of relationships and leisure pursuits. Modern trajectories are more fluid and force young adults to make choices at many critical points at one time. Becoming a parent is a key moment in life which increases responsibility and raises new demands of how to combine educational, work, family, leisure and other trajectories into a healthy and satisfactory balance, and a fulfilling life (du Bois-Reymond, 2009b).

The analysis in this paper is based upon a combination of different sources: a review of academic literature, official statistics and research data from the Transitions project[1] (*Gender, Parenthood and the Changing European Workplace: young adults negotiating the work-family boundary*). Secondary analysis of in-depth interviews with Bulgarian respondents provides the ground for a reflection upon the experiences, meanings and consequences of individual strategies that young prospective and actual parents apply in order to combine work and family, under the conditions of a withdrawal of state support and contradictory company policies and practices in Bulgaria.

---

1 *Transitions* was an eight-country comparative project funded by the 5th Framework Program of the European Commission with the aim to investigate how young people who were employees in private and public organizations negotiated parenthood and work-family boundaries. The research methods included organizational case studies, focus groups and biographical interviews conducted between 2003 and 2006 in Bulgaria, France, the Netherlands, Norway, Portugal, Slovenia, Sweden and the UK. The rich data allowed for the comparison of forms of national welfare provision, forms of employer support in the private and public sector in each country, and traditions of informal help from family and friends. The project analyzed how these dimensions influenced the experiences of young working parents of different gender, ethnic backgrounds, occupational status and household situations.

The social context

In post-socialist Bulgaria youth is no longer a clear cut phase in the life course but has turned into a condition with an uncertain outcome. In only a century our understanding of youth has been significantly challenged at least twice – once through communist modernization, when youth appeared as a social category, and then again with the capitalist liberalization which gave birth to the opposite trend – the *deconstruction* of youth as a social category (Wallace and Kovacheva, 1998). Correspondingly, the condition of youth changed from being only a 'sip of happiness' in peasant society – a brief period before the taking up of heavy family and work responsibilities (Khadzijski, 1943), through the 'driving force of the new society' in the communist construction, when the period of youth was fixed between the ages of Komsomol membership from 14 to 28 (Semov, 1985), to the present state of uncertainty where youth is a prolonged period of waiting and adulthood is losing its self-evident quality.

Young women and men in early 21st century Bulgaria share many common trends and experiences with youth in Europe as a whole, such as the diversification of educational paths by mixing formal with non-formal education and training; the combination of work and study; the growth of precarious jobs and of mobility for studies; the prevalence of work and travel in the enlarged Europe; the rising importance of leisure in the process of identity formation; the spread of consumerism and global cultures; the more individualised forms of religious affiliation; and the more individualised and expressive forms of political involvement. Indeed, the sharp withdrawal of state intervention in youth after 1989 has resulted in more freedom and less control but also in less support, leading to individualization and privatization of youth problems. Social research in the country has described youth as a vulnerable group as social transformation gets underway (Stoilova, 2001; Mitev, 2005; Kovacheva, 2006).

Youth in present day Bulgaria do not benefit much from the pluralisation of schools and universities, the opening up of access to higher education, the democratization of teaching and the new opportunities for non-formal learning. Many young people fall out of the system and the country lags behind the EU average enrollment rates. Thus in Bulgaria in 2010-11 the enrollment in primary school (ISCO-1) was already as low as 91.5%, in secondary school (ISCO-3A, 3C) 80.3% and only 34.6% in university (ISCO-5A). The National Statistical Institute (NSI, 2011a) classified 14% of young people as 'early school-leavers'. Lifelong learning was a rare practice and only 1.2% of the population aged 25-64 was enrolled in some kind of education and training. The liberalisation of the economy and its opening up to world markets have created new modes for the employment integration of the young: to start working in Western-style foreign-owned or mixed companies, to venture into their own businesses, to settle in jobs in the state or private sector as employees or to work abroad for a period of time. Very often young people combine these opportunities or switch between them. Twenty years after the start of reforms, however, the labour market in Bulgaria continues to be unfriendly for the young entrants, although the situation improved significantly in comparison with the 1990s. Statistical data shows that the activity rate in the age group 15-24 in 2010 was only 22%, while it was 59.7% for the whole working age population (15-64) which in turn was 5% lower than the average of the EU (NSI, 2011b). Young people tend to concentrate in the precarious sectors of the labour market, holding insecure temporary jobs, with flexible working schedules, often without employment contracts (Kovacheva, 2006; Sotirova, 2007). With the economic crisis, unemployment in the country rose from 6.3% in 2008 to 9.5% in 2010 and the unemployment rate among young people aged 15-24 reached 23.2% in 2010, which was more than twice the general unemployment rate. In the group of young unemployed those with low or no education are at the greatest risk of long-term unemployment. However, the unemployment rate among youth with higher education is not as high in Bulgaria as it is in southern European countries such as Portugal or Spain. Nevertheless, there is no official data on how many young people with university degrees work in low-skilled jobs, for example in catering and security.

Among the structural factors for youth disadvantage, ethnicity has the greatest influence on the opportunities for social integration of youth in Bulgaria. Most disadvantaged are young people coming from families of Roma and Turkish ethnicity who comprise 4.9% and 8.8% of the population respectively in 2011, according to the last census (NSI, 2011c). Belonging to such a group means several times higher risks for early school-leaving, long term unemployment and poverty. In the Roma group less than one out of ten has completed education higher than basic, and the illiteracy rate is more than 18% and has been rising since 1991 (Simeonova et al, 2007). The same report calculates a ten times higher poverty rate amongst the Roma than amongst ethnic Bulgarians, yet the ratio between the two ethnic groups in unemployment rates is similar. The relevant rates for the Turkish minority have a value between those of the Bulgarians and the Roma.

Gender differences in employment and unemployment comprise a mixed model and are often not as visible in Bulgaria as they are in many advanced economies. Thus Eurostat data shows that women's employment rate in 2010 was 8% lower than that of men, and that the gender pay gap was 15%, which is less than the EU average of 17% (Eurostat, 2011). The average number of hours worked weekly is 41 for both women and men and the predominant employment pattern for households in Bulgaria is still that of full-time jobs for both partners. Flexibility in terms of time, place, and legal conditions for men and women is very low and does not differ much. Thus, only 1.5% of the employed held part-time jobs in 2010. However, what contributes most to the imbalances between women and men in Bulgaria is the unequal division of housework among the partners and the traditional gender ideologies about family roles (Stoyanova and Kirova, 2008). The European Quality of Life Survey (2007) found that women did about 6 hours of housework more than men every week. And respondents from Bulgaria in the European Social Survey (Tilkidziev and Dimova, 2010) scored among the lowest on the scale measuring attitudes to gender equality. The dominant culture assumes women's greater commitment to unpaid care for dependent family members and men's greater responsibility for career advancement and entrepreneurship. Given the long hours spent in the workplace, working mothers commonly alternate between full-time care for their young children and full-time jobs, reducing both the number of children they choose to have and their career achievements.

Transitions to parenthood – forms and meanings

Survey data documents significant changes in the forms, timing and meanings attached to family formation and parenthood by young men and women in Bulgaria. They attest to a growing individualization among youth in the country as well as to a continuing impact of some of the structural limitations of economic constraints and cultural barriers.

One of the most visible changes in young people's experiences attesting to the process of individualisation is the decline of the value of formal marriage in young people's attitudes. Marriage is no longer perceived as a necessary precondition to parenthood (Mitev, 2005). This value change is confirmed by official statistics (NSI, 2011c). Thus in 2010 more children were born to unmarried parents and comprised half of all children born, and this has been a steep rise from 12% in 1990. This change has been accompanied by a trend toward a growth in the number of de facto marriages. It reached 70% among young households in 2010. Cohabitation is a preferred option for many young people as it allows greater freedom for the individual partners. Mitev (2005, p. 75) summarizes this change in the following way – the emancipation of sex from marriage brought about by the young generation in the 1970s is now being replaced by the emancipation of parenthood from state authorisation, expressed in the 'decoupling' of child birth and child rearing from formal marriage.

Another strategy employed by young people to manage the increasing uncertainty of the transition to adulthood is having children later in life. The average age of mothers giving birth for the first time grew from 21 in 1990 to 27.5 in 2010 (NSI, 2011c). Studying this trend, Stefanov and Dimitrov (2003) attribute this to the aspirations of the young to get a higher education, a proper job and to start a career. Another important factor is the high emigration of young people from the country, which, however, has not been studied from the perspective of their transition to parenthood. At the same time young people decide upon having fewer children, although this trend is not linear. The official demographic data shows that the crude birth rate (number of live-born children to 1000 persons of the population) was 12.1 in 1990; it reached its minimal value of 7.7 in 1997 and rose slightly to 8.4 in 2010. The other statistical indicator – the coefficient for total fertility rate measuring the number of children a mother would give birth to – was 1.81 in 1990; it reached its minimum of 1.12 in 1997 and since then it has been slowly rising to reach 1.49 in 2010.

The decrease of the birth rate is mainly a result of avoiding the birth of a second or subsequent child, while childlessness as a choice is very rare. In his studies Mirchev (2009) found that the main reason given by childless respondents was 'poor health'. He argues that risky lifestyles, as well as the widespread practice of abortion, have had their negative effect on the health of both men and women, which leads to various disturbances in reproductive ability. The crisis in the health system due to a lack of funding and inefficient reforms has added to this problem with the declining access to prophylactic examinations (Mihova and Nikolova, 2005). According to their survey data only one out of ten women has visited a gynecologist for the past three years. Young people in Bulgaria are prone to risky sexual styles despite wider knowledge about AIDS and reproductive health (Kozeva and Kostova, 2007).

Many demographic studies (Belcheva, 2004; Mihova and Nikolova, 2005) have found that young people have fewer children than they wish for. Even though practical reproductive ideals are now for fewer children they do not correspond to personal ideals. In surveys and focus groups it is economic reasons that are cited most often as an explanation of this gap – low earnings; bad housing conditions; low child-support benefits; expensive children's food and clothing. Belcheva (2004) argues that the gap between the reproductive intentions and reproductive ideals of the young is mainly caused by the feeling of insecurity in the workplace and insecurity about the development of society general.

The strategies of delaying parenthood and reducing the number of children in the family are not unanimously applied by all young people in the country. Most widely discussed in the media are the diverging patterns between the Bulgarian, Turkish and Roma ethnic groups, although there is not enough reliable research data (Mirchev, 2005; Tomova, 2005). Mitev (2006) provides the following statistical data – at the age of 18 only 4% of Bulgarian women have given birth to a child while 34% of the Roma women have already done so. At the age of 25 half of the young women in the Bulgarian ethnic group have no children, compared to a quarter of those in the Turkish minority and only one eighth in the Roma minority. According to the author, these indicators demonstrate the continuing gender inequality among the Roma and Turkish minorities, where there is a strong adherence to the traditional gender roles and young women are clearly disadvantaged. Similar differences among the ethnic groups have been found in the reproductive ideals (Stefanov and Dimitrov, 2003) – the ethnic minorities wish for more children than ethnic Bulgarians. However, it should be noted that young people in both the Roma and Turkish minorities also have fewer children and later in life in comparison with the previous generations of ethnic parents.

Poverty is another factor influencing the transition to parenthood of many young people in Bulgaria. Having a child raises the risk of falling into poverty (Buhler and Philipov, 2005). However, to our knowledge there are no empirical studies focusing on young parents living in poverty and their coping strategies in Bulgaria. According to Eurostat's measures of poverty (2010), young people in Greece, Spain, Italy and Portugal and the East European countries of Slovakia and Romania are much more disadvantaged, compared to the other age groups within the population of the respective country, than youth in Bulgaria. In Bulgaria young people are protected from this extreme consequence of unemployment mainly by generous parental support rather than by the social protection offered by the state (Biggart and Kovacheva, 2006).

Single mothers are another vulnerable group which, however, has not been the focus of a recent study. They are not present in public debates in the country, unlike in the UK, for example (du Bois-Reymond, 2009a). Mihova and Nikolova (2005) report survey data according to which young women are often discriminated against by employers on the basis of their family status and childcare responsibilities, which forces young mothers in particular to take jobs under their level of qualification. One coping strategy often applied by single mothers in Bulgaria is to live in a common household with their own parents, even if they have been living independently before childbirth (Kovacheva, 2010).

Research data reveals a significant differentiation between young men and young women in their values about family and children. While the two-child model is accepted as the ideal number of children in the family by most young people in Bulgaria, women more often prefer the one-child model, and men are more willing than women to have three or more children. The preference for a family without children is shared by 2% of men and 1.1% of women in the country (Stefanov and Dimitrov, 2003). The authors also found that an urban or rural type of settlement is also a significant factor in people's preferences for the number of children in the family. Thus people living in rural areas wish for more children than those in towns and cities. Paradoxically, young people with no education, or elementary education only, and university graduates share common ideals for the number of children in the family, which differs significantly from those of young people with a medium level of education. Those belonging to the lowest and the highest educational groups more often prefer the multiple-child model (with three or more children per family).

Concluding this overview of statistical and survey data, it should be underlined that from a demographic perspective, population changes in society take decades to be registered as significant. From a generational perspective, however, differences in behaviour between children and parents might look radical. As one interviewee, a 49 year old engineer and father of a 26 year old English studies student put it: *"At his age I had a job and a family while he is only enjoying himself"* (Kovacheva, 2010). In the next paragraph we will look deeper into the strategies that young people in the country employ when making the transition to parenthood and trying to shape their lives in a subjectively meaningful way.

Managing young parenthood

The transition to parenthood in 21st century Bulgaria is no longer perceived as 'self-evident' and 'natural'. The agency of young people is manifested in making reflective choices and social innovation when sequencing transition steps and combining work, childcare and leisure. Qualitative information from the *Transition* project reveals that young people are actively searching for opportunities, and consciously developing capabilities for managing various demands and achieving social integration. In 2005, focus groups were organized with employees in public sector agencies in social care, and then in-depth interviews were carried out with selected participants who were also young parents of children aged up to 7 (Nilsen and Brannen, 2005). This paragraph analyses the agency of young parents in Bulgaria on the basis of two case studies from this project.

Nelly is 28 years old, lives in a big city and is a social worker in the Child Protection Unit of the Agency for Social Assistance. She is living with her partner and three year old daughter. She is from a working class family and left her home town to study in the city at the age of 15. Since then she has been largely autonomous in her life-style and has practiced many of the new forms of behavior that were uncommon for her parents' generation, but which have become widespread among her peers. She combined study and work while in high school and then at university, and changed jobs several times, all in the informal economy. Nelly explained that she valued those jobs for the financial independence and the experience of meeting different people.

She had worked as a waitress for almost a year after graduation when she decided to leave her precarious job and look for a job in her university specialty. She defined this as a critical moment in her life, a moment of self-exploration and key choice.

> One day I told myself: 'Is working at a restaurant... your goal in life? No! Then you should do something to make use of your university degree.' And I quit the job in order to look around and search for an opening for social workers.

Nelly's agency proved successful – she found an open position for a social worker at an NGO dealing with children. She felt highly satisfied with her job, which turned out to 'suit her personality, her understanding of the world'. Later this organization was co-opted in the newly formed state Agency for Social Assistance, which meant that Nelly had to apply for the new position again through a process of written and oral exams just at the time when her daughter was six months old.

Nelly's transition to parenthood was also not very traditional and required choices, reflection and negotiation on her part. She had had a stable relationship since her last year of high school with a young man who was a skilled worker in a construction company, and they started cohabiting after he came back from the one-year military service which was then mandatory for men in Bulgaria. Having lived together with her partner for about seven years, she found herself pregnant. Nelly reflected upon this situation:

> I had always wanted to have a child but tended to see it always in the future tense [laughs]… When I found out [that she was pregnant], I felt that I was ready, that if it comes I will cope with it but it wasn't specially planned, it was not an aim…

Nelly's agency is best manifested in all the negotiations she had to initiate in order to find a satisfactory work-life balance after she became a mother: negotiations with her parents to take care of the baby for two months until it was eight-month old – the age limit required by public crèches; with the managers in the state Department for Child Protection who were reluctant to take her on when they understood that she had a very young baby; with her partner who had to pick their daughter up from the kindergarten in the evenings as Nelly often worked long hours; even with her young daughter who '*was always first on the phone*'. She gradually built a network of neighbors, colleagues and friends on whom she relied in emergencies. She is very proud of her partner who accepted a reduction of his salary in exchange for not traveling on long business trips, so that he was able to look after their daughter in the evenings. This modest accommodation in his career was a big step in the direction of the 'new fatherhood' – which is another area where public debate is silent in Bulgaria, unlike the discourses in the Western countries included in the project (Lewis et al, 2009).

Negotiating new practices and new roles between partners is at the same time a process of biographical learning. The case of Nelly's transition to parenthood demonstrates the significance of both formal and informal learning. In her interview she pointed out the mutual enrichment of her experiences as a social worker and as a mother. She explained that she learned how to deal with critical situations at home in the process of managing conflicts with clients and discussing cases with her colleagues. It worked the other way round as well – the security and the support she felt from her family helped her deal with stressful circumstances at work. She is very pleased with her daughter's achievements and wishes to see her grow up as an '*autonomous and happy person*'.

At present Nelly manages to combine many activities – she works full time at the State Agency, studies part time in an MA programme in Human Resources Management and manages her family life successfully:

> When I don't do anything, when I am in doubt, I do not feel solid ground beneath me, I feel horrible. When I have reached a decision, when I can act, it is exactly the opposite – I am calm, I feel responsible, I feel in charge, I can change the world...

The second case study of young people's agency in their transition to adulthood is an ethnic minority woman. Filiz is 23, and employed on a temporary contract as a 'social consultant' in the Agency for Social Assistance. Roma herself, her job is to help qualified social workers deal with clients from the Roma minority. She is a mother of two children aged six and four. Filiz was born and grew up in one of the most deprived city suburbs in Bulgaria with wide spread poverty and a high unemployment rate. Even though it is very close to the city centre the suburb is highly isolated in a ghetto-like way where about 30,000 people, mostly Roma and Turks, occupy a few square kilometers filled with small clay houses and narrow streets. Filiz started following the traditional life course transitions of the young in her ethnic community – she finished school at 15 and got married the same year. In less than a year Filiz formed a family, moved to live with her husband and his parents, became a housewife and a mother.

> 'I wasn't ready yet for all that, not at all, but it happened... And I had to deal with it.'

In the new family there was a traditional division of labor which meant that Filiz had to take care of the children and all domestic tasks. Her husband is from the Turkish ethnicity and is two years older. He is an unskilled worker, has an insecure low-income job, and that is how she explained his long hours at work and little involvement in childcare. We should, however, take into consideration the role that the more traditional values concerning gender play in ethnic and particularly Turkish minority families (Tomova, 2005).

In these difficult circumstances, Filiz nonetheless found herself capable of agency and social innovation. She managed to mobilize her personal resources despite cultural and economic constraints. When her second child turned three years old – old enough to be placed in a public kindergarten, Filiz decided to take charge of her life and initiated many changes. She signed up as a private student to get a secondary education and found a job at the Agency of Social Assistance. The family moved to a different suburb which was much better than the previous one, occupying one story of a larger house owned by her parents-in-law. All things considered, Filiz thinks that she has done well for herself and has climbed up the social ladder:

> I have always wanted a good home. I have it now. I like the neighborhood a lot. And I don't plan to go anywhere else. But I do hope we have a car one day.

Filiz explained the motivation for change as '*being tired to be looked upon by her husband's relatives*' although she could not point at a definite moment when she took the critical decisions. She is still being traditional in many ways. Her role as a mother is very important for her own identity and her place in society. She misses the opportunity to make nice cookies for her children, to have warm meals every evening. But Filiz has employed agency in many new ways and also considers her job very important for her identity and self-fulfillment:

> I like it a lot that we communicate with people and help people... Some come and complain and argue that we are not doing enough but also there are people who are grateful. There are people who did not like me that much before but are now friendly and respectful.

Her job changed her relationship with her husband as well. Filiz managed to reshape the power relations at home and bring innovation into the gender relations in the family, thus changing the patriarchal gender norms. In her narrative, the young woman underlined that she valued her newly gained freedom very much. She felt more mature and had higher self esteem.

> Before, when I was a housewife, my husband was very jealous. He didn't want me out of the house. Now after I started working, things changed. Now I can go out whenever I want. I often go to cafes with the girls [from the job].

Acting in new ways involves a process of informal learning. Filiz reflected upon how the widening of her contacts broadened the information for practicing motherhood. Previously it was only her mother-in-law to whom she could turn for advice in dealing with her children. At present she exchanged experiences and learnt a lot from her colleagues, as well as from other mothers bringing children to the kindergarten or taking them back home in the evening.

Like Nelly, Filiz has an active stance toward life. Her personal agency allows her to overcome some of the restrictions which are much stronger in disadvantaged groups of young parents.

To make things better for myself, I have to act. This is the truth that I have learnt... But sometimes acting can only hurt you. When you want to do something, to change something, they start piling things against you... I may achieve a little only, but I feel satisfied.'

The two cases presented in this paragraph show important aspects of young people's agency in Bulgaria. As in other modern societies, the competence for negotiating and communicating is widening the space for action and choices, allowing young people to move between constraints and resources. Learning how to balance individual goals and the agendas of various institutions is of even greater value in the post-socialist context, where the reforming state administrations and newly formed private companies still lack enough established and legitimate practices. Under such circumstances effective action depends a lot on the capacities and willingness to cooperate of individual actors within the institutions. Investing in networks and building trust between actors lies at the heart of the concept of social capital, and also proves a significant facilitator of young people's agency.

Policy support for young working parents

Young people's agency develops within the structure of opportunities and constraints on the national and local level. It is strongly dependent upon the access to social rights, which in turn are largely shaped by the model of the welfare state in which youth transitions take place, as well as by company policies, norms of intergenerational support and the activities and engagement of civic organizations with young parents. These constellations are expressions of structured individualization and may advance or inhibit young people's power of agency (Kovacheva, 2006; du Bois Reymond, 2009b).

The welfare state in Bulgaria cannot be clearly defined along the regime typologies as proposed by Esping-Andersen (1990) and Gallie and Paugnam (2000)[2]. In comparative analysis it is usually defined as post-

---

2   In his renowned book 'The Three Worlds of Welfare Capitalism' (1990) Esping-Andersen distinguished between a liberal social policy regime providing minimal state support only for those with a proven need and maintaining the market as the main care provider; a social democratic regime with a well developed welfare state and universalistic access to social rights; and a corporatist or conservative regime based on preserving status differentials and an emphasis on traditions. The liberal type is

socialist. This cluster usually groups together countries with divergent policy characteristics such as Slovenia, the Czech Republic, Hungary and Estonia (Walther, 2006; Kovacheva *et al.*, 2011). What the term says is more about the starting point of the transition than about its current state or future direction.

The diverging and often contradictory trends in social policy reforms in Bulgaria have been widely criticized (Yachkova, 2002; Belcheva, 2004) for their lack of consistency, disregard of research evidence, and reactive instead of preventive approach. One particular weakness relevant here is the total lack of a bridge between the policies assisting the transition from school to work and the transition to parenthood, as well as the lack of recognition of youth as a life stage with specific needs and resources (Kovacheva, 2010). Parenthood is seen by the national legislation as a demographic problem having no bearing on youth and hence the strategy is focused on stimulating fertility.

While spending on families and children is very low in Bulgaria (1.1% of GDP), the national regulation on parental leave and provision of public childcare services are among the longest and well paid in Europe. Thus the statutory leave arrangements for parents in 2011 include 410 days of maternity leave paid at 90% of earnings, followed by 1 year of parental leave paid at a fixed sum and an additional year of unpaid leave. There is an extensive network of subsidised public childcare centres (even though shortages are experienced in big cities), and more than 80% of children between the ages of 3 and 6 are enrolled in them on a full time basis. When parents return to work, they are allowed to take up to 60 days per year of paid leave to care for a sick child. Parental leave presents good opportunities for parents to keep jobs while caring for very young children. At the same time, the long leave policy replicates outlived models of gendered divisions of work and care in the family, as it is almost always women that use the caring leaves. The long absence from the workplace serves as an obstacle for women's occupational development and often acts as a discriminatory factor in employers' recruitment policies.

---

exemplified by the US, Canada, Australia and the UK; the social democratic model is represented by the Scandinavian countries, and the third one, by continental European countries such as Germany, Austria and France. Gallie and Paugnam (2000) later added a forth type of welfare regime in order to account for the specificity of the Mediterranean countries, the "subprotective cluster" which is characterised by the lowest level of state-provided security and by the major role of the family and friends in people's coping strategies.

Attempts to involve fathers to a greater extent in using the parental leave have not yet been successful. When paid maternity leave was prolonged to 315 days in 2007 and then to 410 days in 2009, fathers initially were not allowed to use any part of it. Under pressure from civil society organisations, the law was amended so that fathers are currently allowed to take a 'maternity leave' once the child is six months old. These efforts have been frustrated, however, by the reduction in income families experience when fathers take this leave and the consequent negative effect on family budgets and fathers' careers. Gender stereotyping at the workplace and in society at large is another preventive factor for men's greater involvement in childcare. There is still no evidence as to how many fathers make use of the paid paternity leave of 15 days, which fathers can use or lose upon the birth of a child – a measure which was introduced in 2009.

Company policies are less supportive to young working parents than the statutory measures. Most managers consider that it is not their responsibility to help young people in their efforts to combine job requirements and childcare responsibilities. The new business culture that has started to dominate both state and private companies in Bulgaria also brings about the gap between ideal and real number of children in Bulgarian families. The organization study in the *Transitions* project on two companies in Bulgaria (one private, in the banking sector, and one state social services agency) showed that managers and employees in the country had accepted the values of business efficiency, commitment to work, long-hours culture and loyalty to the company (Kovacheva, 2010) as 'the most relevant' for the country's transition to a market economy. The Human Resources Manager of the private bank claimed that '*there is no private employer caring for the employees*' while the Director of the Regional Office of the State Agency for Social Assistance explained to the interviewer that '*we are supposed to care for the people in need, not for our employees*'.

Trade unions as major actors in the social dialogue in Bulgaria have been more active in wage negotiations and job protection than in measures of support for young employees. The *Transitions* study showed that social networks in the workplace acted as a source of social capital which often filled the gaps in flexibility of work or other company policies (Kovacheva, 2009). Employees relied on 'understanding' line managers and colleagues in cases of family emergencies. Young people and their managers did not see the employer as responsible for creating better conditions for their well-being at the workplace and beyond. Working parents' feelings of entitlement to support were most often directed toward the state, which was expected and perceived to create family-friendly laws and regulations. Parents found the leave policy of the state quite generous in terms of length but were highly dissatisfied with the financial conditions of the leave, and with child benefits as being very low.

Parents' associations and other civic organisations in Bulgaria also provide policy support for young parents (Kovacheva and Kabaivanov, 2009) by insisting on policy changes on the national level, pressuring local authorities and providing information and advice. Using new channels of information in their daily activities and when organising protest campaigns, they seem more open, flexible and responsive to newly emerging problems of young parents than the more traditional policy actors. Young parents themselves form numerous social networks on the Internet, exchanging information on how to deal with state bureaucracy or other pertinent issues.

Conclusions

This paper explored the problematic experiences of becoming and being a young parent in Bulgaria. The analysis showed that radical societal changes in Bulgaria in the first decade of the 21st century have speeded up the process of individualization among young people. They are more mobile and liberalized in their values and behaviours than the previous generations. The diversification of family forms, with greater shares of cohabiting couples, single mothers and couples without children, together with the reduction of the number of children born in the family and the rise of the age of first-time parents attest to this trend. However, the continuing and, in some estimates, growing dependence of young people on their parents for housing, income and childcare limits the opportunities for self-development of the young. Traditional gender stereotypes, low incomes and ethnic inequalities are significant barriers in meeting youth aspirations for parenthood and a fulfilling life. At the same time young people's agency develops their capacities of motherhood and fatherhood in innovative ways, and broadens the scope for choice and actions when balancing work and care, study and leisure.

State institutions make efforts to reform the policies of assistance for youth, but the programs and practices remain largely rigid and unresponsive to young people's individualized needs and interests. Young parents' efforts for a rewarding work/life balance are largely ignored by trade union and company policies. Athough social, income and educational inequalities are rising in the market-oriented society, and cultural differences exist between the ethnic groups within the country, family policy is still highly centralized and uniform. There seems to be a growing recognition among researchers and experts that this policy should be individualized and flexible, accommodating the different life situations and the varying ambitions of young people. Most importantly, such family policy in support of young parents should no longer remain a narrowly defined demographic policy but be based on a strategy for wider support for young people's life transitions, creating conditions for their embodiment as citizens and consumers, students, employees and parents. Policies, where they have existed up to now, have a very thin spread and serve older people more often than youth in need. Niether are they based on research evidence about the young people's aspirations they are supposed to support. No real attempts are made to involve the young in devising such policies, and thus recognising the right to be actors in their own lives and in society as a whole. This short overview of the problematic transition to parenthood in Bulgaria shows that there is a need for a systematic and comprehensive research into the factors influencing youth transitions before adopting a new strategy for the country's youth policy, taking into account the subjective needs of young people.

Bibliography

Alheit, P. (2005) Stories and structures: An essay on historical times, narratives and their hidden impact on adult learning, *Studies in the Education of Adults, 37(2)*, pp. 201-212.

Belcheva, M. (2004) *Socio-Demographic Studies and Analyses,* Sofia, Faber.

Biggart, A. and S. Kovacheva (2006) Social Change, Family Support, and Young Adults in Europe, in du Bois-Reymond, M. and Chisholm, L. (eds) *The Modernisation of Youth Transitions in Europe, 113 (Fall)*, Wiley Periodicals, pp. 49-62.

Buhler, C. and D. Philipov (2005) Social Capital Related to Fertility: theoretical foundations and empirical evidence from Bulgaria, MPIDR Working Paper, WP 2005-016.

Chisholm, L. and Kovacheva, S. (2002) Exploring the European youth mosaic: The social situation of young people in Europe, Strasbourg, Council of Europe.

du Bois-Reymond, M. (2009a) *Young parenthood, agency and social change. Thematic report*, Leiden, University of Leiden.

du Bois-Reymond, M. (2009b) Young parenthood in the Netherlands, *Young – Nordic Journal of Youth Research, 17(3)*, pp. 265-283.

du Bois-Reymond, M. and Chisholm, L. (eds) (2006) Modernization of Youth Transitions in Europe, *New Directions of Child and Adolescent Development, 13 (Fall)*, San Francisco, Jossey-Bass.

Esping-Andersen, G. (1990) *The Three Worlds of Welfare Capitalism*, Cambridge, Polity Press.

Eurofoundation (2007) *European Quality of Life Survey*, http://www.eurofound. europa.eu/areas/qualityoflife/eqls/2007/index.htm (accessed December 10 2011).

Eurostat (2011) *Labour Force Survey*, http://epp.eurostat.ec.europa.eu/portal/page/ portal/statistics/search_database (accessed December 10 2011).

Furlong, A. and Cartmel, F. (1997) Young People and Social Change: Individualisation and Risk in Late Modernity, Buckingham, Open University Press.

Gallie, D. and S. Paugnam (eds) (2000) *Welfare Regimes and the Experience of Unemployment in Europe*, Oxford, Oxford University Press.

Khadzijski, I. (1974) *The Way of Life and Mentality of Our People, 2*, Sofia, Bulgarian Writer.

Kovacheva, S. (2010) *Work Family Balance*, Sofia, East-West.

Kovacheva, S. (2006) Social report: Constellations of disadvantage and policy dilemmas in youth transitions from school to work in Bulgaria, *Social Work and Society*, 4(2).

Kovacheva, S., van Doorne-Huiske, J. and Anttila, T. (2011) Institutional Context of the Quality of Life in Europe, in Back-Wiklund, M. (ed) *Quality of Life and Work in Europe: Theory, Policy, Practice*, Basingstoke, Palgrave Macmillan.

Kovacheva, S. and Kabaivanov, S. (2009) Old and New Actors in Bulgarian Family Policy, in Hristova-Valcheva, K. (ed) *New Actors in a New Environment: Accession to the European Union, Civil Society and Multi-Level Governance*, Sofia, BECSA.

Kozeva, T and Kostova, D. (2007) *Young People and Intimacy in Times of Social Change*, Sofia, Prof. Drinov Academic Publishing House.

Leccardi, C. and Ruspini, E. (eds) (2006) *A New Youth? Young People, Generations and Family Life*, Aldershot, Ashgate.

Lewis, S., Brannen, J. and Nilsen, A. (eds) (2009) *Work, Family and Organisations in Transition: A European Perspective*, Bristol, Policy Press.

Mihova, G. and Nikolova, M. (2005) The Changes in Labour and the Demographic Behaviour, in Ivanov, M. and Atanasov, A. (eds) *Demographic Development of the Republic of Bulgaria*, Sofia, NCCEDPMC, BAS, NSI, UNPF, pp. 149-154.

Mirchev, M. (2009) Social Dynamics and Civilizational Stratification. The Reproduction of the population, Human Capital and Labour Force in Bulgaria, Sofia, M-8-M publishing house in Sofia, p. 542.

Mitev, P.-E. (ed) (2005) *The New Young: Bulgarian Youth and the European Perspective*, Sofia, East-West.

Mitev, P.-E. (2006) *Ethnic Aspects of Youth transitions in Transitional Society*, paper presented at the World Congress of Sociology, Durban, South Africa, 23-30 July 2006.

National Statistical Institute (NSI) (2011a) *Education and Lifelong Learning data*, http://www.nsi.bg/otrasal.php?otr=23 (accessed December 10 2011).

National Statistical Institute (NSI) (2011b) *Labour Market data*, http://www.nsi. bg/otrasal.php?otr=26 (accessed December 10 2011).

National Statistical Institute (NSI) (2011c) *Population data*, http://www.nsi.bg/otrasal.php?otr=19 (accessed December 10 2011).

Nilsen, A. and Brannen, J. (2005) Negotiating Parenthood: Consolidated Interview Study, Report for the EU FP5 study *Gender, parenthood and the Changing European Workplace*, Manchester, Manchester Metropolitan University.

Semov, M. (1985) Changes in Youth, in Mitev, P.-E. (ed) *Youth – Problems and Research*, Sofia, People's Youth Press.

Sotirova, M. (ed) *Flexible Employment and Problems in its Regulation*, Plovdiv, 'Paissii Hilendarski' University of Plovdiv Press.

Stauber, B. (2006) Biography and Gender in Youth Transitions, in, du Bois-Reymond, M. and Chisholm, L. (eds) *Modernization of Youth Transitions in Europe: New Directions of Child and Adolescent Development, 13 (Fall)*, San Francisco, Jossey-Bass, pp. 63-76.

Stefanov, R. and Dimitrov, I. (2003) Planned number of children in newlywed families in Bulgaria under the conditions of social and economic transition, *Health Management*, 2, pp. 8-19.

Stoyanova, K. and Kirova, A. (2008) *Gender Inequality in Paid and Unpaid Work*, Sofia, Prof. Drinov Academic Publishing House.

Tilkidziev, N., and Dimova, L. (2010) *Wellbeing and Trust: Bulgaria in Europe, Comparative Analysis of ESS 2006/2009*, Sofia, East-West.

Tomova, I. (2005) Demographic processes in the large ethno-confessional communities in Bulgaria, in Ivanov, M. and Atanasov, A. (eds) *Demographic Development of the Republic of Bulgaria*, Sofia, NCCEDPMC, BAS, NSI, UNPF, pp. 155-177.

Wallace, C. and Kovatcheva, S. (1998) *Youth in Society: The Construction and Deconstruction of Youth in East and West Europe*, London, Macmillan.

Walther, A. (2006) Regimes of Youth Transitions: Choice, flexibility and security in young people's experiences across different European contexts, *Young – Nordic Journal of Youth Research, 14(1)*, pp. 119-141.

Walther, A., Stauber, B. and Pohl, A. (2009) *Youth – Actor of Social Change, Final Report*, Tuebingen, IRIS.

Walther, A., du Bois Reymond, M. and Biggart, A. (eds) (2006) *Participation in Transition: Motivation of young adults in Europe for learning and working*, Frankfurt a. Main, Peter Lang.

Yachkova, M. (2002) The Family in Bulgaria between the XXth and the XXIst century – Prerequisites, Analyses, Prognoses, Sofia, ASSA-M.

3. Transitions and Shifts in Work Attitudes, Values and Future Orientations of Young Finns

By Helena Helve[1]

The transition from education to employment is, in the life-cycle of young people, the time to develop their adult identities and world views within guiding social structures. Erik H. Erikson (1968) interpreted the transition period between childhood and adulthood as an "institutionalized moratoria", during which a lasting pattern of "inner identity" is formed. This experimentation can take various forms of exploration, including leisure-time hobbies, schooling and education, or even dropping out for a while (cf. Erikson, 1968, p. 157; Côté 2006, pp. 47-48). Erikson also acknowledged that societies vary in terms of the degree to which they structure identity moratoria and in terms of how much conformity they demand to the norms and values of adult society during that moratorium. The circumstances of the transition to adulthood have changed since Erikson's theory. Youth unemployment rates have increased and young people are employed on part-time and/or contractual bases in precarious jobs that make it very difficult to attain financial self-sufficiency. Accordingly, higher-education sectors of universities in post-industrial societies have expanded to include significant proportions of their youth populations. For example the US and Canada have almost one half of their citizens in their early 20s attending educational institutions full time (e.g., Côté, 2006; Côté and Allahar, 2011).

---

1   I would like to express my gratitude to the Academy of Finland Work programme for financing my research project, *The changing lifestyles and values of the young in a context of persisting temporary unemployment in different labour markets of Finland* (Work-Preca). I especially thank Arseniy Svynarenko for his assistance as researcher in this project. The material has been partially analysed and published in Helve, 2012.

Higher education and changing social and economic conditions in Finland

The welfare state supports young Finns during their transition from education to work life by health insurance, social insurance and free higher education. One of the main policy objectives over the decades has been to give everyone the opportunity to study.[2] The Finnish higher education system consists of two sectors: science universities and polytechnics (universities of applied sciences), which are more practically oriented, training professionals for expert and development posts. The number of universities in this country with 5.4 million inhabitants testifies to the value of higher education: there are twenty-five polytechnics in Finland, which have developed as part of the national and international higher education community, with programs that put special emphasis on expertise in working life and its development. There are also sixteen science universities. In 2010 the new Aalto University was opened, combining the former universities of art, economics and techniques in Helsinki. Geographically, the higher education network covers the whole country.

Finnish young people start their higher education later than young people in many other countries: two in three students (circa 159,000 students) have had a break of at least one year before or during current studies. The Finnish student survey 2010 shows that 42% of polytechnic students and 38% of university students spent the gap year working in Finland. 26% of students have studied in another higher education program before their current one. Aproximately 70 % of the students at universities and 68 % from polytechnics have completed their studies (on average at the age of 25 in polytechnics and 27 in universities). (The Finnish Student Survey, 2010; Saarenmaa, Saari and Virtanen, 2010; pp. 21-23; Koulutus ja tutkimus vuosina 2011–2016, 2011).

Students at universities may take a lower (Bachelor's) or higher (Master's) academic degree. It generally takes three years to obtain a lower degree, following which it takes two to three years to obtain a Master's. Students may then go on to study for a licentiate and doctoral degree. In addition to the required studies, doctoral students prepare a dissertation, which they defend in public. The requirement for postgraduate studies is a Master's or corresponding degree. The universities choose their stu-

---

2   In international comparisons the level of education of the Finns is relatively high (cf. PISA studies). Almost 90 % of the group aged 25-34 had attained at least upper secondary education.

dents themselves through entrance examination, and there are enough places to accommodate about one third of each age class.

Over ten years ago, in 1999, 84% of 25-29-year-olds had at least full secondary-level education. Nearly 60% of the population had completed post-primary education, while 27% of the population had a university or college degree or equivalent qualification (Statistics Finland, 2002). These numbers have increased in the past ten years. It has been the Finnish Government's aim to ensure that increasing numbers of people move on to higher education, the biggest sectors being technology, arts and humanities, and the natural sciences.

Finland has experienced intense economic changes, going from a state of economic prosperity where the per capita GDP (gross domestic product) was, in 1989, the third highest in the world (after Japan and Switzerland), to the great recession of the 1990s after the collapse of one of our largest trading partners, the Soviet Union, and on to the explosive growth of the Nokia corporation and other IT businesses in its wake. Finland is currently facing, along with other countries in the world, a global economic recession, with rather different symptoms than the one in 1990s, when unemployment, especially youth unemployment, came to be a regular feature of capitalist societies, and when a new underclass of the unemployed was growing, especially in Western European countries. These global changes are not affecting all citizens in the same way. Migrants and ethnic minorities and young people living in remote rural areas are most vulnerable in contemporary labour markets (Fangen, Fossan and Mohn, 2010).

In Finland much of the squeeze from the earlier recession in the early nineties affected young people in particular and this is the case again. Youth unemployment figures are higher than those of other age groups. Youth unemployment has been characterised by rapid quantitative growth, shorter duration and a higher average level of education among unemployed young people than among the unemployed of other age groups. Young people are also more likely than others to remain outside of the compensation system related to unemployment. In fact, changes in the social support law regarding the labour market, which came into effect in 1996, made young people under 20 years old without vocational education entirely ineligible for labour market support payments. Filtering them into educational programmes has statistically reduced youth unemployment, but it can safely be assumed that hidden teenage unemployment has grown, because it is useless for these young people to register themselves with the employment office if there is no benefit to be received (Aho and Vehviläinen, 1997).

Training sites have increased, for example, in adult vocational training, colleges and open colleges. The selection criteria have also changed. Reforms have led to a growing percentage of students among 20-24 year-olds. Every year, however, tens of thousands of young people are still unable to get into the field of training or education that they apply for. Rationally integrating the student grant and unemployment insurance systems has also been problematic. The risk of becoming unemployed is lower for an educated person than for someone with little education. Repeated periods of unemployment are also rarer among the educated, and the average duration of periods between jobs are shorter. The weakening of the employment situation then has most directly affected young people with little education and work experience.

Young people are now coming out of schools into a less stable and more complicated world than before (cf. youth unemployment levels vary from area to area both vocationally and geographically). Previously it was expected that a young person would go straight from school to work, but now there are far more options – for example apprenticeships, workshops, continuing education, higher education, open college programmes and many other alternatives. Young people's attitudes towards work and education also vary, as do their economic possibilities.

For many unemployed young people, problems are combined; their parents are also unemployed, family relations complicated, and without employment they lack the economic resources to move away from home and establish their independence. Becoming an independent adult while living with one's parents is difficult. The situation is the same when young people work temporarily in so-called precarious jobs. The young person has difficulties planning a longer-term future under such circumstances. The importance of assistance from parents has grown since the student grant reforms of 1992. Student grants alone rarely provide a sufficient income for university students to live from, leading to a longer period of dependence on one's parents. If, on the other hand, employment situations become more favourable for young people again, many students would be able to finance their studies through part-time work.

In 1997 the percentage of the Finnish labour force comprised of those under 25 years old was only 8.1 %, the lowest in Europe (see Table 1). However, most Finns under 25 are still in some form of education at that age[3]. Even so, unemployment rates among Finnish young people were

---

3   Since 1996 unemployed people under 20 with no vocational education, who enter the labour market for the first time, have no longer been granted labour market support

very high by European standards. By August 2009, Finnish unemployment rates had come down to below average for EU countries, but they are still far too high for a healthy economic system.

Table 1. Labour force participation and unemployment percentages among 15–24-year olds in European Union Countries in 1997, 2009 and 2011.

Country:	1997 Youth as % of the labour force	1997	2009	2011(Month 12)
			Youth unemployment rate	
Finland	8.1	27.4	18.8	19.9
France	8.4	28.9	22.3	23.8
Belgium	8.8	22.9	21.3	20.07
Greece	9.1	31.0	24.2	47.2
				(Month 10)
Sweden	9.2	21.1	24.2	22.9
Italy	10.4	33.5	24.9	31.0
Luxembourg	10.8	9.1	19.1	15.2
Germany	11.0	9.9	10.5	7.8
Spain	12.4	41.9	33.6	48.7
Portugal	12.8	16.7	19.6	30.8
Austria	14.7	6.0	9.0	8.2
Great Britain	14.9	15.5	17.9	22.3
				(Month 10)
Netherlands	15.3	11.5	6.0	8.6
Denmark	17.1	10.6	8.9	14.7
Ireland	17.2	18.2	21.5	29,0

Source: Euro Statistics 2009, first quarter; Euro Statistics 2011, month 12; Helsingin Sanomat 19.3.1999, A 14.

Table 1 shows that the youth unemployment situation has changed during the last fifteen years in EU 15 countries. Youth unemployment rates have grown on average in all countries other than Finland, France, Belgium, Italy, Germany, and the Netherlands. Youth unemployment improved from 2009 to 2011 in Belgium, Sweden, Luxembourg, Germany, Austria, and became worse in Finland, France, Greece, Italy, Spain, the Netherlands, Portugal, Great Britain, Denmark and Ireland. The worst youth un-

---

unless they have actively applied for education or participated in a labour market policy measure such as practical training. The right to support will be restored when the applicant shows that he or she has completed a vocational qualification. At the beginning of 1997, the reform was extended to cover those under 25. A young person's living allowance can also be reduced if he or she has refused education.

employment rates are in Southern Europe, in Spain (48.7 %), Greece (47.2 %), Portugal (30.8%), Italy (31.0 %) and Ireland (29.0 %).[4]

Recent public discourse and studies of the sociological aspects of work have raised the issues of short-term employment and longer transition periods (e.g. Manninen and Luukannel, 2006; Palanko-Laaka, 2005). The new short-term employment phenomenon is not comparable to traditional part-time or temporary employment, which was often seasonal or productivity-based (Sutela *et al.*, 2001). Short-term employment in the public sector, particularly in nursing, teaching and social services, is a new trend, typified by the 'chaining' (i.e. repeated renewing) of short-term employment contracts, due to a high level of education among employees and by low unemployment. The issue is therefore no longer confined to 'typically' uncertain careers such as art, new media and communications. Many well-educated young people seem to value short-time jobs and they are not ready to bind themselves to life-long careers (Sell, 2004).

Shifts in work life

Many young people with lower education and who are unskilled are working in precarious non-standard employment which is poorly paid, insecure, unprotected and cannot support a household. In recent decades there has been a dramatic increase in precarious work everywhere due to such factors as globalization, the shift from the manufacturing sector to the service sector and the spread of information technology (cf. Rifkin, 1995). These changes have created a new economy which demands flexibility in the workplace and, as a result, they have caused the decline of the standard employment relationship and a dramatic increase in precarious work.

An important aspect of precarious work is its gendered nature, as women are continuously over-represented in this type of work. Precarious work is associated with the following types of employment: part-time employment, self-employment, fixed-term work, temporary work, on-call work, working from home, and telecommuting. All of these forms of employment are related in that they depart from the standard employment relationship (full-time, continuous work with one employer). Each form of precarious work may offer its own challenges but they all share the same

---

4   These are the EU Member States suffering the most important budget deficits and debt levels. Greece, Ireland and Portugal, collectively, account for only six per cent of the Eurozone's Gross Domestic Product.

disadvantages: low wages, few benefits, lack of collective representation, and little to no job security. The precarization of work is very common among immigrants. From a gendered perspective it is more common in female labour markets than in male labour markets (Miettinen, 2007).

Many of the factors mentioned above are affecting not only young people's transitions to adulthood, but also their identity formation, and they represent a serious challenge for society (Fadjukoff, Pulkkinen and Kokko, 2005). The inability to find a job carries psychological costs, causes frustration and depression, and undermines motivation. Youth unemployment is also often associated with such social problems as violence, delinquency, alcohol and drug abuse, crime, and suicide (UNICEF, 2000).

Identity horizon model

Identity formation is connected to the concepts of identity horizon, which characterises the young person's sense of prospects for the future (Côté *et al.*, 2008). The ability to develop a broad identity horizon can be undermined by the personal and social vulnerabilities associated with 'identity anxiety', a psychological state that can inhibit personal and moral development (Stålsett, 2006).

Studies into education can predict that certain family backgrounds produce different levels of academic achievement, which in turns produces different levels of academic engagement (Salmela-Aro, 2009). Optimally, family influences are positive, but some are problematic, and along with other negative influences can produce alienation and underachievement, which in turn lead to disengagement/dropout and ultimately to socio-economic exclusion.

This study exploits the identity horizon model of James Côté (Côté *et al.*, 2008) The hypothesis is that prior experiences will broaden or narrow the future horizon that a person perceives for him/herself, and that this perceived horizon is anchored in the subjective realm of identity. Those with broader horizons should have more positive assessments of the returns in terms of the relationship between benefits and costs because they can anticipate their future involvement in target environments. In contrast, those with narrower horizons will have less positive assessments because of a blockage in their ability to visualize their involvement in environments that are sensed as 'foreign'.

Those with broader identity horizons should thus have more positive perceptions of the potential returns on investments of time, effort, and money devoted to achieving certain goals, and an important source of these perceptions would be parental influences: parents who themselves have broader horizons would promote broader horizons in their children as they grow up. Conversely, a source of a narrowing effect on horizons may come from parents with low levels of educational and occupational attainment. In addition to having fewer role models for estimating cost and benefit for their own futures, those from such backgrounds may be particularly prone to 'identity anxiety' (a non-monetary 'personal' cost of change in one's life) because they do not perceive a goodness of fit for themselves in current and future educational or work settings, and they lack the level of personal agency necessary to rectify that problem them-selves. Moreover, they might have deep-seated apprehensions that they will experience tensions with parents and peers and that they will have to change in ways that are unacceptable to these significant others (Côté *et al.*, 2008, pp. 77-78).

Narrow horizons are more likely to include 'local' goals, while broad horizons include more 'global' goals. Thus, those with narrow horizons will not want to study or work far from where they grew up, while those with broad horizons will have goals that take them away from their local comfort zone into the world at large.

Research questions and data

This paper will present views of the research project *The changing life-styles and values of temporarily employed young people in the different labour markets of Finland* (WORK-Preca 2008-2011[5]). It is based on comparative mixed methods approach studies of shifts of values for young people (Helve, 1993, 2002 and 2005). Analyzing new case study interview data (N=20) gathered in 2009-2010 from young people work-ing temporarily in tourism in Lapland and from an online survey about work attitudes, values, identities and future expectations gathered from university students in 2010-2011, this study focuses on young people's transition from education to work in local and global labor markets. The

---

5   The researchers involved in the project were PhD candidates Arseniy Svynarenko and
     Marjaana Kojo, and post-doctoral researcher Jaana Lähteenmaa.

results will be discussed within the framework of youth transitions, as well as taking into consideration the agents of socialization relating to the expected patterns of value preferences regarding work.

The hypothesis is that short-term and temporary employment is changing the identity, future expectations, work attitudes and values of young people. The value shift extends to attitudes towards employment politics and life-styles of young people.

In brief, I will examine in this paper the following research questions:

– How students in higher education start their working life in the age groups 18-22, 23-25 and 26-30? Are they combining employment and study? What kind of jobs do they have and how many employers have they had?

– What kind of attitudes do they have towards education and work, and how are these influenced by their parents and friends? Do they have short or broad future orientation and are they positive or negative?

– How is short-term employment affecting the attitudes, lifestyles and worldviews of young adults?

Quantitative and qualitative data was gathered in 2009-2011 from 709 young people aged 17 to 31 in different areas of Finland. The in-depth narrative interviews and ethnographic observations were conducted in 2009-2010 among twenty (N=20) young people working temporarily in tourism in Lapland. Almost all were skilled workers. They were professionals with degrees (such as a Bachelor of Hospitality), restaurant workers and managers, skiing instructors, wilderness nature guides, and so on. The survey data was gathered online from 15th November 2010 to 15th February 2011 from students of Finnish Universities and universities of applied sciences (polytechnics). A link to the questionnaire was posted on the recruitment websites of the universities. In total, 689 young people filled in the questionnaire, which included attitude scales from my earlier value studies (1989, 1992-93 and 1995-96; Helve, 1993 and 2002), from surveys of economic, political and social attitudes conducted by the Council of Economic Organizations in Finland (EVA), and from the identity horizon scales of James Côté, translated into Finnish. The questionnaire also used open-ended questions. The attitude scales measured attitudes towards working life and society, and the meaning of work. Basic socio-demographic data was also gathered.

Almost all of the 18-22 (N=171) and 23-25 (N=244) year old online questionnaire respondents were enrolled in education (95% and 96% respectively). The situation was different among 26-30 year olds (N=255);

some 15% of them were not studying any more. They were looking at Career Services recruiting webpages from the universities where they found the questionnaire. Most of the respondents were females (81%). It could mean that more females than males were interested in the question-naire, and/or that the females were following the universities' recruiting websites more than males[6].

The online survey was targeted to students of higher education in the process of transition from education to work. The hypothesis was that the recruiting websites of universities are one of the first places students or graduates access when searching for a job. Students of higher education are experienced Internet users. Hypothetically, users might have experienced technical problems when completing the survey, but in this case the respondents were very conscientious when filling in the question-naire, which had 174 variables. The amount of missing data was very small. The long survey was divided into several topic sections.

Our intention was to collect as many responses to our online ques-tionnaire as possible without using a commercial online panel and to use this quantitative data side by side with our qualitative data to explore the trends and tendencies in the value systems of young people. Therefore we were constrained to using sampling without specific predetermined quo-tas.

Starting working life

My study supports the Finnish student survey of 2010 (Saarenmaa, Saari and Virtanen, 2010, pp. 50-53) regarding the high proportion of students in higher education who work and study at the same time (46.1%, N= 627). The majority studied and worked part-time (56.2%) but also every fifth (21.5%) worked full-time and studied at the same time. Every tenth of those who had finished their studies were unemployed and searching for a job, while 85.4% of those who did not study already worked full-time (See Figure 1.)

---

6   In my earlier studies of world views (1987; 1993a) and values (2002) females were also over-represented.

Figure 1. Cross tabulation: "Do you study?" and "Do you work full time, ½ time, part time, or other arrangement" (total % from 689 respondents).

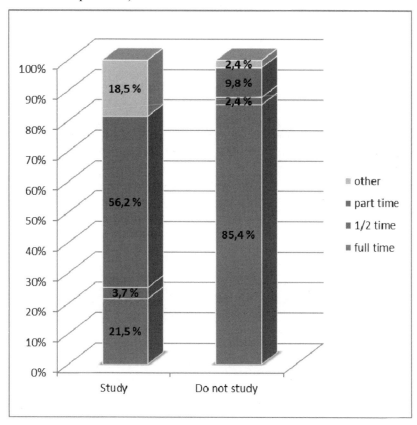

The study shows that almost all of the 18-22 and 23-25 year old respondents were enrolled in education (95% and 96% respectively). 84.7% in the age group 26-30 were still studying. The great majority (74.5%) of employed students in the youngest cohort (18-22) had a part-time job; every fourth (21%) employed student had other work arrangements, most likely hour-based non-contractual or occasional employment. Older students (aged 23-25) tended to have more stable jobs; every tenth (11:6%) had a full time contract, two thirds (63%) had part time contracts, and 21% had other work arrangements. The rate of full-time employment increased with the age of the students: among 26-30 year olds, 36.8% had full time contracts and 45.6% had part time contracts, while only 14% had other arrangements. The Finnish student survey of 2010 showed that out of all students 30% worked regularly and 30% occasionally during term-time (Saarenmaa, Saari and Virtanen, 2010, pp. 50-53.)

Political discussions in Finland in recent years have been concerned with young people starting higher education earlier and entering the labour market earlier, while decreasing the time spent in education programs. My study shows that almost one third (28.5%) of the youngest respondents already combine education with work. Among 23-25 year old students, the percentage of employment is even greater, with some 46.3% of students in this age cohort combining study with work. By the end of their professional training students become engaged in the labor market. More than half (60.4%) of 26-30 year olds still both study and work (See Figure 2.).

Figure 2. Cross tabulation: "Are you employed?" and age groups (total % from 689 respondents) (%).

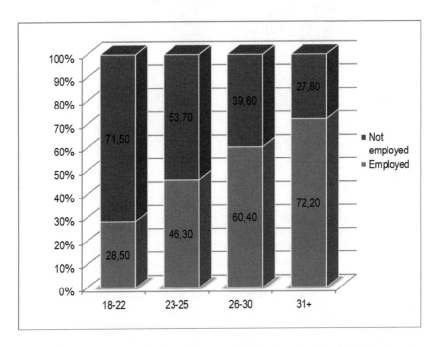

In the younger age cohort (18-22) some 69% of young people had already had from one to four employers, while every fourth (25.6%) had had from five to nine employers. About half of all young people in the age groups 23-25 and 26-30 have had from five to nine employers (45.1% and 50.2% respectively). A very remarkable fact is that 16.5% of 26-30 year olds have already had more than ten employers (13.3%: 10-14 employers; 2%: 15-19 employers; 1.2%: over 20 employers) (See Figure 3.).

Figure 3. Cross tabulation: "How many employers have you had?" and age groups (total % from 689 respondents).

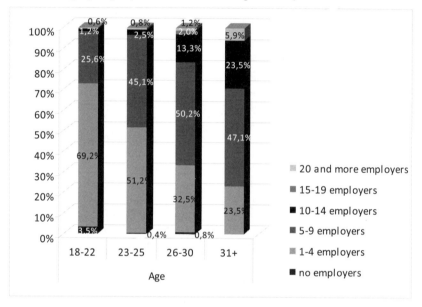

In Finland, it is typical for students to have one or more gap years before the beginning of higher education study. This is one reason why debates around Finnish higher education policy have been concerned about the delay in starting higher education study, as well as the extended duration of the studies. My research into young people in higher education shows that almost half of them studied and worked at the same time. Working became more common in older cohorts, which means that they might progress more slowly in their studies than usually expected. There are also many other different life situations and various personal reasons for slow progression (Saarenmaa, Saari and Virtanen, 2010, pp. 50-53).

This study of Finnish higher education students gives evidence that they do enter the labour market during their studies. A third of the 18-22 year olds already combine study with work. Many of them may have had a gap year before they reached university. They might have continued the job they had during the gap year after starting their studies. The number of those who are combining study with work is increasing in older cohorts. More than half of 26 to 30 year olds still both study and work.

The time dedicated to paid work varies according to the age of the student and the stage of studies. Working alongside study slows down higher education students' progress. Especially for students at universities of applied sciences (polytechnics) one major reason for slow progression could be the reform which has resulted in people under 25 who are not in education or employment finding their living allowance reduced if she/he refuses to pursue education or training. This push towards education could be a reason for poor study motivation or a sense of having chosen the wrong field of education.

Even though the time spent in education is long in Finland, young people have been able to work and study at the same time, thus acquiring important work experience. They have a wide range of experience from several employers. In the beginning of their studies young people work mostly part-time. The money they receive then allows them a more independent life from their parents. Finnish young people also move out of their family homes quite early because of government education allowances. These facts have given them independence quite early, as in all Nordic countries, compared to their counterparts in Southern European and post-communist East-European countries. In the Anglo-Saxon liberal countries the policy has been to get young people to the labour market early and to economic independence as soon as possible (McNeish and Loncle, 2003; Walther and Pohl, 2005; Walther, 2006; Walther et al., 2006; Pohl and Walther, 2007). In comparison, the transition from education to the labour market for Finnish young people is easier after their studies, particularly when employment has been part of their studies, than, for example, the same transition for young people in Britain, where they come to the labour market earlier and without work experience (Lindberg 2008).

Work attitudes and future orientations of higher education students

This study used the identity horizon attitude scales of James Côté, and measured attitudes towards work, job opportunities, career and education with the scale *Strongly agree* and *Agree* (Yes); *Difficult to say*; *Disagree* and *Strongly disagree* (No) (see Figure 4).

Figure 4. Identity horizon attitude scales.

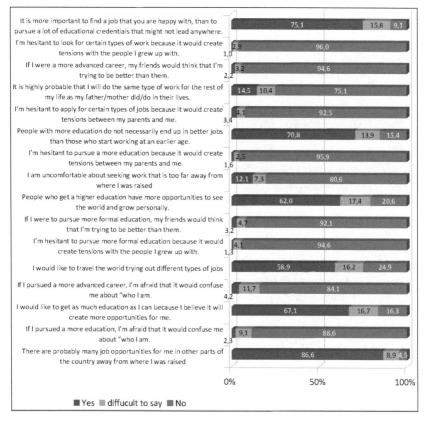

| | Yes | diffucult to say | No |

Over half of the respondents (67.1%, N=683) would like to get as much education as they can because they believe it will create more opportunities for them. Well over half of them thought that people who get a higher education have more opportunities to see the world and grow personally (62%, N=684). Most of them (70.8%, (N=684) agreed with the claim "People with more education do not necessarily end up in better jobs than those who start working at an earlier age". This attitude might get support from an individual's employment situation. Of all new jobs under half are permanent (Statistics of Finland, 2011). The number of temporary jobs has increased by 4% from 2009 to 2010.[7] It is nowadays not certain that young academics who have studied for many years can get a better job, or even a permanent job, compared to their peers who have started to work at an earlier age.

Almost all respondents (88.6%, N=683) disagreed with the claim "If I pursued more education, I'm afraid that it would confuse me about "who I am". They (94.6%, N=684) also mostly disagreed with the claim "I'm hesitant to pursue more formal education because it would create tensions with the people I grew up with" as well as disagree with the claim "If I were to pursue more formal education, my friends would think that I'm trying to be better than them" (92.1 %, N=682). Almost all (86.6%, N=685) believed that they have many job opportunities in other parts of the country away from where they were raised, and every second respondent (58.9%, N=684) would like to travel the world trying out different types of jobs. They did not experience tensions with parents and peers (75.1%, N=683), and for most, it is highly probable that he/she will not do the same type of work for the rest of his/her life as their parents did. A more advanced career compared to friends would not lead to those friends thinking the young person was trying to be 'better' (94.6%, N=683), and almost all of the studied university students (96%, N=684) agreed with the claim "It is more important to find a job that you are happy with, than to pursue a lot of educational credentials that might not lead anywhere".

We can summarize that Finnish young people in higher education have a positive attitude towards education and work. Regarding the future they seem to have a broad horizon, including 'global goals'. They do not feel uncomfortable in searching for a job far away from their home environments. They want to see the world and grow personally. They are ready to travel the world to try different types of jobs. These young people seem to have a lot of self-confidence, which may either be a result of an academic education or of upbringing. They seem not to be limited by their parents' or friends' education or work attitudes and values. However, we have to remind ourselves that these results might be skewed by the gender balance of respondents (81% of the respondents were women).

Here, it is not possible to account for the narrowing effect on horizons of having parents with low levels of educational and occupational attainment. Young people in higher education were ready to change their life

---

7   Women are working temporarily more often than men. In 2010, 62% of women in new jobs had employment of limited duration, while the same situation affected about 49% of men in new jobs (Finnish Statistics).

and future education or work settings. Their attitude to the future was positive with a broad identity horizon

Short-term employment and attitudes, lifestyles and worldviews of young adults

Although Finnish young people are joining the labour force armed with more education than their parents had, and with a rather broad and optimistic identity horizon, the status of many entering the labour market involves greater risk and uncertainty. Many factors point to how this process may not be functioning as quickly and easily as in the past: young people take more time to make the transition to employment, fall back on jobs for which they are often overqualified and receive less pay, and delay forming a family of their own. In a context where the economy is undergoing rapid transformations that favour the expansion of jobs requiring advanced education, the young people particularly at risk are those without at least a secondary education certificate.

Some young people already seem to be used to the lifestyle of short-term employment. For example, many of the professionally skilled young people I interviewed who were working temporarily in tourism in Lapland seemed to value the lifestyle of short-term jobs, and they were not ready to commit themselves to life-long careers. Below is a quote from Anna, a nineteen-year-old girl who works in a ski shop at a ski resort. I was asking her about her future expectations:

> Anna: I don't know, I am quite satisfied here. I like this kind of seasonal [i.e., temporary] work, even if I can't be sure if I'll get another job after this. I like being up on this mountain [a ski resort in Lapland]. When others go south for the summer I like to stay here. I haven't done anything else than these mountain jobs. This place has its own magic. I'll be coming back here. [...] I think I'll always find some sort of work here, even if there are a lot of unemployed people. [...] I don't think they've really tried to find work. [...] I know unemployed people who live off of what they get from unemployment. [...] I don't like it that we pay our taxes for these people. I am annoyed by their attitudes [...] I found this job myself from the website at an employment office.

Even though the young people in higher education had an optimistic future orientation, the biographies of the young people interviewed seemed to have lost a 'life-course' perspective, and the dimension of continuity associated with it. Young people's narratives have fragmented into episodes – each of which has its own past and future. Many still have other professional ambitions for the future. Adult life for many of the interviewed young people did not necessarily mean a family of their own. Friends were more important. Temporary, short-term work gave many of them the possibility to be active in their hobbies with their friends. For example, in ski resorts in Lapland, young temporary workers get free passes to the ski slopes. For many of them the future was seen as cyclic, from one winter season to the next. During the summer, when they were unemployed, they travelled and lived with their parents, who helped them if needed. They have formed their own individual concepts of time. This is also part of the identity construction and plurality of identities of new youth (Wyn and White, 1997).

For older generations working patterns have coordinated social rhythms with biographies that are constructed around this linear time: eight hours work, eight hours leisure time with family and friends, and eight hours for sleep each day. Now young people are living virtual lives, where time and space have lost meaning in their world views. Youth does not necessarily mean preparation for adulthood, work and family life anymore. The research supports the Northern model characterized as an extension of living away from home and yet not starting an adult life with one's own family (cf. Chisholm, 1995, p. 6; Côté and Bynner, 2008, p. 254). The transition to adulthood has been extended or prolonged (see more discussion and criticism of the emerging adulthood concept by Arnett, Côté and Bynner, 2008, pp. 251-254).

Discussion

In my research (Helve, 2002) into young people's changing values, I asked what sort of professions they aspired to. These ambitions turned out to still be largely gender-based. Most girls aspired to teaching or caretaking professions, which have traditionally been considered suitable tasks for women. Boys in turn aspired to traditionally masculine professions. Boys seemed to have more ambitions, entrepreneurial spirit and imagination in their professional aspirations than did girls, who perhaps in turn tried to think more realistically in relation to such hopes. Boys had more hopes for academic careers that girls did.

When asked to list the three most important things in their lives, young Finns identified health as the highest, followed by loved ones:

family, home and close friends. Work came third in the list (Helve, 1998). In another study, Finns aged 18-30 were asked about the things they valued most: they put social relationships with friends and family at the top of the list, followed by good manners and traditions, with work coming third (Nurmela and Pehkonen, 2000). In yet another survey of those aged 15-24 years old, very similar values were recorded: most important were home and family, followed by leisure time and friends, with work in third place (Elinolot/Official statistics, 1996, p. 223). In the Finnish Youth Barometer survey of 1998, nine persons out of ten in the 15-19 year old age group prioritised quality of life over material well-being and resources. In my own study (Helve, 1996), young people aged 16-19 placed more value on interesting work rather than on salary. Work has thus been consistently important in young people's value systems.

In the Finnish Youth Barometer of 2009 (Nuorisobarometri, 2009, p. 107) nine out of ten 15-29 year olds believed that education is helpful in finding a job. Trust in education among young people is still at a high level, and even unemployed young people seem to be optimistic too, when arguing for education as a means of improving their possibilities of entering the labour market. Yet new flexible types of work for young people – which are temporary, short-term and/or part-time – are changing young people's values. Italian sociologist Carmen Leccardi (2006) says that there is a crisis of 'time experience' which can be seen in young people's understanding of time. Finnish researcher Matti Kamppinen (2000) has written about social transformations which involve changes in people's socially constructed temporal profiles; drawing distinctions between cyclical, linear, absolute and relative conceptions of time. It could be predicted that, in this new information society, with the appropriation of information technology, our conceptions of time will be radically transformed. The Digital Revolution means a new generation of cell phones, wireless Internet and handheld computers, which allow us to work anywhere, anytime, 24/7. However, Kamppinen refutes the claim that in a digital information society we are moving into 'timeless' time, where modern people work in computer-based jobs and where individual life projects have lost their temporal order. Instead, he concludes that time is transformed in the digital information society but not radically, and that our lives and related processes are temporally ordered even though the processes are speeded up and reshuffled.

Have these changes, brought on by the digital information society and virtual environments, influenced young people's life-styles and values, and their transitions into adulthood? Young people still socialize on the institutional level in their families and in schools; and there is still a linear time of transition into adulthood, from school to work.

Impacts of social change on young people are seen in their changing attitudes and values. We have some evidence from interviews with young people working with short-term employment contracts, or who are temporarily unemployed, that they are not doing much long-term planning. Leisure activities, such as skiing during winter, are very important to them. These leisure activities and hobbies have become important means of building up their identities. Labour markets are structured so that younger generations have to be satisfied with temporary unemployment and short-term low-paid employment. Institutionalized society will lose this young generation if they are not brought into labour markets. Yet the young people we interviewed gave us the message that they could be happy in the sort of work which older folk would see as precarious.I think, therefore, we should have flexible jobs for young people and we should accept their viewpoints regarding temporary jobs, an uncertain future and an extended present.

In this study I have examined the situation in Finland, an affluent Nordic welfare society where the State and families are both able to subsidize the low wages corporations pay, and are able to provide young people with many opportunities to 'be' rather than 'do'. For example, working for low wages at a ski resort is not so bad; neither is working for low wages anywhere when one can have a good time and have basic needs met. For those not amenable to taking on responsibilities, this situation is a godsend. But surely, most of the world's youth do not face such benign circumstances. Even within the entire youth population of welfare societies, there are many young people who want to establish a stable sense of identity and experience a life based on responsibilities and full participation in society.

The tentative signals of new attitudes toward working life – with new lifestyles, relationships and ethical principles – have a two-part relation to young people's world views, influencing the way they balance themselves between a collective world view and an individual one. In their world view, past, present and future each have individual/cyclic and collective/institutionalized/linear temporal dimensions (see Leccardi, 2006). In this process of world view formation, life planning and future planning in the post-modern risk society (Beck, 1999) seem to be in crisis (cf. Leccardi, 2006). In the world views of young people I have interviewed, the future is unpredictable and subject to change.

Flexible and temporary world views help them to accept temporary jobs and even to value them as part of their lifestyles. They seem to want to keep their future unknown. My interpretation is that many of today's young people in Finland are in no hurry to reach adulthood. Maybe we should listen to young people who, in their transition to adult work life, emerge from a vague and prolonged youth and stumble on towards a vague and prolonged adulthood – perhaps even an arrested adulthood (see Côté, 2000).

What seems to be happening is that a period of 'youthhood' is being institutionalized in welfare societies, where it is comfortable for some young people to delay adulthood and live fully and freely as 'youth', free from commitments or responsibilities and with little need to plan for the future. According to Erikson's theory, the 'identity moratorium' has become extended. However, at some point those young people who live an extended transition need to plan for the future because they will not be 'taken care of' forever, even in a welfare society. From the point of view of identity formation, ignoring it for too long can be detrimental for long-term development and the opportunities people can realize later in life. Establishing a family and other long-term commitments requires a positive trust in the future. Also, life management is based on having a regular income, a steady social situation and a predictable future (see Kuure, 2006). In these regards having a future orientation is particularly important for young people going through developmental and transitional periods where they should be preparing themselves for future adulthood challenges.

Bibliography

Arnett, J. (2004) *Emerging Adulthood: The Winding Road from Late Teens through the Twenties*, New York, Oxford University Press.

Beck, U. (1992) *Risk society: Towards a new modernity*, London, Sage.

Chisholm, L. (1995) Conclusion: Europe, Europeanization and young people: a triad of confusing images, in Cavalli, A. and Galland, O. (eds), *Youth in Europe*, London, Pinter.

Côté, J. and Allahar, A. L. (2011) Lowering Higher Education: The Rise of Corporate Universities and the Fall of Liberal Education, Toronto, University of Toronto Press.

Côté, J. (2000) *Arrested Adulthood: The Changing Nature of Maturity and Identity*, New York, New York University Press.

Côté, J. (2006), Emerging adulthood as an institutionalized moratorium: Risks and benefits to identity formation, in Arnett, J.J. and Tanner, J. (eds) *Emerging adults in America: Coming of age in the 21st century*, Washington DC: American Psychological Association.

Côté, J. E. and Bynner, J. (2008) Changes in transition to adulthood in the UK and Canada: the role of structure and agency in emerging adulthood, *Journal of Youth Studies, 11(3)*, pp. 251-268.

Côté, J. E., Skinkle, R. and Motte, A. (2008) Do perceptions of costs and benefits of post-secondary education influence participation? *Canadian Journal of Higher Education, 38(3)*, pp. 73-93.

Erikson, E.H. (1968) *Identity: Youth and Crisis*, New York, Norton.

Eurostat (2012) *Harmonised unemployment rate by sex – age group 15-24*, http://epp. eurostat.ec.europa.eu/tgm/table.do?tab=table&init=1&language=en&pcode=teilm 021&plugin=0 (accessed June 15 2012).

Eurostat (2008) *Key figures on Europe 2009* Luxembourg, Office for Official Publications of the European Communities, http://epp.eurostat.ec.europa.eu/cache/ITY _OFFPUB/KS-EI-08-001/EN/KS-EI-08-001-EN.PDF (accessed June 15 2012).

Fadjukoff, P., Pulkkinen, L. and Kokko, K. (2005) Identity Processes in Adulthood: Diverging Domains, *Identity: An International Journal of Theory and research, 5(1)*, pp. 1-20.

Fangen, K., Fossan, K. and Mohn, F.A. (eds) (2010) *Inclusion and Exclusion of Young Adult Migrants in Europe*, Aldershot, Ashgate.

Statistics Finland (2010) *Kansantalouden tilinpito 1999–2008* Statistics Finland, http:// ilastokeskus.fi/tup/julkaisut/tiedostot/vtp_2008_en.pdf (accessed June 15 2012).

Helve, H. (2012) (forthcoming) From Higher Education to Working Life: *Work Values of Young Finns in Changing Labour Markets*, in Helve, H. and Evans, K. (eds) *Youth, Work Transitions and Well-being*, London, Tufnell Press.

Helve, H. (2006) Values, world views and gender differences among young people, in Helve, H. and Bynner, J. (eds), *Youth and Life Management. Research Perspectives*, Helsinki, University Press, pp. 171-187.

Helve, H. (ed) (2005) *Mixed methods in Youth research*, Finnish Youth Research Society, Publications 50.

Helve, H. (2002) *Arvot, muutos ja nuoret* [Values, Change and Youth], Helsinki, Helsinki University Press.

Helve, H. (1998) Perspectives on Social Exclusion, Citizenship and Youth, in Helve, H. (ed) *Unification and Marginalisation of Young People*, Finnish Youth Research 2000 Programme, Helsinki, The Finnish Youth Research Society, pp. 211-221.

Helve, H. (1993) The World View of Young People: A Longitudinal Study of Finnish Youth Living in a Suburb of Metropolitan Helsinki, Helsinki, Annales Academiae Scientiarum Fennicae, Ser. B, Tom. 267.

Innocenti Social Monitor (2009) *Child well-being at a crossroad: Evolving challenges in Central and Eastern Europe and the Commonwealth of Independent States*, available at: http://www.unicef-irc.org (accessed September 2009).

Kamppinen, M. (2000) The transformation of time in the information society, *Foresight, 2(2)*. pp. 59-162.

Koulutus ja tutkimus vuosina 2011–2016 (2011) Report by the Ministry of Education and Culture, Helsinki, available at: http://www.minedu.fi/export/sites/efault/ PM/Koulutus/koulutuspolitiikka/asiakirjat/Kesu_2011_2016_fi.pdf

Kuure, T. (2006) Tuotettua epävarmuutta, in Hoikkala, T. and Salasuo, M. (eds) *Prekaariruoska? Portfoliopolvi, perustulo ja kansalaistoiminta.* http://www. uorisotutkimusseura.fi/julkaisuja/prekaariruoska.pdf (accessed April 11 2007).

Leccardi, C. (2006) Uncertainty, Temporality and Biographies in the New century, in Leccardi, C. and Ruspini, E. (eds) *A new youth?: Young people, generations and family life*, Aldershot, Ashgate.

Lindberg, M. (2008) *Diverse Routes from School, via Higher Education, to Employment: A Comparison of Nine European Countries*, Turun yliopisto, Koulutussosiologian tutkimuskeskuksen raportti 70.

Manninen, J. and Luukannel, S. (2006) *Maisterit ja kandidaatit työmarkkinoilla. Vuonna 2000. Helsingin yliopistosta alemman tai ylemmän korkeakoulututkinnon suorittaneiden sijoittuminen työmarkkinoille viisi vuotta tutkinnon suorittamisen jälkeen*, Helsingin yliopisto, Koulutus- ja kehittämiskeskus Palmenia, Ura- ja rekrytointipalvelut. ttp://www.helsinki.fi/urapalvelut/materiaalit/aisteritja_kandit_ yomarkkinoilla.pdf (accessed June 15 2012).

McNeish, W. and Loncle, P. (2003) State policy and youth unemployment in the EU: rights, responsibilities and lifelong learning, in López Blasco, A., McNeish, W. and Walther, A. (eds) *Young people and contradictions of inclusion: towards integrated transition policies in Europe* (pp. 105–126), Bristol, Polity Press.

Miettinen, A. (2007) *Pätkätyön tulevaisuus?* E27. Väestöliitto, Helsinki, Väestöntutkimuslaitos.

Nuorisobarometri 1/1998. Selvitys 15-29-vuotiaiden suomalaisten nuorten koulutukseen, työhön, työelämän muutoksiin ja julkisen talouden säästöihin sekä syrjäytymiseen liittyvistä käsityksistä, NUORAn julkaisuja Nro 7, Opetusministeriö, Helsinki, Nuorisoasiain neuvottelukunta.

Nurmela, S. and Pehkonen, J. (2000) *Nuoret ja presidentinvaalit 2000*, Raportti 18-30-vuotiaiden osallistumisesta vuoden 2000 presidentinvaaleihin. NUORAn julkaisuja 16. Helsinki, Opetusministeriö, Nuorisoasiain neuvottelukunta.

Myllyniemi, S. (2009) *Taidekohtia. Nuorisobarometri 2009,* Nuora, Youth Research Society.

Palanko-Laaka, K. (2005) Määräaikaisen työn yleisyys, käytön lainmukaisuus ja lainsäädännön kehittämistarpeet, Työhallinnon julkaisuja 359. Helsinki, Työministeriö.

Pohl, A., and Walther, A. (2007) Activating the disadvantaged: Variations in addressing youth transitions across Europe, *International Journal of Lifelong Education, 26(5)*, pp. 33–553.

Quintini, G., Martin J. P. and Martin, S. (2007) *The Changing Nature of the School-to-Work Transition Process in OECD Countries,* Discussion Paper No. 2582, Bonn, IZA.

Rifkin, J. (1995) *The End of Work: the decline of the global labor force and the dawn of the post-market era*, New York, Putnam.

Ryan, P. (2001) The School-to-work Transition: a cross-national perspective, *Journal of Economic Literature, 29 (March)*, pp. 34–92.

Saarenmaa, K., Saari, K. and Virtanen, V. (2010) *Opiskelijatutkimus 2010. Korkeak-ouluopiskelijoiden toimeentulo ja opiskelu.* Opetus- ja kulttuuriministeriön julkai-suja 2010:18, Helsinki, Opetus- ja kulttuuriministeriö.

Salmela-Aro, K. (2009) Personal goals and well-being during critical life transitions: the 4 C's – channeling, choice, coagency and compensation, *Advances in Life Course Research*, 14, pp. 63-73.

Sell, A. (2004) *Pätkätyöttömyys osana elämäntyyliä. Nuoria aikuisia pidentyvien siirtymien aikakaudella.* Sosiologian pro gradu -tutkielma, Helsingin yliopisto, Sosiologian laitos.

Stålsett, S.J. (2006) *Ethical dimensions of vulnerability and struggles for social inclu-sion in Latin America*, http://www.urbeetius.org/newsletters/23/news_23_stalsett. pdf (accessed June 15 2012).

Statistics Finland (1998) *Suomen tilastollinen vuosikirja*, Statistics Finland, Helsinki, Tilastokeskus.

Statistics Finland (1997) *Labour force Finland* , Helsinki, Statistics Finland, Ministry of Labour.

Statistics Finland (1996) *Suomen tilastollinen vuosikirja*, Statistics Finland, Helsinki, Tilastokeskus.

Sutela, H., Vänskä, J. and Notkola, V. (2001) *Pätkätyöt Suomessa 1990-luv*ulla, Hel-sinki, Tilastokeskus.

UNICEF (2000) Young People in Changing Societies: Regional Monitoring Report No. 7 – 2000, Florence, The MONEE Project, CEE/ CIS/ Baltics, UNICEF Inno-centi Research Centre.

Walther, A. and Pohl, A. (2005) *Thematic study on policy measures for disadvan-taged youth in Europe: Final report to the European Commission*, Tübingen, IRIS, http://ec.europa.eu/employment_social/social_inclusion/docs/youth_study_ en.pdf (accessed June 15 2012).

Walther, A., du Bois-Reymond, M. and Biggart, A. (eds) (2006): *Participation in Transition: Motivation of young adults in Europe for learning and working.* Frankfurt a. Main, Peter Lang.

Walther, A. (2006) Regimes of Youth Transitions: choice, flexibility and security in young people's experiences across different European contexts, *Young – Nordic Journal of Youth Studies, 14(1)*, pp. 119-141.

Wyn, J. and White, R. (1997) *Rethinking Youth*, London, Sage.

4. Migrant and minority youth in the U.S.: rights, belonging, and exclusion

By Sunaina Maira

Fantasies and fears of youth as simultaneously threatening and hopeful, or deviant and liberating, are fundamentally tied to the conceptualization of adolescence as a transition between 'childhood' and 'adulthood.' This cultural notion of adolescence as a liminal stage is at the heart of the ambivalence with which youth are often viewed, and also the exceptionalism that sometimes overdetermines this category, i.e. youth are viewed as exceptionally unstable, or especially vulnerable to intense political commitments and social experimentation. The romanticization of young people as agents of social change often co-exists with the fear of that very change (Lesko, 2001; Shepard and Hayduk, 2002). This duality underlies what scholars of youth studies have critiqued as 'moral panics' about youth, which are often driven by an anxiety about threats to the status quo that young people are presumed to embody (Cohen, 1997).

Youth is a key site in which processes of nation-building and state-craft can be explored, given the construction of youth as a transitional category in relation to the social order and civic personhood (Maira and Soep, 2005). Young people are the focus of socializing processes by the state and civil society; for example, in institutions such as public high schools where national culture and history are inculcated into students for the purposes of producing "good citizens" (Cole and Durham, 2007, p. 10). Young people themselves express notions of national belonging in various ways, in the contexts of popular culture, schooling, work, immigration, policing, social services, the military or the prison-system.

If the category of 'youth' has been viewed as a liminal stage in the development of political and national identity (France, 1998), then immigrant youth are perceived as doubly liminal, for their national allegiances are often seen as shifting or divided. Imaginaries of 'otherness' are intertwined with imaginaries of youth and youthfulness, which generally represent the edge of 'difference' and symbolize new temporalities, the next generation or 'the future.' For Muslim youth in the U.S., this perception is even more acute, especially after 9/11; they are constructed in mainstream discourse as culturally or religiously alien, and as potential threats to the nation, but also as symbolizing future threats to national security in the next phase of the War on Terror.

The issue of exclusion and integration of youth, especially of migrant youth, is deeply bound up with the question of citizenship. Citizenship is a central question that connects pressing issues of nationalism, globalization, immigration, cultural pluralism, democracy, and human rights. An analysis of citizenship is crucial to understanding the ways in which the state manages, integrates, and controls its subjects, including young people. The possibilities and limitations of citizen rights have been shaped by the evolving form of the nation-state, the administrative practices of colonial (and postcolonial) regimes, the demands of the market, and supranational institutions, such as the United Nation or World Bank (Hindess, 2005). Yet until recently the issue of 'youth citizenship' has not received enough attention by scholars, for it falls between the cracks of literature on children's rights and adult citizenship. In both scholarship and public discourse, young people's ideas of citizenship are viewed as not fully formed, or unstable, and more susceptible to shaping by external forces than for adults.

In general, the political subjectivity of young people is viewed as something not to be taken seriously, on the one hand, and as potentially threatening, on the other. It is certainly true that youth are engaged in an ongoing process of social and cognitive development and they do acquire more legal rights and responsibilities as they move into adulthood. But the traditional literature on the political socialization of youth often suggests that youth need to be drawn into 'consensual citizenship,' inherently maintaining the status quo and leaving the very definition of citizenship or national belonging largely unchallenged (France, 1998, p. 105). The implications of such approaches are that young citizens must be socialized into adult norms of political involvement, rather than considered as thinking agents who may express important critiques of citizenship and national identity, even if their rights are limited (Buckingham, 2000, p. 13).

I focus here on the ways young people themselves grapple with ideas of citizenship, using ethnographic methods to highlight the everyday experiences of young people in considering policy implications and strategies for meaningful integration, equality, and social justice.

Cultural Citizenship

My research focuses on young Muslim immigrants from South Asia living in the U.S. and explores how they make sense of citizenship, particularly cultural citizenship, after September 11, 2001, at a time when there is increasing scrutiny and suspicion of Muslim Americans. Scholars have increasingly focused on the importance of everyday understandings of belonging and exclusion, or cultural citizenship, that centrally shape the experiences of immigrant communities and underlie their relationship to the nation-state (Coll, 2010; Rosaldo, 1997). Cultural citizenship is a critical issue for multi-ethnic societies, for the idea of national belonging is based not just on political, social, and economic dimensions of citizenship but is also defined in the cultural realm of belonging. Cultural definitions of citizenship and dominant understandings of who is truly 'American' mediate the rights afforded to citizens and immigrants, particularly in moments of national crisis. The issue of cultural citizenship is a critical one for it goes to the heart of issues of equality and exclusion, rights and justice, and extends beyond official definitions of citizenship. At the same time, there are still important legal distinctions between citizens and non-citizens and pressing issues of immigrant rights that cannot be overlooked in discussing the cultural dimensions of citizenship.

This chapter draws on the research for my book, *Missing: Youth, Citizenship, and Empire After 9/11* (Maira, 2009), which is based on an ethnography of working-class Muslim immigrant youth from South Asia conducted in 2001-2003. These Pakistani, Bangladeshi, and Indian immigrants were students in a public high school in a small city in the northeast and had recently arrived in the U.S. While doing research in the school, I was also working as a volunteer with the South Asian Mentoring and Tutoring Association (SAMTA), a support program for South Asian immigrant students that offered workshops on social, cultural, and academic issues. Using field work and interviews, I examined how these young immigrants understood cultural citizenship in their everyday lives after September 11, 2001 in the context of school, work, family, and youth culture.

Education is an important site where ideas of national identity and citizenship are produced, but I also explored the ways in which national belonging or notions of civic participation are shaped by young people's experiences of popular culture and of labor, especially for these youth who had part-time jobs in the service sector, in stores or fast food restaurants. The research literature has not sufficiently focused on Muslim

American youth as cultural consumers or workers, however, generally focusing solely on issues of religious identity and political orientation, narrowly defined.

Exploring expressions of cultural citizenship by youth who are from
communities targeted with suspicion after 9/11 allows us to understand
some of the paradoxes of national belonging, exclusion, alienation, and
political expression for a generation of immigrants coming of age at this
particular moment. It also sheds light on larger cultural and political debates about citizenship for minority youth in the U.S. and elsewhere. The
national allegiances of Muslims, Arabs, and South Asians in the U.S.
have come under intense scrutiny for signs of betrayal to the nation since
2001. Discussions of the political views of Muslim youth in the U.S. are
shaped by deeper social anxieties in the U.S., not just about 'radical Islam' but also about national culture, race relations in the U.S., and
American policies and military interventions in the Middle East and
South Asia. In my research, I connect the experiences of young immigrants to issues of state policy, domestic and foreign, to show how their
lives are shaped by larger political forces and how their experiences illu-
minate the paradoxes of cultural citizenship in the post-9/11 era.

The "War on Terror"

In the War on Terror launched by the U.S. after 9/11, there were mass detentions and deportations of Muslim and Arab Americans who were in-
nocent of terrorist charges and were largely immigrant men rounded up
on public suspicion or for immigration violations. The USA-PATRIOT
Act, passed by the Bush administration, violated basic constitutional
rights of due process and free speech and, in effect, sacrificed the liberties of specific minority groups in exchange for a presumed sense of
'safety' of the larger majority. This had an impact on Muslim and Middle
Eastern youth whose national allegiances were viewed as potentially suspect. Muslim Americans were scapegoated for the 9/11 attacks and there
were numerous incidents of harassment, assaults, and discrimination,
based on racial, religious, and also political profiling. After 9/11, Muslim
American youth began experiencing the 'disappearances' of their fathers,
brothers, and friends, for none of the detainees were identified publicly
and the locations where they were held remained secret (Chang, 2002,
pp. 69-87). As part of the domestic 'War on Terror,' at least 1200 and up

to 5000 Muslim immigrant men were detained in the immediate aftermath of 9/11, none of them with any criminal charges, and some in high security prisons (Cainkar and Maira, 2006). Foreign policy interests were encoded in the PATRIOT Act since its counterterrorism provisions principally targeted foreign nationals, especially from Arab and predominantly Muslim nations (such as Pakistan) linked by the Bush administration to Al-Qaeda, but not those from Spain, Germany, France or Britain, all countries where alleged Al Qaeda suspects had lived.

The state created new policies of surveillance to collect information after 9/11 that officially targeted Muslim immigrants, particularly young men and adult males. In 2002, the National Security Entry-Exit Registration System (NSEERS) – or 'Special Registration' – was established, requiring all male nationals over sixteen years of age from 24 Muslim-majority countries, including Pakistan and Bangladesh, as well as North Korea, to submit to interrogation at federal immigration facilities. Over 80,000 men, youth as well adults, complied with Special Registration, even though information about the process was badly disseminated among the target communities, heightening the climate of fear for Muslim immigrants and youth. Many of these men, including youth, however, never came out; 2,870 were detained and 13,799 were put into deportation proceedings (Nguyen, 2005, xviii).

The anxiety about Special Registration and the chilling effect of the surveillance, detentions, and deportations permeated Muslim communities in the US, creating a pervasive fear of speaking out and of political mobilization. Attention to the infringements of civil and immigrant rights for South Asian, Arab, and Muslim Americans has largely receded in the mainstream U.S. media (except in a few sensationalized cases) but these communities continued to be targeted for surveillance (for example: Maira, 2007). There are ongoing cases of FBI informants infiltrating Muslim communities and mosques and targeting young Muslim men, in particular, and there have been several extraordinary incidents of entrapment of Muslim American youth by undercover agents, leading to a heightened anxiety about involvement in the public sphere, whether on college campuses or in the community.

The political participation of Muslim American youth has been deeply impacted by this exceptional scrutiny and suspicion of their religious beliefs, political views, and social networks. In the post-9/11 discourse of the national security state, Middle Eastern and Muslim youth are viewed as inherently opposed to Western notions of liberal democratic citizenship. Young Muslim men are perceived through an Orientalist lens as inherently militant, fanatical, and anti-American and young Muslim women as inherently oppressed and in need of saving from their cultural and religious traditions. This makes the relationship of these young people to cultural citizenship a charged one, given the pressure to prove that they are loyal citizens or 'good' Muslims who support the War on Terror. The post-9/11 culture wars have led to a charged debate about Islam, gender, and cultural citizenship that often focuses on Muslim youth through an Orientalist framework of 'clashing civilizations' and identity conflict. Neoconservatives (and also sometimes liberals) have used a reductive cultural discourse to emphasize the 'radicalization' of Muslim youth alienated from 'Western' values and Western notions of liberal or secular democracy. Yet the policy aspects of this issue are not sufficiently explored, for in asking whether Muslim immigrant youth are becoming radicalized, not enough attention is paid to the impact of state policies, domestic and global, that have radically altered the lives of youth, families, and communities or generated outrage and dissent.

The War on Terror has rested not just on policing the legal, but also cultural, boundaries of citizenship through defining the behavior required of 'good' citizens in the context of the "coercive patriotism" after 9/11 (Park, 2005, p. 6). It is also important to keep in mind that the War on Terror is an extension of the 'war on immigrants,' revived by right-wing and anti-immigrant groups since the late 1980s, for it has stripped civil rights from non-citizens and led to raids and mass deportations of undocumented immigrants, who provide cheap labor for the U.S. economy. The 'war on terrorism' was waged primarily against immigrants, heightening the distinction between citizens and non-citizens and making citizenship a key issue in the post-9/11 crackdown. Working-class and undocumented immigrants are thus much more vulnerable, since they have fewer economic and legal resources for support if detained or deported.

In response to these experiences of exclusion and challenges to belonging in the War on Terror, my research found that some Muslim immigrant youth in the U.S. developed complex forms of cultural citizenship. I found that these youth had three major ways of expressing cultural citizenship, often simultaneously:

• Transnational or flexible citizenship: National belonging connected to the U.S. as well as to countries in South Asia from where they migrated (India, Pakistan, Bangladesh). These youth were connected to South Asia through satellite TV and films/music circulating transnationally, but simultaneously trying to immerse themselves in mainstream American culture and society, mainly through the school and their part-time jobs (which is where they primarily interacted with other immigrant and minority youth, since they had little time or money for leisure activities);

- Multicultural citizenship: Emerging in response to multicultural policies in education and to their everyday experiences of interacting with other racial minorities, with whom some felt a greater affiliation since 2001. Some Muslim youth began to feel a political affinity with young people from groups historically excluded from cultural citizenship, such as African Americans or Latinos;
- Dissenting citizenship: Based in these young Muslim immigrants' experiences of racial profiling within the U.S., on one hand, and on the other, in response to U.S. foreign policy, the invasion of Afghanistan and Iraq, and U.S. support for Israel's occupation of Palestine.

Some of these forms of cultural citizenship may overlap with the experiences of immigrant youth from other groups, for though these tensions in national belonging were felt more dramatically by Muslim minority youth at a particular moment in the U.S., they are also shared by minority youth before and after 9/11. To illustrate some of these concerns, let me draw on an excerpt from an interview with Ismail, an Indian Muslim immigrant from Gujarat in western India:

> "My relatives came to America twenty years ago; both my father's sisters are here and they live in Medford. My father works in a factory, he makes car parts... My family is from Valsar, in Gujarat... Now, there are a lot of people coming from villages around there...

> We would like to come more to the SAMTA meetings, but we have to leave school right after it ends and go to work. I do a phone card business with my brother, where I sell phone cards to these Indian stores and convenience stores, and I also work at the university doing tech support. One of my friends is working at Dunkin' Donuts, the other one is now working with his father in a store. The other boys, Pakistani boys work at security jobs, and they work from five to twelve at night. So we don't really have the time to do things, every one's busy with their own thing, no one has the time. We don't have the time to go to the Gujarati events in Billtown, or to do the dandiya raas [Gujarati folk dance]... I'm just occupied with work, and with helping my mother... I have to do the house work, shopping, laundry.

> I'm thinking that after I finish school, maybe I'll go to India for six months and then I'll come back here for six months and work. Maybe I'll buy a gas station or a convenience store. I might do a business with my uncle, who works in McDon-

ald's… Actually, the thing is I'd like to stay here but this place doesn't need me more than my country, because in India there's a lot of poor people who need our help and our education. If we study here, then we'll go back to our country, open up some kind of company or something, that'll be really good for them there because our economy is really down right now, you know. So most people are unemployed in India right now.

Here, in my building, it's very international, there are Chinese people, Korean, Cambodian, Moroccan, black… But for blacks and others who live here, it's not a problem that we are Muslim. I had just come here to this country when I met a black person and he said, "For me, it makes no difference that you are a Muslim, I don't care." … [African American political leader] Jesse Jackson came to our school one time, when there were people from the International Center and some lawyers and Muslims talking to us after September 11. And he was talking about peace and saying, "It's not right for the American government to go crazy after September 11, you should first understand what is happening in other countries." I've talked to some friends of mine about the war [in Afghanistan], and they said this is all wrong, the American government is just causing more violence and we don't want this war, we should solve the problem peacefully."

Ismail's reflections illustrate all three forms of citizenship, and demonstrate his sense of agency in trying to respond thoughtfully and critically to larger processes of migration, globalization, labor, racism, and warfare. Ismail seems to offer a transnational perspective on national belonging linking his home country and its developing economy to the U.S. (flexible citizenship). He understands his experience of racial profiling in relation to other minorities who have historically experienced discrimination, particularly African Americans, and has a differentiated view of American national identity and political culture based on his interactions with diverse groups (multicultural citizenship). Ismail also expressed a dissenting critique of state policies of invasion and occupation in the War on Terror, alluding to the importance of international human rights (dissenting citizenship). There is, of course, an emotional and sometimes painful aspect of the politics of cultural citizenship; Ismail is clearly frustrated with the pressures of having to work in a part-time, low-wage job; with not having time for leisure; and with exclusion from civil rights. These issues of labor, immigrant, and civil rights need to be central to policy discussions regarding not just Muslim immigrants, but migrant youth in general.

My work also examines the ways in which the discourse of rights has become the dominant paradigm for politics. Randall Williams observes that critiques of the regime of human rights responds to the "contemporary ascendancy of rights as the privileged discourse for the symbolic articulation of international justice" (2010, xv). My current research explores how Muslim American youth politics uses a language of rights that bridges the national and the transnational. Young Muslim American activists are making linkages between their experiences after 9/11 and a domestic history and discourse of civil rights struggle and are invoking the notion of human rights to connect to the experiences of Muslims elsewhere, in Iraq, Afghanistan, Pakistan, or Palestine.

Transnational citizenship

Cultural citizenship is necessarily intertwined with transnational labor and education, issues that are interrelated for immigrant youth. Many earlier South Asian immigrants were highly educated professionals who were buffered from the most extreme forms of racial exclusion in the U.S. For these upwardly mobile South Asians the often brutal experience of discrimination after 9/11 was a shock because they were long perceived as a 'model minority.' Increasingly, youth from South Asia, and also Latin America, Africa, the Middle East, and other parts of Asia, come to the U.S. with their families as migrant workers, and work in low-wage, part-time jobs. As such, these young workers provide the flexible labor that the globalized U.S. economy relies on for maximum profit. However, opportunities available to migrant workers through immigration and citizenship policies discriminate between U.S. and foreign-born workers, and after 9/11, also between Muslim and non-Muslim workers as employment discrimination has been on the rise. These experiences shatter the promise of the American Dream for migrant youth. Soman, an Indian immigrant student who worked in his family's restaurant after school, said, "Here, you live in a golden cage, but it's still a cage... my life is so limited. I go to school, come to work, study, go to sleep." So while some youth and their families come to the U.S. in search of freedom, they find that this freedom is limited or comes at a price, making them acutely aware of issues of inequality and exclusion from citizenship.

The paradox of transnational citizenship in the current moment is that it is considered desirable for some and dangerous for others: the rights to 'freedom' and 'mobility' are unevenly distributed. Transnational ties have been encouraged, and produced, by global capitalism and viewed as not just positive, but necessary and even glamorous. Yet while in some cases, flexibility of citizenship is considered favorable and supported by the state, in other cases practicing flexible citizenship is seen as a threat. After 9/11, ties to Muslim organizations, charities, businesses, or movements outside the nation cast Muslim immigrants as potential security threats to the U.S., or at least as immigrants whose political loyalties were suspect. Travel across national borders; money transfers, including donations to Islamic relief organizations; and connections to transnational businesses and political or religious groups have all been used to monitor or detain Arab and Muslim immigrants, as the state has broadened its definitions of involvement with terrorism. This has affected the livelihood of families and youth, and so Ismail's goals for a transnational business may not be easy to achieve in the current climate. Yet academic discussions, and sometimes even policy debates, about Muslim American youth often ignore these issues of labor and class, focusing only on issues of religion or cultural conflict, as though Muslim youth are outside of the labor market and class relations, not to mention state policies.

Multicultural citizenship

The liberal discourse of multiculturalism in the U.S., in the arena of policy as well as everyday culture, promotes the notion that inclusion and exclusion is shaped primarily by issues of cultural belonging and difference, generally evading issues of class inequality and structural exclusion. While racial and ethnic identity, as well as gender, class, and religion, certainly affects processes of integration, the question of belonging is fundamentally bound up with the political and material contexts in which different groups are positioned in relation to the power structure. In the U.S., multiculturalism was intended to expand the notion of 'American' culture but it has often been reduced to symbolic displays of culture, such as through food, clothing, or festivals, ignoring deeper issues of integration and exclusion in favor of a politics of recognition. Diversity has become something to be celebrated and consumed, disconnected from a politics of redistribution. In recent years, there has also been an increasing trend to promote a liberal religious multiculturalism in the U.S., inviting token Muslim representatives or young people to talk about Islam but often avoiding difficult issues of discrimination, detention, deportation, and surveillance, not to mention foreign policy.

Multiculturalism has become a significant component of educational policy, both in high schools and colleges, and has shaped the experiences of Muslim immigrant students. While high school curricula promote a notion of cultural citizenship based on diversity, cultural, racial, and religious difference, as well as political views, continue to be the basis for discrimination, even in schools, and for exclusion in the larger public sphere. There is often a contradiction at work as right-wing political actors generally oppose multiculturalism while liberal proponents often evade complex issues of state power. However, Muslim American youth have increasingly tried to link issues of cultural and racial exclusion to state policies of surveillance and warfare after 9/11, building alliances with other minority youth who face discrimination and policing. In my research, I found that the South Asian Muslim students began to realize they shared experiences of racial exclusion with African Americans, who have a much longer history of profiling and incarceration, and many activists have worked in coalition with other Asian Americans or Latinos who have faced deportation and discrimination.

In my current research in California, I have found that Muslim American college students of South Asian, Arab, and Afghan backgrounds have increasingly formed cross-ethnic coalitions, mobilizing with other communities and movements against discrimination in the U.S. and also in opposition to U.S. wars and interventions in the Middle East and South Asia, as well as U.S policies in Israel-Palestine.

Dissenting Citizenship

While none of the youth in my study were political activists in the traditional sense, or belonged to formal political organizations, they expressed their political views and dissent in a range of everyday contexts, and forged affiliations with other communities across racial and religious boundaries. For example, Ayesha, a young Indian American woman, belonged to the Black student club in the high school, and had been involved with planning Black History Month. A week after the attacks in New York, Ayesha chose to write the words 'INDIA + MUSLIM' on her backpack. She said, "Just because one Muslim did it in New York, you can't involve everybody in there, you know what I'm sayin.' Just because a couple of Muslims did it, they gotta blame everybody for it." For her, this was a conscious gesture of defiance, for she knew the possibility of repercussions for those publicly identified as Muslim after 9/11 but was not afraid of backlash. She said staunchly, "I'm hard-headed, that's how I am."

Despite the surveillance and scrutiny of the political views of Muslim Americans after 9/11, I found some youth, such as Ayesha, publicly challenged racial and religious profiling and critiqued the War on Terror at large. Some students spoke at public events in the school and used the discourse of civil rights to critique anti-Muslim incidents in the school and community. They challenged the scapegoating of Muslims and America's war in the name of human rights, what some call 'humanitarian imperialism,' expressing a dissenting citizenship in the face of a dominant patriotic nationalism. Yet many Muslim Americans were also afraid to express dissenting views, especially in the immediate aftermath of 9/11. In general, it has been difficult for young people, especially immigrants who do not have legal citizenship and are afraid of being detained or deported, to engage in political movements and formal activism.

However, my current research explores the ways in which a new generation of Muslim American youth has become increasingly involved in political organizing around issues of civil, immigrant, and human rights in domestic and international contexts. Many South Asian, Afghan, and Arab American youth have become involved in mobilizing in response to the War on Terror and forging alliances with political movements in the U.S. and also transnationally. This is not easy, because U.S. policies since September 11, 2001 have increasingly focused on Muslims American youth as an internal threat to be surveilled and contained and have simultaneously tried to promote the notion of 'good' Muslims, who are pro-U.S., vs. 'bad' Muslims, who are critical of U.S. policies. This binary framework suppresses complex political critique and makes it difficult to for Muslim and migrant youth to engage in political mobilization critical of the state but many are courageously doing so nonetheless.

Conclusion

In my research, I have found that young people who are from communities struggling with political, economic and social exclusion are deeply aware of the role of the state in shaping national belonging. Muslim migrant youth in the U.S. are concerned about whether the state's promise of democracy, civil rights, and multicultural inclusion applies to them or whether there are different sets of rights for different groups. Do they have the right to have rights? Particularly in the War on Terror, the notion that certain groups of people can be excluded from rights has made the question of citizenship a tenuous one. Immigrant youth are deeply aware of the impact of state policies, and the discrepancy between policy and practice, on their everyday lives. There are indeed movements in the U.S. that have been challenging these contradictions and excesses in state policy, and migrant youth are variously involved in these. Yet stereotypes of disaffected or 'radicalized' Muslim youth abound: often the everyday experiences of young people get buried in hysterical rhetoric or fear-mongering, which is bound up with larger concerns about shifts in social demographics, challenges to the racial and class order, and the (declining) status of the U.S. as a superpower. For policy makers, then, it is imperative to understand the genuine concerns of immigrant youth, their needs, hopes, fears, and uncertainties, and the root causes of their frustration or alienation, whether it is tied to issues of education, labor, civil and immigrant rights and questions of economic, social, and political exclusion in national and global contexts.

Bibliography

Buckingham, D. (2000) The *Making of Citizens: young people, news, and politics*, London and New York, Routledge.

Chang, N. (2002) Silencing Political Dissent: How post-September 11 anti-terrorism measures threaten our civil liberties, New York, Seven Stories/Open Media.

Cohen, S. (1997) Symbols of trouble, in Gelder, K. and Thornton, S. *The Subcultures Reader*, (pp. 149-62), Routledge, London.

Cole, J. and Durham. D. (2007) Introduction: Age, Regeneration, and the Intimate Politics of Globalization, in Cole, J. and Durham, D. (eds) *Generations and Globalization: youth, age, and family in the new world economy*, Bloomington and Indianpolis, Indiana University Press, pp. 1-28.

Coll, K. (2010) Remaking Citizenship: Latina immigrants and new American politics. Stanford, Stanford University Press.

France, A. (1998) 'Why Should We Care?': Young people, citizenship and questions of social responsibility, *Journal of Youth Studies, 1(1)*, pp. 97-111.

Hindess, B. (2005) Citizenship and Empire, in Hansen, T. B. and Steputat, F. *Sovereign Bodies: Citizens, migrants, and states in the postcolonial world*, (pp. 241-256), Princeton, Princeton University Press.

Lesko, N. (2001) Act Your Age! A Cultural Construction of Adolescence, London and New York, Routledge.

Maira, S. (2009) *Missing: Youth, Citizenship, and Empire After 9/11*, Durham NC, Duke University Press.

Maira, S. (2007) Deporting Radicals, Deporting La Migra: The Hayat Case in Lodi, *Cultural Dynamics, 19(1)*, pp. 39-66.

Maira, S. and Soep, E. (eds) (2005) Introduction, in *Youthscapes: The Popular, the National, the Global*, (pp. 15-35), Philadelphia, Temple University Press.

172   Sunaina Maira

Nguyen, T. (2005) We Are All Suspects Now: Untold Stories from Immigrant Communities After 9/11, Boston, Beacon Press.

Park, L. S. (2005) Consuming Citizenship: Children of Asian immigrant entrepreneurs, Stanford, Stanford University Press.

Razack, S. H. (2008) Casting Out: The eviction of Muslims from Western law and politics, Toronto, University of Toronto Press.

Rosaldo, R. (1997) Cultural Citizenship, Inequality, and Multiculturalism, in Flores, W.F. and Benmayor, R. (eds) *Latino Cultural Citizenship: Claiming identity, space, and rights*, Boston: Beacon Press.

Shepard, B. and Hayduk, R. (eds) (2002) From ACT UP to the WTO: Urban protest and community building in the era of globalization, London, Verso.

Williams, R. (2010) *The Divided World: Human Rights and Violence*, Minneapolis, University of Minnesota Press.

5. Migrant youth in Europe: challenges for integration policies[1]

By René Bendit

Globalization, modernisation and migration processes are changing the 'social map' of Europe: they are radically influencing the world of work, of culture and of social life. In the context of these changes, it can be observed that young migrants and young people of migrant origin are in the process of becoming part of modern youth in the European countries in which they live. During this process, they have to cope not only with the classical psychological developmental tasks of adolescence and of the youth phase but also with the social and cultural challenges late modernity presents to modern youth life.

In order to be successful in coping with these challenges, young migrants have to overcome the different constellations of social inequality and disadvantage in which they grow up; constellations in which a structural lack of resources and opportunities interacts with cultural aspects, and individual orientations and coping (agency) strategies.

In the present article we will consider the integration process of young migrants into youth life in European Union (EU) member states from three different perspectives: from a social integration perspective; from a cultural perspective and from a biographical (agency) perspective. For this purpose, we will present data from official statistics and empirical research referring to the performances of young migrants and ethnic minority youths confronted with integration challenges at these three levels.

---

1   This article was originally prepared in 2010/2011 so that the European data analyzed in it cover the period from 2005 to 2009. We are aware that over the recent years the EU landscape has changed considerably (there are now 27 EU Member States) and with it, the structure of the total and migrant populations. Nevertheless the general tendencies observed and discussed in this chapter with regard to young migrants' integration processes continue to be roughly the same.

Finally, the analysis of integration processes of young migrants must also consider the role of European migration policies in supporting the social and cultural integration of these groups, and contributing to the development of a new concept of social cohesion and citizenship based on the acceptance of cultural differences (CDMG, 2002). For this purpose, the chapter will analyze official policy documents concerning the different strategies being implemented by EU-Member States that aim to integrate migrant youth and those with a migrant or ethnic minority origin (Council of Europe, 2006).

Migration in Europe: an overview

At the beginning of 2006, the European Union (EU 25) had 462 million inhabitants, 389 million (84 %) of which were either citizens or foreign residents of the EU 15. The other 73 million were citizens or foreign residents of the 10 new EU Member States (Münz 2006). Of a total of 3.5 million immigrants to the EU 27 Member States in 2006, about 3 million (86%) were foreigners, i.e. they were not citizens of the country to which they migrated. More than half (1.8 million) of these immigrants were not citizens of any EU Member State. However, this does not mean that all non-EU immigrants were newcomers to the EU since this number includes immigrants coming directly from outside the EU and those having first immigrated to other Member States before moving to the country where they were living in 2006. Slightly less than half of all immigrants, 1.7 million, were EU citizens, of whom nearly half a million were nationals returning to their country of origin (Eurostat 2008a).

In 2007, the EU 27 population continued to grow, and reached 497 million, but eight of the EU 27 Member States saw their populations continue to decrease. It is important to note that 80% of population growth in the EU 27 was due to migration (Eurostat 2008b). By 2007, the immigrant population in the EU had reached 28 861 974 (Eurostat 2008a).

During 2008 the population of the twenty-seven EU Member States grew by 2.1 million, at an annual rate of 0.4%, due to a natural increase of 0.6 million and a net migration of 1.5 million. At the very beginning of 2009, the total population of the 27 EU Member States was of about 499 million inhabitants (Eurostat 2010). In 2008, immigration from non-EU countries and mobility between Member States became stronger and the proportion of the working-age population that was either born abroad or had at least one parent who was born abroad continued to grow (Eurostat 2010). On 1 January 2009, a total of 31.9 million persons with citizenship of a country different from their country of residence were living on the territory of the EU 27 Member States representing 6.4% of the total EU 27 population. Of these non-nationals, more than a third (11.9 million) were citizens of another Member State (Eurostat 2010).

From the total population living in EU 27 Members States at the beginning of 2009, more than 94 million were children and adolescents under the age of 18 (18.8%), and over 62 million (12.4%) were young people aged between 15 and 24 years. In sum, the proportion of persons under 25 years old was 31.2%; according to Eurostat projectons, in 2050 the proportion of young people in reference to the total population will decrease considerably (Eurostat 2010).

The age structure of the EU-born and migrant populations shows some similarities and differences (Eurostat 2006). While the ratio for the age group 0-19 years was almost equal for those born in the EU and migrants (23% vs. 20%), for young adults and adult groups, significant differences exist. Among migrants, 22% were aged 25-29 years while only 14% of those born the EU were of this age group. These figures were similar for 30-34 year olds. Taken together, 41% of migrants were in the 20-39 age group (e.g. 'post- adolescents' or young adults and adults), while the rate was 28% for EU-born residents. Nevertheless, the largest differences in the age structure of both population groups existed for those over 65, who represented 17% of those born in the EU and only 9% of those born outside the EU. The differences in the higher age categories indicate that EU-born residents form an increasingly older population and that immigration contributes only in the short term to reduce the average age of the total EU population (*ibid*). The role of migration with regard to demographic changes in Europe has attracted attention in recent years because of growing concerns about the demographic ageing of the population, the future labour supply caused by shortages of working-age populations, dependency ratios and the sustainability of pensions. There are countries where population growth is attributed entirely to migration, such as Germany, Sweden and Greece (Haug, Compton and Courbage, 2003).

Composition of the Migrant Population

The composition of the migrant population is mainly determined by geographic, historic and economic factors as well as by political situations and traditional international relationships. The migrant population also reflects different waves of post-war migrations associated with labour shortages, family reunion and formation, and refugees within and outside Europe. Therefore, in all EU Member States, migrants and ethnic minorities constitute a diversified group that includes:

- Long-term and temporary 'guest' workers;
- Workers and merchants along the EU borders (among them are unskilled workers and highly educated people);
- Students and highly qualified immigrants;
- Migrants from former colonies with British, French, Portuguese or Spanish citizenship;
- Migrants from Eastern Europe;
- Asylum seekers and refugees;
- Illegal or irregular migrants (Niessen, 2000).

During the last decades a global migration market has emerged that particularly refers to those with high levels of expertise and skills. By bringing highly skilled migrants (especially in the information and communications technology sector) into their countries, national governments expect to obtain economic benefits by increasing national expertise or by countering specific skills shortages. Finally, it is important to note that illegal migration has led to the introduction of strict controls on the borders of European countries. Due to its clandestine nature, no one knows exactly the size of the illegal population across Europe or in individual countries.

Distribution and origin of the 'migrant/foreign[2]' population in EU Member States

The distribution of migrants is uneven across Europe. In absolute terms, in 2009 the largest numbers of foreign citizens were living in Germany, Spain, the United Kingdom, France and Italy (Eurostat 2010). Non-nationals in these five countries represented more than 75 % of the total EU foreign population. Germany has about a third of the total, while France registers about 15% and the UK about 12%. Other countries with significant proportions of 'foreign' people are Luxembourg, Switzerland, Italy, Austria, Belgium and Spain. In relative terms, the EU Member State with the highest percentage of non-nationals was Luxembourg (43.5 %). In Austria and Germany, the proportion was around 9%, while Belgium's was slightly lower. In Denmark, France, Ireland, the Netherlands, Norway, Sweden and the UK it was around 4 to 5%. In the rest of the Western European countries, the proportion of foreigners was less than 3%. By comparison, the proportion of recorded migrants in Central and Eastern Europe is much smaller (Eurostat, 2007). In 2009, a high proportion of non-nationals (10% or more of the resident population) was also observed in Latvia, Estonia, Cyprus, Spain and Austria, while the countries with the lowest share of non-nationals (less than 1 %) were Poland, Romania and Bulgaria (Eurostat 2010).

Luxembourg, Ireland, Belgium, Cyprus, Slovakia and Hungary were the only countries where the majority of non-nationals were citizens of the 27 EU Member States. In all other Member States, the majority of non-nationals were citizens of non-EU countries (Eurostat 2010). So, for example in Austria, most migrants came from the former Yugoslavia (Slovenia, Croatia, Serbia and Kosovo) but also from Romania and Turkey. In Finland, immigrants came mainly from Somalia, Russia, Pakistan, Turkey and some Arab countries while in France, most immigrants came from former French colonies, especially from North Africa (Algeria, Tunisia and Morocco) and Sub-Saharan francophone countries. In Germany, Denmark and the Netherlands, Turkish immigrants form the largest immigrant groups. In Germany also, citizens from the ex-Yugoslavia, Italy,

---

2   Here, we differentiate these two categories since certain groups of migrants in Europe, e.g. 'Aussiedler' (ethnic Germans emigrating from East European countries to Germany) or citizens of former British colonies or from French 'Territoires d'Outremer' having emigrated from their countries of origin, might possess a German, British or French citizenship and can therefore not be considered legally as 'foreigners'.

Greece and Poland represent important immigrant groups, while in Italy, most non-EU immigrants come from Albania, Croatia, Egypt, Eritrea, ex-Yugoslavia, India, Morocco, Tunisia, Senegal, other Sub-Saharan African countries, Romania and Sri Lanka. In Portugal, immigrants are mostly citizens of former colonies, like Angola, Brazil, Cap Verde Islands and Mozambique; finally, in Spain, the largest immigrant groups come from the Dominican Republic, Ecuador, Morocco, Peru, Tunisia and some Sub-Saharan African countries but also from Poland and Romania (Bade, Bommes and Münz, 2004).

The challenges of social and cultural integration for young people with migration backgrounds in Europe

The main challenges 'new European youth' has to cope with are linked to: the requirements and high expectations linked to educational and vocational training standards established in their country of arrival; the development of individual strategies to obtain access to the labour market; learning to live with tensions and contradictions stemming from the requirements of very complex and differentiated societies and their transition processes towards knowledge- based societies and their 'post- modern' values and from cultural norms; and the values and lifestyles anchored in traditional socialisation patterns of their families, communities and other social contexts. Young migrants also have to learn to cope with differences and with intercultural conflicts between majority and minority cultures (managing diversity) and they have to construct their own cultural identities in the context of tensions and contradictions between their own self-understandings and the cultural labelling and stigmatization processes present in the majority society (Bechmann Jensen and Mørch, 2006; Bechmann Jensen et al., 2007; see also Walther, Stauber and Pohl, 2009).

Educational and vocational training: how do migrant youths perform?

We first draw on data presented and analysed in the context of the *Up2 Youth* project (see different National Reports by: Bendit et al., 2007; Blasco et al., 2007; Ferreira and Pais, 2007; Marcovici et al., 2007; Mørch et al., 2007; Salovaara and Julkunen, 2007), and also other reports on the situation of migrant youth (Alitolppa-Niitamo, 2004; Reißig et al., 2006; Mørch et al., 2008; Großegger, 2008; Machado, Matias and Leal, 2005; López Sala and Cachón, 2007). This data shows that in most EU Member States, migrant youth of first and second generation (those born outside the EU and those born of parents who migrated to the EU) show lower school achievement than majority youth[3]. This is particularly the case for Arab and Turkish youth in Scandinavian countries; Turkish and Balkan youth in Austria; North Africans in Belgium; Moroccan and Sub-Saharans youth in France; Turkish and other migrant youth (e.g. Italians) in Germany; Turkish and North African youth in the Netherlands; and finally for young Africans in Spain and Portugal. The main difficulties for migrant youth, youth with migration backgrounds and ethnic minority youth in school and in vocational training are associated with language problems, learning difficulties, school interruption and abandonment, social and family problems and difficulties in accessing and succeeding in vocational training (see Bendit et al., 2007; Blasco et al., 2007; Ferreira and Pais, 2007; Marcovici et al., 2007; Mørch et al., 2007; Salovaara and Julkunen, 2007; Alitolppa-Niitamo, 2004; Mørch et al., 2008; Großegger, 2008; Machado, Matias and Leal, 2005; López Sala and Cachón, 2007).

Most European countries demonstrate the importance of family support when it comes to educational achievement. Even if migrant families want their children to have a better education than their parents, they often do not have the time or the competencies to help their children with homework or with educational advice. At the same time, most migrant parents are insufficiently informed about the professional perspectives offered to their children by the various types of educational institutions.

Particularly problematic is the educational situation of young Roma and Sinti, in different Central and East European countries (in Austria, Bulgaria, the Czech Republic, Hungary, Portugal and Romania), of young Gypsies in Portugal and Spain, and of young Gypsies and Travellers in Ireland. Analysed data show high rates of early school abandonment while their school trajectories in general tend to be more problematic and misleading (Walther et al., 2002).

In these situations, gender plays an important differentiating role. The national reports of the Up2Youth project describe the following trends:

• In most EU Member States young migrant and ethnic minority girls achieve better results at secondary school than migrant boys;

---

3   In most EU countries, important differences can be observed between first, second and
     third generations of migrants and ethnic minority youth.

- Female youth of Sinti or Roma origin, in countries like Bulgaria, Italy, Portugal, Romania and Spain, are often hindered in secondary education by their families;
- Male youths of migrant origin in Austria, Belgium, Germany, Great Britain, Portugal, the Netherlands, Spain and the Scandinavian countries have a strong orientation towards professional/vocational training institutions but are often unmotivated by the discriminatory practices of employers or institutional representatives;
- In most EU Member States more male than female youths of migrant origin have access to vocational training and gain corresponding certifications (see Bendit *et al.*, 2007; Blasco *et al.*, 2007; Ferreira and Pais, 2007; Marcovici *et al.*, 2007; Mørch *et al.*, 2007)

Furthermore, different studies indicate that the possibilities for young migrants and ethnic minority youths to develop self-determined biographic careers are lower than those of other young people of the same age and social class (Bendit *et al.*, 2007; Walther, Stauber and Pohl, 2009). Exceptions to such lower educational achievement can be found among young migrants from Eastern European countries and certain groups of Latin American students in Spain (Blasco *et al.*, 2007) and Portugal (Ferreira and Pais, 2007). Their educational performances are often better than those of other young people. The same can be observed in the case of Eastern European youth living in Finland (see Salovaara and Julkunen, 2007).

Access to the labour market

Secondary analysis of labour market statistics and specialized studies in different EU Member States confirm the fact that low-qualified youth face many difficulties in labour market integration in countries with high educational standards and post-industrial labour markets. This is mostly the case for young migrants in countries like Denmark, Finland, Germany, Norway and Sweden, but it also occurs in most other EU Member States.

In most EU countries, the occupational trajectories of young people with migrant backgrounds are characterized by precarious employment situations. They mostly perform unqualified jobs and receive short-term contracts. In Southern Europe, many of them work in the informal sector of the economy without any kind of social security. In some cases, young people occupy these jobs in parallel to secondary school attendance. For example, 25% of young migrants from African origins in Portugal, aged from 14 to 19 years, are working in such jobs.

Data further shows that young migrants with informal vocational qualifications become jobless more often than majority youths in the same situation. Some studies demonstrate that migrant youths commonly obtain unqualified jobs in 'ethnic enterprises' (e.g. young Italians in Italian restaurants, Turkish youths in Turkish restaurants and shops, etc.) (Zentrum für Turkei Studien, 2004). In other cases, they are supported in looking for jobs by parents and family networks. This happens mostly by asking for jobs in the same enterprises where parents, relatives or family friends are already working. In other cases, they are integrated into the family business (Schittenhelm, 2005; Bendit, 1997)

Summing up, young migrants and ethnic minority youths living in the EU Member States face more difficulties during their school careers than other young people in the same countries. They may have troubles with language, school attendance, and the learning process in school trajectories, and often experience discrimination in school life. The result seems to be that ethnic minority youth are disadvantaged in the education system and tend to have lower achievement levels than average[4].

Analysis of successful educational trajectories shows that, under the rather marginalizing circumstances in which they are living, the conscious decision of many young migrants to take up vocational training seems to be the most appropriate and promising coping strategy available to them. Vocational training not only serves the purpose of long-term material reproduction, but also enhances the possibilities of participating in modern youth life in late modern European societies. It is a valuable support in the process of emancipation from their families of origin; it stabilizes self-esteem, fosters social contacts, and opens up perspectives for the future. In other words, being successful in secondary education and in vocational training opens the road to individualization, social integration and biographisation (see Badawia, 2002).

---

4   In particular, Roma, Sinti and Gypsies in Central European and in South-East European countries like Bulgaria and Romania, but also in Italy, Portugal and Spain, leave school early and without any educational certification. Gender differences are also very visible. Roma girls often have to stay home to take care of younger siblings. When they are allowed to attend school however, they have better results than boys (Marcovici *et al.*, 2007). For their part, boys may try to get some vocational education but they often experience discrimination when they are applying for vocational training programs.

Cultural challenges and behaviours

Social and cultural integration takes place in everyday life. Families, schools, neighbourhoods, peers, youth centres, NGOs and youth associations, but also mass media are the psychological '*base-camps*' in which young migrants and ethnic minority youth, like all other young people, learn to develop agency and their own cultural identities. But in these spaces, migrant and ethnic minority youths are also confronted with discrimination and other problems that, in some cases, lead to social labelling and/or to an ethnicisation of social relations (Skrobanek, 2007).

Different empirical studies on migrant youths in Austria (Großegger, 2008), Denmark (Mørch *et al.*, 2008), Germany (Bendit *et al.*, 2007), Finland (Salovaara and Julkunen, 2007; Alitolppa-Niitamo, 2004), Portugal (Ferreira and Pais, 2007; Machado, Matias and Leal, 2005) and Spain (Blasco *et al.*, 2007; López Sala and Cachón, 2007) show that a significant number of migrant parents consider it important to transmit their own cultural identity to their children. From this perspective, some parents also pressure their children to accept and reproduce their own lifestyles and traditions. This is particularly the case for religious beliefs and practices. Furthermore, traditionally-oriented migrant families perceive late modern lifestyles as problematic and dangerous for their family life. In these families, the idea that social contact for a non-married woman should only take place in the context of her own family networks is a dominant one. Girls and young women growing up in this type of family mostly become wives and mothers at a relative young age.

Participation in everyday contexts influences individualization in many ways. Young people can learn about late modern life by participating in many informal groups and activities. In inter-ethnic peer groups, youth centres and associations, young migrants and ethnic minority youths get in touch with values, norms and behavioural patterns of late modernity and learn, step by step, to be part of modern youth life and youth culture.[5] Nevertheless, certain groups of young migrants and ethnic minority youths prefer social contacts inside informal or organized intra-ethnic groups (e.g. peers; sport clubs; religious and political organiza-

---

5   In these open spaces of informal peer-learning, they can develop new inter-personal contacts and new life perspectives. In inter-ethnic groups, they might also learn to develop strategies to cope with ambivalences, contradictions and conflicts between the traditional lifestyles of their families and the modern lifestyles prevailing in the host society.

tions, etc.). These groups and organizations are viewed sceptically by the majority society and are sometimes characterized as 'parallel societies' inhibiting social integration and endangering social cohesion.

In different EU Member States, migrant and ethnic minority girls and young women of traditional family origins have relatively low chances of participating in modern youth life. They remain excluded from inter-gender peer groups and youth associations as well as from other forms of expression in the context of youth cultures. In this way, they also are excluded from different informal learning situations and youth specific life-styles relevant for social and cultural integration in late modern societies.

Young migrants and ethnic minority youths from Roma and Sinti communities with low formal education, who are practicing unskilled jobs or who are unemployed, seem to reproduce 'traditional' adult life-styles early on in their biographical development. They marry early; the girls remain without jobs and have children very early. For many of these ethnic minority youth groups, ethnic and low socio-economic conditions become interwoven and are determining factors in the construction of such traditional life trajectories (Walther, Stauber and Pohl, 2009; Weiss, 2007a, 2007b, 2007c; Machado and Matias, 2006; Singla, 2004).

Summing up, for young migrants and ethnic minority youths, learning to adopt active coping strategies relevant for their social and cultural integration in late modern societies is facilitated through processes of informal learning in different social spaces of everyday life. Also, the individualization of ethnic minority youth appears to be more gendered than in the general processes of late modern individualization. Therefore, direct and indirect social integration initiatives in schools and jobs are clearly important.

Overview of strategies for the integration of young migrants

Policies and measures aiming at the social integration of disadvantaged groups (and thus trying to strengthen social cohesion) can be categorized as either 'indirect' or 'direct' strategies.[6] Based on this categorization and

---

6   Both those that are aimed at the population as a whole, and those focusing on specific groups, such as migrants. Authors like Heckmann and Bosswick (1995) are of the opinion that 'indirect' strategies, such as promoting the access of disadvantaged youths to professional training, are more significant and effective than 'direct' measures

considering the different welfare and transition regimes prevailing in the different EU member states (Esping-Andersen, 1990; Gallie and Paugam, 2000; EGRIS - Research Group, 2005, 2006; Walther, du Bois-Reymond and Biggart, 2006), as well as different integration modes (Schnapper, 1990; Kastoriano, 2002; Heckmann and Schnapper, 2003; Heckmann and Bosswick, 1995), we shall provide a short overview on some relevant strategies practiced in several EU member states. These strategies aim to respond to the social exclusion of young people in general[7] and also focus their attention on the integration of young migrants and ethnic minority youths in education, vocational training and employment.

Indirect Strategies: the integration of disadvantaged young people living in 'social hotspots' and inter-departmental programmes against social exclusion.

In Europe, many children and adolescents grow up with multiple disadvantages, often in *'disadvantaged'* and *'socially problematic areas.'* In countries like Bulgaria, Romania, the Czech Republic and *Lithuania*, it is mainly ethnic minorities (e.g. Gypsies) who suffer from many deficiencies. These children and adolescents often live in peripheral areas and in 'communities' of their own; they are often 'travellers' and, on the whole, are exposed to general conditions that make it difficult for them to integrate into their respective majority societies. A significant portion of these children, adolescents and youths are immigrants themselves or have a migration background. To cope with this situation, the EU Member States have developed general integration strategies against social exclusion. Since these problems are not merely a national phenomenon, the EU Commission itself has developed an Action Plan against poverty and social exclusion (2005), including the promotion of National Action Plans in the member states as well as equal opportunities programs (2007). In this EU Plan, 'integration strategies' refer to different aspects of social discrimination: education, employment, health, security, multicultural coexistence, social infrastructure, cooperation and networking.

In the context of indirect strategies, inter-departmental programs against social exclusion have also been implemented in different EU Member States. They are particularly well-developed in France, Ger-

---

(promotion of access for specific sub-groups among the disadvantaged, such as young migrants).
7   Information in this chapter on these strategies stems from contributions presented at the EU convention 'Children and Adolescents in Social Hot Spots – New Strategies of Cohesion', Leipzig, June 2007 (see DJI Bulletin, 2007, p.32).

many, England and the Netherlands. Social integration, security, health, employment and housing are the core issues of the respective national programs and strategies. In some EU Member States, educational strategies for migrant and ethnic minority children and youth, including those living in 'hot spots', are at the core of these programs. Local authorities attempt to achieve cooperation among all relevant governmental and social actors (youth offices, voluntary agencies, educational institutions, employment agencies, the health sector). Prototypical strategies and programs have been introduced in France (*Politique de la Ville* (Urban Policy)[8]); in Germany (Development and Chances of Young People in Social Problematic Areas ("Social Hot Spots"[9]); and in Great Britain (Every Child Matters). In France and Germany, the programs have a strong socio-environmental orientation, whereas the program in Great Britain is regionally administered and directed at all children and adolescents under 19 years old.

Direct strategies: specific programs and measures aimed at the social integration of migrant youth

A variety of efforts are carried out in most EU Member States in order to socially and culturally integrate young people with migrant or ethnic minority origins. Most of the programmes and measures developed for this purpose focus on education (in most countries learning national languages is seen as crucial), vocational schemes/training, enlarging opportunities for apprenticeships, fighting crime, etc. Activation policies play a major role in some countries, as well as guaranteed minimum income as a means for supporting disadvantaged groups. In most countries, municipalities, regions or autonomous states/counties are required to carry out their own specific plans, which blurs the overall picture of the success of these interventions. What follows is a short summary of the programs and measures:

8   See: http://www.ladocumentationfrancaise.fr/dossiers/politique-ville-index.shtml/politique-ville-lutte-discriminations.shtml and Agence nationale pour la cohésion sociale et l'égalité des chances: http://www.lacse.fr/wps/portal/internet/acse/accueil/noschampsdaction/politiquedelaville/education/!ut/p/c5/04_SB8K8xLLM9MSSzPy8xBz9CP0os3iTsGADI09LYwMDVy9nA09Tv0BjVwNfQ2dTQ6B8pFm8AQ7gaICi293R39XAM8DCyN_DzdfA29MMotv LIsjZwsnQ0cA9wBIo7-PvaextYWoY7G1CjN14TMev288jPzdVvyA3NDSi3FERABP0   EQE!/dl3/d3/L2dBISEvZ0FBIS9nQSEh/.
9   See: http://www.eundc.de/pdf/00902.pdf.

Primary and Secondary schools

Programs and measures aiming at better achievement in school and the social integration of migrant and ethnic minority children and youth at the primary and secondary levels of education exist in most EU countries. They might include: promoting education in national languages at pre-school institutions (Kindergarten, École Maternelle etc.); anticipating schooling age and school matriculation; standardized early testing of host country language skills; flexible school-entering phases; remedial teaching in the context of preparatory courses in the national language, as well as in mathematics and other subjects for adolescents entering the host country's educational system at a later age (for example, in Austria, Germany, the Netherlands); compensatory courses in national languages as a second language for students with migration backgrounds; introduction of educational standards and monitoring for special target groups; extending/constructing 'all day' schools (especially in Germany where they are almost non-existent); introducing social work and social workers into schools; strengthening school autonomy to enable the development of integration projects along with internal and external evaluation; improving teacher training and further qualifications needed in pedagogic work with disadvantaged pupils and in the field of intercultural pedagogy; and finally developing quality standards and quality management for multicultural or intercultural teaching. One important aspect of young migrants' school integration refers to adolescents entering the educational system at the secondary level, in grades 7, 8 or 9. In some German Federal States, for example, these students are sent to preparatory classes where the main aim is to put emphasis on teaching the German language, and fostering the adaptation of young migrants to the educational system and to a problem-solving-centered teaching style (see Bendit et al., 2007).

Education/vocational training

Alongside policies implemented in general education, the main strategies in different EU Member States aim to improve vocational training. This is being done in the context of very different existing legislations and training systems. Central elements of these strategies, programmes and measures are: internships or work placements in companies during the last year of secondary school education; job-preparation courses; school-based pre-vocational education; and basic courses offered by employment agencies outside the formal educational system. Besides formal and informal instruction and qualification, the emphasis of these programs is on vocational orientation, apprenticeship searches, job preparation, leisure time activities and socio-pedagogical support. Local educational institutions, specialized NGOs, and private institutes are responsible for their pedagogical implementation. Meanwhile, a large number of successful programs and measures for occupational integration can be found in Austria, England, France, Germany, Ireland, Italy, Luxemburg, the Netherlands, Portugal, Spain, and in most Scandinavian countries.

Conclusion

Young people from migrant origins are standing at the threshold of late modern individualised youth life. As newcomers to Western societies, many of them are suddenly propelled into late modern youth life, and as minority youth they are under pressure to participate in this life against barriers they must confront. If young migrants and ethnic minority youth successfully participate in modern 'structures of activity' offered to all young people in European societies, this form of individual agency may be in conflict with the cultural background of their families and family networks, where social integration may be expected to follow the logic of social or cultural 'traditional' integration, where social categories refer to family, kin, local dependencies, etc. Therefore a first aspect of the challenge of social and cultural integration and individualisation points to a contradiction between *categorical* social integration and *late modern individual* social integration (Mørch *et al.*, 2008).

The road to successful integration and agency in late modern society takes time. Data shows that in most countries great differences exist between first, second and third generation migrants and ethnic minority youth. Also, ethnic minority youth individualization seems more gendered than late modern individualization. Furthermore, from data provided by different studies, we may also conclude that for adolescent migrants not yet fulfilling the requirements to participate in an adequate form in modern youth life, transitions from school to work and to adult life have to be interpreted rather as trajectories (as the concept is employed by Roberts, 1968; 1977; 1995; 1997)[10] than as 'biographisation'.

10 The concept of "trajectories" is derived from a larger explanatory model that was proposed by Roberts in 1968, the "opportunity structure" model, and which he developed in later years (see Roberts 1977, 1995 and 1997). According to this model, school leavers of different social origins pass from school to employment and to adult life through different transition routes or trajectories that are essentially predefined by the

In this perspective, their transitions are largely determined by structural factors, and opportunities in the job market depending mostly on social and ethno-cultural factors rather than on individual action or control. For this group of youth and young adults, choices are still limited and their access to the job market depends strongly on local situations.

The decision of many young migrants and ethnic minority youths to take up vocational training in the labour market segments open to them (even if they do not correspond to their vocational preferences) seems, under the rather marginalising structural circumstances in which they grow up, the most appropriate and promising coping strategy available. Vocational training not only serves the purpose of labour market entrance and long-term material reproduction, but also enhances the possibilities of participating in various late modern European societies. It is a valuable support in the process of emancipation from their families of origin, it stabilises their self-esteem, fosters social contacts (including the choice of a partner), and it opens up perspectives for the future.

More reflexive perspectives (i.e. post-structural), which describe successful transitions in terms of individual skills, such as the ability to 'negotiate' one's own biography, to construct alternatives, and to evaluate social and job-related opportunities and risks, may apply only to the few better-qualified migrant youths. For the majority of adolescents and young adults from migrant backgrounds, if biographisation takes place, it will most likely be on a cultural level, in building and negotiating 'patchwork identities'(Keupp 1988; Atabay 1991). In summary, the transitions from school to apprenticeship and work still carry the traditional characteristics of classic industrial societies.

It has been also shown that, in late modern European societies, social inequality creates different 'constellations of disadvantage' (Bendit & Stokes 2003) in which structural lack of resources and opportunities interacts with individual orientations and coping strategies. Ethnic minority

structure of job opportunities. Roberts argued that entry into employment in different social contexts requires different explanatory frameworks, and that entry into employment does not take place in a similar manner amongst all groups of young people, even within the same society. Roberts thus challenged the relevance of the concept of choice embedded in psychological theories, by emphasizing the structure of constraints. Nowadays, an extended transition period from education to employment touches almost all young people, who are able to exercise some choices at some stage of this process, although the available choices differ markedly from one social group to another. This stands in contrast to complete "biographisation" of transitions in which all young people may be considered as equally able to negotiate life choices.

youth and young migrants are especially affected by such constellations. Therefore, different policies, measures and programmes in Europe, developed in the context of different 'modes of integration', have focused on several of these structures of disadvantage in order to promote social, educational, vocational/professional and cultural integration among these groups.

Even though the goals and the intentions of integration are positive, and even though policies, measures and programs are extremely differentiated, the overall results do not seem too positive. Although there are promising agendas and a variety of policies and programmes that have been carried out, the general impression is that no country is truly in a position to affirm that their efforts to integrate young people from migrant origins and those belonging to ethnic minorities have been successful. This is not to say that strategies and specific programs fail, but merely that the problem remains. Even though young migrants and ethnic minority youths of the second or third generation are performing better educationally, do not have severe problems in transition processes and are increasingly integrated into different societies, disadvantaged young migrants must still face big obstacles and odds.

The big challenge from a European perspective seems to be to find effective strategies of providing better opportunities for young migrants and ethnic minority youths. In this respect, the lessons we can learn from each other is highly dependent on the ways in which transition processes and youth life are organised and conceptualised in each country. Furthermore, if one recognizes the positive consequences of overcoming marginalization, both on the personal and societal levels, through successful general education and professional training, one must reach the conclusion that, in the future, measures in these fields have to be further intensified.

Most integration policies continue to have an ethnocentric orientation as they expect migrants to assimilate into the majority culture, thus implying that their own culture is less valuable and that their practices are dysfunctional to the host societies' cohesion. Therefore, the strengthening of individual capacities and agency, as well as the social acceptance of an individual's right to be culturally different, are necessary pre-conditions of the successful integration of migrants.

For the time being, none of the countries involved in the EU studies can convey the impression of having integrated young migrants and members of ethnic minorities successfully into modern youth life. Only a partial success can be verified. The situation of young migrants can still be characterised as being in a precarious balance between partial inclusion and partial marginalisation (regarding labour market and vocational training). In spite of all efforts, integration problems continue to exist in all societies and these are becoming problematic in countries where immigration is new.

Bibliography

Alitolppa-Niitamo, A. (2004) *The Icebreakers: Somali-speaking youth in metropolitan Helsinki with a focus on the context of formal education*, Helsinki, The Family Federation of Finland, The Population Research Institute.

Atabay, I. (1991) *Die Identitätsentwicklung türkischer Migrantenkinder und Jugendlicher in der Bundesrepublik*, Arbeit zur Erlangung des Magistergrades an der Universität München, Munich, Institut Für empirische Pädagogik und pädagogische Psychologie.

Badawia, T. (2002) 'Der Dritte Stuhl'. Grounded Theory-Studie zum kreativen Umgang bildungserfolgreicher Immigranten-Jugendlicher mit kultureller Differenz, Frankfurt a. Main and London, IKO-Verlag für interkulturelle Kommunikation.

Bade, K. J., Bommes, M. and Münz, R. (eds) (2004) *Migrationsreport 2004: Fakten – Analysen – Perspektiven*, Frankfurt a. Main, Campus Verlag.

Bechmann Jensen, T., Mørch, S., Hansen, B. and Stokholm, M. (2007) Transitions to work of young people with an ethnic minority or migrant background, in *Up2Youth. Youth – Actor of Social Change*, Synthesis of National Reports, available at: http://www.up2youth.org (accessed June 15, 2012).

Bendit, R. & Stokes, D. (2003): 'Disadvantage': transition policies between social construction and the needs of vulnerable youth, in López Blasco, A., McNeish, W. and Walther, A. (eds.) *Young People and Contradictions of Inclusion. Towards Integrated Transition Policies in Europe* (pp. 261-281), Bristol (UK), The Policy Press.

Bendit, R. (1997) "Wir wollen so unsere Zukunft sichern". Der Zusammenhang von beruflicher Ausbildung und Lebensbewältigung bei jungen Arbeitsmigranten in Deutschland, Aachen, Shaker Verlag.

Bendit, R., Wilhelm, M., Rink, B. and Skrobanek, J. (2007) Transitions to work of Ethnic Minority Youth: National Report (Germany), in *Up2Youth. Youth – Actor of Social Change*[11].

Blasco, A., Rodríguez, G.G., Minués, A. M., Errea Rodriguez, J., López, F. and Gil, M. (2007) Transitions to work of Ethnic Minority Youth: National Report (Spain), *Up2Youth. Youth – Actor of Social Change*[12].

---

11 This 'Up2Youth' project report was produced by the EGRIS network (European Group for Integrated Social Research). Available at: IRIS e.V. – Fürststr. 3, 72072 Tübingen, Germany – Telephone: +49 7071 79520-60. http://www.iris-egris.de/.

12 This 'Up2Youth' project report was produced by the EGRIS network (European Group for Integrated Social Research). See previous note for access to this report.

CDMG (European Committee on Migration (2002) *Current Trends in International Migration in Europe*, Strasbourg, Council of Europe.

Council of Europe (2006) Achieving social cohesion in a multicultural Europe: concepts, situation and developments: Trends in Social Cohesion No. 18, Strasbourg, Council of Europe.

DJI Bulletin. (2007) Kinder und Jugendliche in sozialen Brennpunkten – Neue Strategien der Kohäsion [Children and Adolescents in Social Hot Spots – New Strategies of Cohesion], *DJI Bulletin of the German Youth Institute, 79*, Munich, German Youth Institute.

Esping-Andersen, G. (1990) *The Three Worlds of Welfare Capitalism*, Cambridge, Cambridge University Press.

Eurostat (2010): *Demography report 2010. Older, more numerous and diverse Europeans,* Commission staff working document, European Commission. Directorate General for Employment, Social Affairs and Inclusion, Unit D.4, Eurostat, the Statistical Office of the European Union, Unit F.1.

Eurostat (2009): European demography – 5.4 million children born in EU 27 in 2008: EU 27 population reaches 500 million, in *Eurostat News Release 113/2009*, http://www.lex.unict.it/eurolabor/documentazione/altrestat/eurostat030809.pdf (accessed 15 June 2012).

Eurostat (2008a) Population in Europe 2007: first results, in *Eurostat Statistics in focus 81/2008* (author: Giampaolo Lanzieri), http://epp.eurostat.ec.europa.eu/cache/ITY_OFFPUB/KS-SF-08-081/EN/KS-SF-08-081-EN.PDF (accessed June 15, 2012).

Eurostat (2008b): Recent migration trends: citizens of EU-27 Member States become ever more mobile while EU remains attractive to non-EU citizens, in *Eurostat statistics in focus 98/2008* (author: Anne Herm), http://epp.eurostat.ec.europa.eu/cache/ITY_OFFPUB/KS-SF-08-098/EN/KS-SF-08-098-EN.PDF (accessed June 15, 2012).

Eurostat (2007) *24-25 March: Youth Summit in Rome - Young Europeans through statistics,* Eurostat news release STAT/07/44, Luxembourg, Eurostat Press Office, http://europa.eu/rapid/pressReleasesAction.do?reference=STAT/07/44&format=HTML&aged=1&language=EN&guiLanguage=en (accessed June 15, 2012).

Eurostat (2006): Non-national populations in the EU Member States, in Eurostat Statistics in focus 8/2006, http://www.cefmr.pan.pl/docs/sif_06-008_en.pdf (accessed June 15, 2012).

European Commission – EU Research on social sciences and humanities (ed) (2005) *Families and Transitions in Europe (FATE) - Final Report*, Brussels, EU Directorate General for Research, http://cordis.europa.eu/documents/ documentlibrary/100124161EN6.pdf (accessed June 15, 2012).

Ferreira, V. S. and Machado Pais, J. (2007) Transitions from school to work of young people with an ethnic or migrant background: National Report (Portugal) *Up2Youth. Youth – Actor of Social Change*[13].

---

13 This 'Up2Youth' project report was produced by the EGRIS network (European Group for Integrated Social Research). See two previous notes for access to this report.

Gallie, D. and Paugam, S. (2000) Unemployment, welfare regimes and social exclusion, *Presentation of results of the TSER Project 'Employment Precarity, Unemployment and Social Exclusion'*, Brussels, 9-11 November.

Großegger, B. (2008) Jugendliche mit Migrationshintergrund: Die '2. Generation' in Zahlen und Fakten: Expertise erstellt im Auftrag des Bundesministeriums für Gesundheit, Familie und Jugend, Vienna, Institut für Jugendkulturforschung, http://www.jugendkultur.at (accessed June 15, 2012).

Haug, W., Compton, P. and Courbage, Y. (2003) The Demographic Characteristics of Immigrant Populations, Population studies No. 38, Strasburg, Council of Europe.

Heckmann, F. and Schnapper, D. (2003) The Integration of Immigrants in European Societies: National Differences and Trends of Convergence, *Forum Migration 7 – European Forum for Migration Studies*, Bamberg, Lucien & Lucien.

Heckmann, F. and Bosswick, W. (1995) *Migration Policies: A Comparative Perspective*, Stuttgart, Enke Verlag.

Kastoriano, R. (2002) Negotiating Identities: States and Immigrants in France and Germany, Princeton, Princeton University Press.

Keupp, H. (1988) Riskante Chancen. Das Subjekt zwischen Psychokultur und Selbstorganization. Heidelberg, Asanger.

López Sala, A. M. and Cachón, L. (eds) (2007) *Juventud e inmigración: Desafíos para la participación y para la integración,* Las Palmas (ES), Dirección General de Juventud de la Consejería de Empleo y Asuntos Sociales del Gobierno de Canarias.

Machado, F. L. and Matias, A. R. (2006) Jovens descendentes de imigrantes nas sociedades de acolhimento: linhas de identificação sociológica, CIES e-Working Paper, n.º 13/2006, Lisbon, CIES.

Machado, F. L., Matias, A. R. and Leal, S. (2005) Desigualdades sociais e diferenças culturais: os resultados escolares dos filhos de imigrantes africanos, *Análise Social, XL, 176*, pp. 695-714.

Marcovici, O., Voica, I., Stefanescu, I., Popa, D. and Marcovici, D. (2007) Transitions from school to work of young people with an ethnic or migrant background: National Report (Romania) *Up2Youth. Youth – Actor of Social Change*, available at www.up2youth.org.

Münz, R. (2006) Europe: Population and Migration in 2005, in *Migration Information Source. Newsletter of the Migration Policy Institute*, June, https://secure. migrationpolicy.org/o/6170/donate_page/source10yr (accessed June 15, 2012).

Niessen, J. (2000) *Diversity and cohesion: New challenges for the integration of immigrants and minorities,* Strasbourg, Council of Europe Publishing, http://www.coe.int/t/dg3/migration/archives/Documentation/Series_Community_Relations/Diversity_Cohesion_en.pdf (accessed June 15, 2012).

Payet, J.-P. (2004) Schulerfolg, Staatsbürgerschaft und Diskriminierung: Migrantenfamilien im französischen Schulsystem, in Fröhlich, M., Haag, F. *et al.* (eds) *Interkulturalität in europäischer Perspektive. Jugendliche aus Migrantenfamilien und ihre Integrationschancen* (pp. 79-92), Frankfurt a. Main, Brandes & Apsel.

Reißig, B., Gaupp, N., Hofmann-Lun, I. and Lex, T. (2006) *Schule – und dann? Schwierige Übergänge von der Schule in die Berufsausbildung*, Munich, Deutschen Jugendinstitut, http://www.agjae.de/pics/medien/1_1168602067/06.1_Schule-und_dann.pdf (accessed June 15, 2012).

Roberts, K. (1997) Prolonged Transitions to Uncertain Destinations: the implications for careers guidance, *British Journal of Guidance and Counselling, 25 (3)*, pp. 345-360.

Roberts, K. (1995) *Youth Employment in Modern Britain*, Oxford, Oxford University Press.

Roberts, K. (1977) The social conditions, consequences and limitations of career guidance, *British Journal of Guidance and Counselling, 5 (1)*, pp. 1-9.

Roberts, K. (1968) The entry into employment: an approach towards a general theory, *Sociological Review, 16*, pp. 165-84.

Salovaara, V. and Julkunen, I. (2007) Transitions from school to work of young people with an ethnic or migrant background: National Report (Finland), *Up2Youth. Youth – Actor of Social Change*[14].

Schittenhelm, K. (2005) Soziale Lagen im Übergang. Junge Migrantinnen und Einheimische zwischen Schule und Berufsausbildung, Wiesbaden, VS Verlag für Sozialwissenschaften.

Schnapper, D. (1990) La France de l'integration: sociologie de la nation, Paris, Gallimard.

Singla, R. (2004) Youth Relationship and Ethnicity: a social psychological study and implications for psychosocial intervention, New Delhi, Books Plus.

Skrobanek, J. (2007) Wahrgenommene Diskriminierung und (Re)Ethnisierung bei Jugendlichen mit türkischem Migrationshintergrund und jungen Aussiedlern, *Zeitschrift für Sozialisationsforschung und Erziehungssoziologie 27 (3)*, pp. 265-284.

Walther, A. et al., (ed) (2002) Misleading Trajectories: integration policies for young adults in Europe, Opladen, Leske + Budrich.

Walther, A., du Bois-Reymond, M. and Biggart, A. (eds) (2006) *Participation in Transition: motivation of young adults in Europe for learning and working*, Frankfurt a. Main, Peter Lang.

Weiss, H. (2007) Wege zur Integration? Theoretischer Rahmen und Konzepte der empirischen Untersuchung, in Weiss, H. (ed) *Leben in zwei Welten: Zur sozialen Integration ausländischer Jugendlicher der zweiten Generation* (pp. 13-69), Wiesbaden, VS Verlag für Sozialwissenschaften.

Zentrum für Türkei Studien, (2004) Türkei – Jahrbuch 2004/2005 der Stiftung Zentrum für Türkeistudien, Münster, LIT Verlag.

14 This 'Up2Youth' project report was produced by the EGRIS network (European Group for Integrated Social Research). See previous notes for access to this report.

6. Preparation for work in the trajectories of youth from low socioeconomic backgrounds

By Claudia Jacinto and Veronica Millenaar

The social construction of young people's careers is the result of complex interactions both at a structural and macro-social institutional level, as well as at micro-social institutional and individual levels. One of the most interesting debates relating to this refers to the way in which the different structural, institutional and individual dimensions link up and also to the strength of the impact of each of these on careers. Drawing on a research project, this paper starts off with a specific question referring to how work training programs have an impact on young people who have completed compulsory secondary school education careers and who come from low socioeconomic backgrounds. The study covers the suburbs of the city of Buenos Aires, Argentina.

The initial labour trajectories of young people who have attended different training programs are compared and analysed as to whether or not they have achieved better inclusion (than could have been predicted) from a social or work point of view.

1. The relationship between secondary school diplomas and programs: a comparative perspective

The current job market in Argentina presents a scenario of great reactivation, with a strong decrease in unemployment; nevertheless, 40% of the active population have precarious work. The work situation of young people has also improved but high levels of inequality persist. The strengths and limitations of Argentina's model of development and production, as well as market segmentation, represent important structural conditioners of the inclusion of young people in the world of work.

The system that links education, the job market and training (Verdier and Buechteman, 1998) is mainly based on formal academic education (only 20% of students pursue secondary level technical education) and vocational training, which has historically been perceived as having poor social value, including in the job market.

The secondary school diploma used to be an important factor in differentiating educational paths. However, the expansion of secondary school, along with the weakening of educational institutions and the persisting informal job market, are keys to understanding the loss of the value of this level of qualification. Today, it has become the minimum requirement to obtain a quality job. However, secondary education is not reaching all segments of the population: only one-half of adolescents manage to complete secondary school within the normal time frame, while many millions of workers have not completed their secondary schooling.

Furthermore, recent studies show that the ones who find it most difficult to 'make their secondary school diploma worth something' on the job market are those who come from low-resource homes or who have less educational capital (Salvia, 2008; Jacinto and Chitarroni, 2009). For example, according to statistics from the Permanent Survey of Households (Encuesta Permanente de Hogares, 2006), non-poor young people who hold a secondary school diploma are those with the lowest rate (33%) of employment in the informal labour market. However, among poor young people who have graduated from secondary school, this figure goes up to 81%, which is very near to those living in poverty who have not completed high school (89%). As far as unemployment is concerned, graduation from secondary school for the poor in fact leads to higher unemployment than for those who have not graduated (49% vs. 30%). Nevertheless, this situation is very different from the rate of unemployment among the non-poor (around 11%) who have or have not graduated from secondary school.

There is abundant empirical evidence about the strong impact of family educational capital on young people's employment inclusion (Siteal, 2007; Perez, 2008, among others). This evidence shows that the educational efforts made in low-resource sectors are far from being reflected in terms of better labour market inclusion and working conditions. Thus, social reproduction trends take precedence over educational qualifications. From the point of view of public policies in education, vocational training and employment, it is paramount to consider how secondary level qualifications, considered to be basic today, can be revalued. Within this context, we ask how specific programs oriented to work preparation can generate better employment opportunities and more social participation among young people in Argentina.

In our research into youth trajectories, we studied not only the impact of diplomas and certificates, and of skills that have been acquired in jobs, but also the ways in which individuals absorb their experiences, how they are motivated by them and the way they use them to obtain other resources such as social capital, economic support, social participation, etc. From this more comprehensive view, we undertake a comparative analysis of work inclusion in different moments of careers, and take into consideration the testimony of individuals in order to fully understand the processes at play. By examining program impacts on three moments of their trajectories (before, immediately after and one year after their training), we are able to identify ruptures in the biographical settings of young people, for example in the opening of new horizons and work projects, including educational ones.

We turn also to sociological variables whose relation to work inclusion has been pointed out in the previous paragraphs, such as the educational capital of households, gender and level of education (basically graduation or not from secondary school). As far as institutional dimensions are concerned, the emphasis is placed on the type of institution (regular secondary school, technical school, Vocational Training Centre or NGO), as well as on the institutional dynamics of the program (e.g. curricular integration, actors involved). In terms of the job market, it must be remembered that the study was carried out in a socio-structural context of lower unemployment and of rising demand for skilled workers.

We start off from the following working hypotheses: 1) For low-resource young people who have graduated from secondary school, providing programs to approach the world of work, such as internships or basic or continuing vocational training, could mean a rise in their conditions of employability and/or an improvement in their chances of obtaining good jobs. 2) However, programs may also have an impact on the processes of subjectivation which are reflected in social participation, in the subjective relation with employment, and in career decision making. 3) The technical or general training provided by the secondary school works in tandem with different ways of training for employment.

In terms of methodology, the study provides a quantitative – qualitative (and exploratory) analysis of 106 cases of young people between 19 and 29 years of age, of both sexes and from low resource homes, who had graduated from 12 institutions which offer various kinds of work training (in particular internships through secondary school and courses of vocational training) one year prior to the study. The young graduates responded to a closed questionnaire and a semi-directed interview focussing on their careers before, during and after their program of study. Career types are reconstructed according to the profiles of typical young people and programs, and are based on the qualitative data which provides greater comprehension about how subjective and objective factors are combined in careers, and also about fractures which occur during careers (Longo and Bidart, 2007).

The programs under study are very different according to the type of institution, their relation to secondary school and the emphasis they place on the type of knowledge and social and technical skills they intend to teach:

a. Internships during secondary technical school (INTERNSHIP). Three schools which provide internships for their students were included: two predominantly technical and another with training in the service industry. The internships consisted of periods in companies of between one and four months under the supervision of the schools. The internships which are linked to a technical occupation focus on complementing the training of the most traditional work apprenticeship; however, the ones linked to the service sector provide a more unspecific training experience and are linked to the development of general labour skills (social, interactive, etc) (Jacinto and Dursi, 2010).

b. Vocational training courses (with recognized certificates) or work-specific training. In Argentina, vocational training has developed in a similar way to the school model and according to social demands. Generally speaking, it is a marginal sector of the education system that provides no linkages with other educational tracks, and is reputed historically for its lack of resources and scarce teacher training. This training generally offers very basic qualification courses for trades. However, the centers where these programs are offered have achieved an important social role by providing tools for the creation of self-employment as well as channels of social participation for wider sectors of the population (Jacinto, 1998). Three institutional models of Centers of Vocational Training have been observed in the framework of the research:

b.1. Union Vocational Training (UVT): these are courses developed in Vocational Training Centers which depend on their respective provinces but at the same time are associated with trade unions. Their certifications are valid within the recognized qualifications of companies in each trade sector, and the institutions themselves usually participate in sector networks. The UVT graduates that were interviewed are almost all males aged over 22 years. Many have parents working in the same trade for which they were taking a course.

b.2. Vocational Training with a local community/religious approach (NGOVT): These are courses provided by NGOs, but in tandem with Vocational Training Courses, which are public, free and depend on the respective educational structures of the provinces. This sub-group comes from homes with comparatively low educational capital: approximately 7 out of 10 come from homes where neither of the parents graduated from secondary school.

b.3. Public Vocational Training (PVT): These are courses developed by Centers of Vocational Training which generally depend on the respective educational structures of the provinces, but that do not hold partnership agreements with other parties, as in the two previous cases. From the point of view of family educational capital, nearly all these interviewees come from homes of low educational capital.

c. Training and Career Guidance (TCG). This type of program is also set up by a NGO (but without local community approaches or coordination with Vocational Training Courses) and focuses particularly on orientation and career guidance in the inclusion process. Above all, it responds to logic of 'activation' aimed at new graduates or pupils in the last year of secondary school. It is characterized by the emphasis it places on training for social competencies more than technical ones, and by the importance it attaches to 'the self-management of the young person' in their transition processes.

2.   Quality of the jobs one year after the training programs

What was the work situation of the young people at the third moment (T3), that is when they were interviewed one year after attending the training program? Job quality indicators generally used in follow-up studies of graduates and/or of impact of training, such as size of company and job insecurity, are used to measure the objective impact.

    The first piece of evidence related to objective impacts, is that there is a strong heterogeneity among the graduates according to their program of study. A kind of continuum is found where young people who attended internships generally appear to have more formal and quality jobs in productive sectors of the economy. Vocational training is seen to have a positive impact on the greater presence of self-employment, while the TCG program shows a strong impact on the quality of jobs, particularly in the service sector.

Secondly, there is also intra-program heterogeneity. In particular, the different models of Vocational Training reflect different kinds of impacts. The Union Vocational Training, where enrollment is higher than in the other two cases, tends to lead graduates to enter medium-sized companies. Intra-program heterogeneity is also present in the fact that, in all programs, there are at least some graduates who have low quality jobs.

In general, it can be observed that although the programs have some impact on employment, they cannot of themselves explain the differences between young people's trajectories. The following sums up the trajectories according to program type:

Internship: those who followed this program tend to be employed in establishments of more than 40 employees (70%). Almost 40% of them work in jobs as technical analysts (this coincides with their technical school studies). Among the others, some work in services or have jobs as technical operators. In contrast with all the other groups (except TCG), the great majority of these respondents work in registered jobs (83%). They receive the comparatively highest salaries (average of 1997.83 pesos per month) in spite of belonging to the youngest group in the sample.

Union Vocational Training (UVT): The young people who attended this program have the highest rates of self-employment and family work (42%). Those that are salaried workers work in small companies (42%) although companies employing from 6 to 40 people carry weight (31%). Jobs such as electrician, plumber, mechanic, skilled operator and construction worker stand out. There are no cases of young people in unskilled jobs. The level of job insecurity is shown to be polarized: while 52% have all benefits, 42% have none. The latter situation is especially linked to family work. Over-employment, that is, working more than 45 hours a week, is also important in this group (42%). It is the group with the second highest average income (1578.95 pesos per month).

Vocational Training with a local/religious approach (NGOVT): Those belonging to this group tend to be salaried in companies of up to 5 employees (42%) but they also have a presence in the category of more than 40 employees (28%), and a few are self-employed. One-half (50%) of the interviewees are factory operators; more than a third have unskilled jobs in different trades, mainly in business and personal services. There are few skilled jobs. Nearly 60% have an informal and precarious job, which is one of the highest rates among the groups. Finally, this group tends to work less hours (nearly 43% in 'sub-employment' of less than 35 hours per week) and have low income levels – the average salary is the lowest (1157.78 pesos per month).

Public Vocational Training (PVT): One out of every 4 young people in this group is self-employed, mostly in unskilled work (40%). This group has the highest rate of informal work: 7 out of 10. At the same time, there is a high proportion of over-employed and a similar proportion of persons who work less than 35 hours a week (in both cases, 4 out of 10). Their income places them among the lowest salary groups (average of 1238.64 pesos per month).

Training and career guidance (TCG): These participants are mainly employed in companies, particularly those with between 6 and 40 employees. In accord with the training provided, the hotel, restaurant, and fast food trades are predominant, and jobs are often linked to the food industry, such as waiter and cook. It stands out as the group with the highest percentages of registered employment (90%) which is a result of institutional efforts to link them with this type of job. According to household surveys, they are in a better position than groups of the population with a similar level of education and age. These young people also stand out due to the fact that more than half come from homes with low educational capital. Nevertheless, most of these interviewees work more than 45 hours a week and their average monthly salary is 1286.45 pesos.

In general, the data we have just presented reflects the strong influence of social reproduction which can be seen not only in the type of program that these young people have access to, but also in the quality of later work inclusion. The inequality of access to programs persists. Nevertheless, when examined from the perspective of careers, it is evident that a multiplicity of objective factors (diploma, home educational environment, type of neighborhood) and subjective dimensions (school experience and previous work, motivation towards program and job) encourage paths of career inclusion when the mediation of the program produces 'breaks' in predictable trajectories (Jacinto and Millenaar, 2010). This issue is analyzed in the following section.

3.   Typical trajectories of young people who attend training programs

The analysis of the qualitative data concerning youth trajectories enables us to consider in articulation the multiplicity of dimensions and to identify 'typical' paths. The analysis of the initial careers of the participants showed that 'types' are linked to socio-demographic conditions (whether or not they have graduated from secondary school, the type of secondary school they attended, the work situation before and after, as well as situational issues such as at what moment of their trajectory they attended the program) and to 'subjective' issues, which guide decision making as far as careers are concerned (perceptions of secondary school, motivation for attending the program and one's self-appraisal). In the framework of these careers, the path through the program holds different places and meanings.

a) *Applying at work what I have done at school:* trajectories where the program complements technical training
A first trajectory type is one which was followed by both male and female interviewees aged between 18 and 20, who attended a technical secondary school and who took part in an internship through the school before graduation. These young people come from homes of medium and high educational capital, attend secondary school without any interruptions and, through their internship, gained access to their first job in a medium or large sized company that offered all benefits and a high salary. The internship took place at the beginning of the career path and enabled access to a quality job where tasks were related to school knowledge as well as knowledge and skills acquired during the internship. Those who follow this typical path possess positive perceptions of both what was learnt at school and the quality of the teaching and the institution; they value the fact that the classroom knowledge was intended to complement their work experience and the chance they had to apply this knowledge during their internship.

The motivation to attend their program was centered on acquiring practical experience and on the possibility of getting a quality job after secondary school. The internship gave the youngsters an opportunity, either to gain useful experience or to obtain more specific useful knowledge.

The value of the program is also positive, since the internship helps the actual career to begin in 'good conditions': obtaining a higher income (the young men's incomes are higher than the young women's), paying for further university studies and improving the quality of life in their homes of origin. The main feature of this typical trajectory is that it is strongly centered on a work project in the technical production sector, which begins to be imagined by the participants in the last years of secondary school and is realized after attending the program.

b) Working in the formal market: trajectories in which the program acts as a 'bridge' to the world of quality work

This refers to young males and females of between 18 and 20 years of age who attended a general secondary school with general orientation and who took part in a TCG course or in an internship during the last year of secondary school. They are from homes of low educational capital and have had limited work experience (generally during weekends or the holidays). After the course, these youth accessed jobs in the service sector in medium-sized or large companies, with all benefits. Nevertheless, the women received lower salaries than the men. The course takes place at the beginning of the trajectories and forms a direct 'bridge' to inclusion in a quality job due to the mediation provided by the training institution, which is key in these cases. It is likely that these young people would not have gained access to these jobs based on their own social capital.

These young people have a negative view of the training they acquired at secondary school as far as the quality of the teaching and the institution are concerned. The criticism is focused on the lack of preparation to enter the labour market. Therefore, the motivations to attend a training program are based on their desire to learn to work and/or to acquire practical work experience.

The appreciation of the program is positive precisely because of the content of the training which enables the participants to acquire occupational knowledge, as well as behaviors as workers, while experiencing a real work environment (in the case of the internships). Also, although these young people were already motivated to work, they learned to attach new significance to the value of work, recognizing it as a central activity in their lives. They have a will to continue their studies as one of their future projects. In this way, the guidance component of these programs enables young people to start their careers with a clearer work horizon as the specific training they receive assists them in their future job searches in a particular area of the job market. Therefore, this trajectory is characterized by the reinforcement of willingness towards work and is accompanied by a first inclusion into quality work, provided by the program.

c) To be able to endorse what you know: trajectories in which the program certifies skills

A third type of path characterizes young men, older than 21, who have also attended a technical school and who began working independently in trades connected to home maintenance or mechanical or electronic appliances when they were still students. These young men come from homes with either low or average educational capital and their parents or another relative work in these trades. Their work is carried out in informal conditions but continuously. After a few years of work they decide on their own, or following a recommendation by a worker in the same trade, to attend a UVT course. This experience enables them to systematize their knowledge and to obtain an official certificate in a work specialty which they had not achieved with their secondary schooling. They continue to be self-employed after obtaining this certificate, or work in informal family ventures and, in some cases, in small or medium-sized companies with all benefits. In these cases, the program takes place later in the young people's careers and often leads to improvements in working conditions, whether through an increase in the clientele thanks to the certificate or through access to formal employment.

Although these participants usually value what they have learned in their technical school, they believe that work training is learned, in fact, *by working*; and so they particularly appreciate the practical components of school and their own work experiences.

The motivations which lead these young people to the program were of acquiring a certificate for what they had learned in their field of work. In their later careers a strong link can be seen between the jobs to which they have access and the contents of the UVT course. In this way, the program enables the acquisition of some kind of technical-operative qualification which, added to the knowledge of the technical school, professionalizes their careers. This not only allows work conditions to improve but also contributes to the development of professional identity.

d) To feel part of a Project: trajectories where the program acts to broaden social capital

A fourth typical path that we have identified is that of young males and females of fewer than 21 years, who come from low educational homes and who live in poor neighborhoods. In this context, the limitation of resources and opportunities are paramount in conditioning their lives.

These young people approached an NGOVT program where they had participated in different activities since their adolescence. They had achieved a secondary school certificate with a general orientation in a local school thanks to support from the NGOVT in the form of scholarships, teaching support and encouragement. After graduating from secondary school or while still there, they took part in a work training course in the same program and were able to obtain a job through the same organization, either by working in the institution itself or on a social or cooperative project organized by the NGO. The participants had had some work experience (mainly in temporary or unstable jobs in the informal sector) before the program. After the program, again with strong institutional support, some of them managed to improve their income and even their work conditions.

These young people interweave their appreciation of school with a perception of the great personal effort that they would have to make to continue with their studies. They consider that the fact they have a diploma is thanks to *one's performance,* to the will to learn and to the effort in itself to stay on in school. Their words reflect the institutional weakness of their secondary school. They are aware of their willpower and even their leadership roles, which they have assumed many times. Their initial motivation to attend the training course was a consequence of the existing bond between the course and the NGO. The appreciation of the program is positive and highlights the environment of the course, the classmates, the class dynamics and the warmth of the teaching staff. Within this appreciation, emphasis is always placed on the networking component which the course encourages and not so much on the technical aspects of the training. The chance to be included in the NGO's activities is seen as more positive than the course itself. In this way, this path is characterized by the strong support provided by the organization.

e) Thinking more about the future: trajectories where the program acts as a guide to social and labour market integration.

A fifth typical trajectory is that of young men and women of different ages, who did not finish their compulsory secondary school studies and who come from homes of low educational capital. These young people drop out of school at a very young age and begin to work in jobs in the informal sector of the economy with a low salary. They attend a VT, NGOVT or PVT course at a later stage of their path. After the course, no changes can be observed in their careers; they continue on in small or medium-sized companies in the informal sector or work independently.

What stands out among these youth is their negative appreciation of the school they attended which, according to them, neither trained nor guided them as far as work was concerned. Nevertheless, they show strong regret for having dropped out of school. They all recognize the value of the secondary school certificate as a 'minimum' requirement in the job market.

Their motivation to attend a course is focused on specific training as a way of obtaining better job prospects; they also mentioned the chance to do something 'more recreational' and that this course was valued in their neighborhood. These young people tend to share a positive perception of the usefulness of the course as a form of career guidance. More knowledge on how to look for work, how to present oneself at a job interview, as well as learning about the attitudes necessary to perform as a worker were stressed.

Another strong mark of the course in this path is the revaluing of the importance of the secondary school certificate for their forthcoming career paths. The chance to *think more about the future* leads some youth to go back to a 'second chance' secondary school.

f) Doing something for myself: trajectories where the program provides a space for social participation

The last path is that of young women of different ages who come from homes of low educational capital, who drop out from school at very young ages and who have one or more children. They have had prolonged periods of inactivity. It is in these conditions that they attend the program (either NGOVT or PVT). What prevails prior to the program is housework and reproduction. After the course, these young women turn to work because they are motivated by the course they attended. However, their later paths are marked by employment intermittency and precariousness.

Their perception of school is negative, partly because the young women feel that their school did not think or care about them. Some of them became mothers at an early age and prevented them from continuing their studies.

The motivation to attend the course proved to be a combination of expectations of improving their job opportunities in case they need to work, and of a desire to participate socially in an activity which provides them satisfaction. The young women perceive that, in the past, when they had to work, they did so because it was necessary and in bad conditions due to their lack of schooling and their situation as young mothers. In this respect, their evaluation of the courses is negative in relation to their expectations concerning job prospects; but it is positive in relation to the social experience of the course as it enabled new relationships to be made. The course enabled these young women to revalue work outside the home so that it is no longer thought of as a task to be carried out only when necessary. The new meaning given to work also involves revaluing their own knowledge as well as questioning the division of labour in their own homes. The chance to think as workers means a deeper subjective modification with respect to their self-perception as women.

Final comments

A central conclusion of this paper is that these programs are an addition to secondary school and contribute to breaking the social reproduction patterns for some young people from homes with low educational capital. The situation of these young people in relation to their jobs one year after attending the program is proven to be better in terms of quality (registered employment and level of salary) than the same group in the job market as a whole. The programs have objective and subjective impacts on careers which go from providing certification, to giving an intermediary step towards obtaining a job (or a better one), and to broadening social capital and/or the participation in education and/or the community. On examining the place and meaning of attending a program, it is observed that the trajectories vary not only according to whether young people have or have not graduated from secondary school and to the educational capital in the home, but also according to secondary school experiences, gender, motivations for attending, etc. A multidimensional approach is clearly needed to understand the impacts of the programs.

In conclusion, when added to a secondary school certificate, vocational training programs have the potential to provide knowledge and specific skills, as well as act as 'bridges' to quality jobs. In sum, they provide 'resources' for young people. The range and representativeness of the data in this study are limited and should lead to a wider population sampling. However, the analysis thus far provides a clear sign that further research in this area could make important contributions to secondary, post-secondary and vocational training policies.

Bibliography

Jacinto, C. and Chittaroni, H. (2009) *Precariedades, rotación y acumulación en las trayectorias laborales*, 9° Congreso Nacional de Estudio del Trabajo, Asociación Argentina de Especialistas en Estudios del Trabajo, Buenos Aires, Facultad de Ciencias Económicas.

Jacinto, C. and Dursi, C. (2010) La socialización laboral en cuestión: las pasantías ante las incertidumbres de las transiciones laborales de los jóvenes, in Jacinto, C. (comp.) *La construcción social de las trayectorias laborales de jóvenes. Políticas, instituciones, dispositivos y subjetividades*, Buenos Aires, Teseo.

Jacinto, C. and Millenaar, V. (2010) "La incidencia de los dispositivos en la trayectoria laboral de los jóvenes. Entre la reproducción social y la creación de oportunidades" in C. Jacinto (comp.) *La construcción social de las trayectorias laborales de jóvenes. Políticas, instituciones, dispositivos y subjetividades*, Buenos Aires, Teseo.

Jacinto, C. (1998) ¿Qué es calidad en la formación para el trabajo de jóvenes de sectores de pobreza? Un análisis desde las estrategias de intervención, in Jacinto, C. and M. A. Gallart (coords.) *Por una segunda oportunidad. La formación para el trabajo de jóvenes vulnerables*, Montevideo, CINTERFOR-RET. pp. 311-341.

Longo, M.E. and Bidart, C. (2007) Bifurcations biographiques et évolutions des rapports au travail, in Giret, J-F. et al. *Rupture et irréversibilités dans les trajectoires*, Marseille Relief n°22.

Pérez, P. (2008) *La inserción ocupacional de los jóvenes en un contexto de desempleo masivo*, Buenos Aires, Miño y Dávila.

Salvia, A. (comp.) (2008) *Jóvenes promesas. Trabajo, educación y exclusión social de jóvenes pobres en la Argentina*, Buenos Aires, Universidad de Buenos Aires-Miño Dávila.

SITEAL. (2007) *Informe sobre tendencias sociales y educativas en América Latina*, Buenos Aires, IIPE-OEI.

Verdier, E. and Buechteman, C. (1998) Regímenes de educación y de formación profesional: evidencia macroinstitucional, in J. Gautie and J. Neffa (comps.) *Desempleo y políticas de empleo en Europa y Estados Unidos, Trabajo y Sociedad*, CEIL PIETTE, CONICET, Buenos Aires, Lumen-Humanitas.

7. Young Migrant Workers in China: Plausible Integration Strategies

By Ngan-Pun Ngai

Since the 1980s, China's economic reform has transformed the rural labor force into urban workers in the cities, particularly in the Special Economic Zones and coastal areas. This has led to the large influx of young migrant workers or "floating population" to the cities where large numbers of workers are needed (Chan, 1993; Xu Qingwen, Guan Xinping and Yao Fangfang, 2011). According to the 1% National Population Sample Survey in 2005, the floating population was of 147.35 million persons at the end of 2005 (National Bureau of Statistics of China, 2006). However, in 2010, the total population of migrant workers had reached 242.23 million (National Bureau of Statistics of China, 2010). They were mainly engaged in manufacturing, construction and service jobs.

China has become a world center for producing cheap manufactured goods. On the one hand, the migrant workers have become an important force for the country's economic and social development, and make significant contributions to the modernization of China. On the other hand, due to migrant workers' subservient and powerless position, they are situated at the bottom of society with low status and limited resources for life choices and mobility. They suffer from numerous forms of exploitation, discrimination, and unfair treatment which have created growing social discontent among them and have gradually turned them into a force that threatens social stability. Thus there is a need to explore some effective integration strategies or social inclusion policies which can deal with the vulnerability of migrant workers and promote social harmony.

This paper attempts to examine several integration strategies which are useful for tackling various issues related to migrant workers. They include: improving rules, regulations, policies and legal procedures, eliminating the rural-urban dichotomy in the social structure, improving the migrant workers' consciousness about their personal qualities and rights, recognizing civil society's supporting role and services, and reforming the social security system.

Young migrant workers: 'Second class citizens'

In China, the concept of 'the young migrant worker' is almost the same as that of 'the migrant worker' because the vast majority of them are young people aged below 35. The terms 'floating population', 'foreign population', and 'peasant-worker' are also used to identify the same group of people who share a number of specific characteristics: 1) young and with low education; 2) no official urban residence under the household registry system; 3) official residence status as peasant and land owner in their home village, with a mixed identity of being farmer and worker; 4) high degree of mobility and unstable labour situation, but mainly engaged in manual labor and manufacturing work; 5) lack of adequate protection of citizen rights and labor rights; and 6) situated at the bottom of the social class structure in cities. (Li Si-ming and Siu Yat-ming, 1994; Li Peilin and Li Wei, 2007; Chen Yingfang, 2005; Geng Li and Kao Zhongjian, 2009; Wang Xiaozhang, 2009). Therefore, 'young migrant workers' refers to a special group of young peasant workers who were born after the mid-1970s and moved from the countryside to the urban area, while shifting from work in the agricultural sector to the industrial and service sectors; they are also 'second class citizens' in the city facing various discrimination and exploitations. This definition reveals that young migrant workers are pseudo-urban dwellers who do not have full residential status in the city and are continuously suffering from conditions of vulnerability and from serious political, social and economic discrimination. Solinger (1999) defines them as un-rooted non-citizens. The following sections review the crux of the problems.

Exploitation and violation of rights

In 2006, China published an official document titled State Council's Several Views on the Settlement of the Issue of Migrant Workers, in which it acknowledged a series of problems for migrant workers: low wages, serious delay of salary payment, long working hours, poor safety conditions, lack of social security, severe occupational diseases and industrial accidents, lack of job placement and training, unsatisfactory schooling for children, poor living and housing conditions, etc. It explicitly acknowledged the fact that the development of contemporary China is moving ahead at the expense of migrant workers whose labor rights have become an issue of public concern. It is reported that nearly 60% of migrant workers do not sign labor contracts with employers or working units (National Bureau of Statistics of China, 2011). Thus, difficulties in enforcing the practice of labor laws are clear. This situation may induce violations and the infringement of the rights of migrant workers. For example, claiming compensation for work injuries of migrant workers is very difficult because of various reasons: 1) many injured migrant workers do not sign labor contracts and use false identities; 2) they use pseudonyms when admitted to hospital; 3) they work in unregistered illegal factories; 4) they can face lengthy struggles with their employers due to complicated judicial procedures; 5) their access to external help is limited; and 6) litigation costs are high (Zhou Lingang and Zhu Changhua 2009). As a result, migrant workers might end up going home without any gains or be forced to accept 'under the table' negotiations for compensation (Zheng Guanghuai, 2005).

In recent years, due to the rising awareness of human rights and civic consciousness, an increasing number of migrant workers use legal means to seek justice when their rights are infringed by employers or supervisors. According to official statistics, from 1996 to 2008, the total number of labor dispute cases had increased from 48,121 to 693,465 cases (National Bureau of Statistics of China, 2009). In reality, these official statistics are only the 'tip of the iceberg' of all migrant workers suffering from violation of rights because many more choose to keep silent or accept private settlements from employers. Furthermore, government departments appear ineffective in protecting workers' rights. For example, many labor dispute cases demonstrate that migrant workers are unable to recuperate their wages or compensation for injuries for many years (Zhang Yunhao, 2005; Zheng Guanghuai, 2005).

The unfair household registry system and 'second class citizens'

China distinguishes its citizens' official residence (hukou) using the notions of agricultural and non-agricultural household. The hukou in the existing household registry system has a very important function in the allocation of social resources. The country's 9-year free compulsory education, public health care, social security, and other living resources are allocated in accordance with the hukou of the persons involved (Cai He and Wang Jin, 2007). Local governments use the hukou to control its political activities, financial expenses and distribution of living resources. As a result, the hukou scheme upholds two different citizenship rights, even though people are of the same nationality. It also creates adverse effects on the strange political and social status of migrant workers who appear to be 'both workers and peasants', 'both urban and rural', and 'non-workers and non-rural' (Zhang Sheng Li and Sung Liang, 2008).

Under this dichotomous urban-rural dual system, though the migrant workers contribute to the development of the city by taking up the 'dirty, heavy, tired, bitter and dangerous work', they do not gain the city's recognition and are unable to obtain an official resident status for the place where they live and work for years. They are identified as the city's 'second-class citizens' who are discriminated against by urban residents and cannot enjoy the same status, rights and entitlements in the areas of education, welfare benefits, public participation, political life and other living opportunities (Liu Jing ming, 2001; Zhang Sheng Li and Sung Liang, 2008; Solinger, 1999). Research has shown that the migrant workers' experiences of discrimination have a direct significant negative effect on their quality of life (Zhang Jintao, Li Xiaoming, Fang Xiaoyi and Xiong Qing, 2009). Recently, due to social and economic changes, elevated education and civic consciousness, the awareness of citizenship rights have increasingly strengthened among migrant workers, especially among the second generation of migrant workers (Zhang Sheng Li and Sung Liang, 2008). The unfairness of the dual social class system and the legitimacy of the hukou scheme under the household registry system are being questioned, and are often criticized as policies against equality and of discrimination based on citizenship identity.

The trans-generational discriminatory 'Non-local peasants' identity tag

Given the continuous emphasis on the dichotomous urban-rural dual system, the migrant workers have developed a sense of being 'non-urban residents' and they often identify themselves as 'non-local peasants' so as to differentiate themselves from the local 'urban residents'. This reveals that migrant workers generally accept their status as the city's 'outsiders' who do not develop a sense of belonging to the city and lack a feeling of home and social identity (Wang Chunguang, 2001). This 'non-local peasant' identity tag has a direct negative impact on the migrant workers' self image and their ability to assert their rights to be legitimate city dwellers. More importantly, these detrimental personal and social identities have not only created a dual class society, but have gradually forged the emergence of a damaging hereditary effect on the personal identity system of migrant workers' children, who are generally labeled with the discriminatory 'peasant' identity, and become known as the 'children of migrant workers'. As a result, the extension of the peasant status identity tag to the younger generation is problematic in that it allows for the transgenerational transmission of discrimination in Chinese society (Chen Yingfang, 2005).

The lack of political participation channels

China's election law provides that in local grass-roots elections, the representatives of the People's Congresses at local levels are elected by the local people with official residence status (hukou). In accordance with this provision, migrant workers cannot participate in the city elections. The only way to exercise their right to political participation is to return to their place of origin. However, for the majority of migrant workers, this is practically impossible due to high transportation costs, lack of leave from work, unemployment risks, family finances, and expenses related to such travel (Zhang Sheng Li and Sung Liang, 2008; Pun Ngai, 2010). Thus, their political rights are neglected under the current law. They do not have the opportunity to participate in the political life of the city to which their daily activities and immediate interests are most closely related. However, the younger generation of migrant workers has generally grown up in a social context significantly different from that of the previous generation and holds a higher level of education than their parents. They are more aware of their rights and welfare benefits entitlements, and demand greater political and social participation. If this expectation cannot be met, tension, social conflicts, and social instability will accumulate (Pun Ngai, 2010).

Plausible integration strategies

As the growing number of disputes concerning migrant workers puts pressure on the stability of society and affects the international image of the country, the significant problems of migrant workers have attracted official attention in recent years. A series of integration strategies or social inclusion policies have been proposed in the academic field which have aroused public concern and facilitated advocacy for policy changes. Conceptually, we refer to integration policy as strategies, means or measures by which migrant workers can be integrated into the urban system and the country as a whole, and which can achieve a higher level of social harmony. The following discussion provides a brief account of the key strategies or policies which might have a significant impact on the social inclusion of migrant workers.

Protecting migrant workers' labor rights through improving rules, regulations, policies and procedures

In order to address the increasingly prominent issue of migrant workers and to improve the laws that protect their rights, the state government has promulgated a series of policies, laws and regulations (Geng Li and Kao Zhongjian, 2009). Since the 1990s, the central and local People's Congresses, the State Council, and the judiciary at various levels have introduced a variety of laws, regulations and policies to protect the interests of migrant workers. In the early 1990s, the State Council issued the Prohibition of Child Labor Law (1991) and The People's Republic of China Labor Law (1994). In 1996, the Ministry of Labor issued the Interim Measures for Enterprise Employees Injury Insurance, and in 2003, the central government announced a series of important policies aimed at protecting the legitimate rights and interests of migrant workers through the abolition of administrative approvals for the employment of migrant workers, and of restrictions on the types of work they can perform. At the same time, the state also raised the importance of the occupational safety of workers and issued the Safety Production Law, the Coal Mine Safety Supervision Ordinance and The People's Republic of China Occupational Disease Prevention Law (Tan Shen, 2003). Then, in 2007-2008, the state government promulgated The People's Republic of China Labor Contract Law and The People's Republic of China Mediation and Arbitration of

Labor Disputes Law. Besides this, over the past 20 years, these and other laws were adopted to prevent the violation of the rights of migrant workers.

However, these laws, regulations and policies have in practice failed to play their role of defending the rights and interests of migrant workers. This is because migrant workers who want to begin litigation to defend their rights and interests in labor disputes or work injuries have to face the huge economic and psychological costs entailed by this process. First, the employer, the labor department, and the judicial system usually take quite a long time to investigate and collect evidence of the work-related injuries or disputes; this always results in the delay of the judicial procedures and brings with it tremendous psychological and economic pressure for the workers. Second, it is rather difficult for migrant workers to provide evidence of the injuries or violation of labor law because some employers have not registered their factories officially or signed labor contracts to recognize labor relations, and the migrant workers themselves may have used forged identity cards. In effect, this means that injured workers cannot quickly apply for work relief assistance and begin judicial procedures. Third, since the amount of compensation is often not worth the trouble of obtaining it, many migrant workers choose to give up their legal right of action.

Thus, simply resorting to the rule of law, policy and legal procedures to protect the rights and interests of migrant workers is definitely inadequate. More importantly, specific actions are needed to plug loopholes, such as identifying the violations that occur in these processes, and then amending the related laws, policies and procedures to establish a clear mandate practice of labor law. Substantial support has to be provided in order to remedy the above deterrents and to prevent migrant workers from giving up their claims because of the risks of financial hardship, unemployment, and psychological stress. The government may also consider expanding the legal aid system to provide professional counseling and special funds to support migrant workers' reasonable litigation.

Safeguarding the political rights of migrant workers through the elimination of the dichotomous urban-rural social structure

At present the social structure of urban-rural residence registration within China explicitly violates the political rights of its citizens, resulting in contradictions, divisions, and tensions between urban and rural people. The Chinese election law stipulates that citizens over 18 years of age, regardless of nationality, race, sex, occupation, family background, religious belief, education, property status or length of residence, have the right to vote and to stand for election (Zhang Sheng Li and Sung Liang, 2008). However, in practice, migrant workers are marginal voters in politics. They face difficulties in participating in political activities in their home towns or villages because of their work in faraway cities where they are not allowed to exercise political rights. This leads to discontent among migrant workers. Thus there are voices demanding the abolition of the social structure that divides urban and rural and discriminates against the 'second-class citizens' system from the perspective that the citizenship rights of migrant workers in the cities need to be recognized, and that changes need to be brought to the existing household registration system. The government should therefore review the existing voter registration system and the eligibility of voters by eliminating the dichotomous urban-rural social structure and by changing the official original residence to current place of residence, so that migrant workers can participate in political activities as any other urban dweller does.

So far, some provinces have eliminated the rural residence registration system and changed to a simple residence registration system (Xie Guihua, 2007). Of course, this structural change may result in significant impacts on cities regarding various aspects of services, and these must be handled cautiously. A series of interim measures and a list of eligibility criteria such as family relationships, permanent residence, stable employment, and number of years of residence, need to be developed and implemented in order to achieve a smooth transition.

Moreover, migrant workers have accumulated grave grievances in various areas such as employment, social security, children's education, housing, health care, and others. Thus there is a need to consider setting up some formal mechanisms for migrant workers to communicate, participate and express their voice within the political structure so that their discontent can be channeled to various government departments in a timely manner in order to resolve social conflicts in their early stages. Cai

Wo, Li Chaohai and Feng Jianhua (2009) have suggested that the benefit appeals mechanism, the benefit appeals capacity and the institutionalization of labour relations are the three preconditions for guiding the settlement of migrant workers' conflicts and complaints within the current system. A public consultative system might provide migrant workers with a proper channel to exercise their right to political participation at lower levels, and will provide support in their fight for their legitimate rights and interests, while providing a channel for the expression of some social discontent.

Improving the personal quality and rights consciousness of migrant workers

The majority of migrant workers are growing up in the relatively conservative and undeveloped rural areas of China. They have attained a low level of education and have little knowledge and skills to deal with technical issues. According to the China Development Report 2011, the distribution of the educational level of migrant workers are: illiteracy (1.3%), primary school (12.3%), junior secondary school (61.2%), senior secondary school (15%) and college and above (10.2%) (National Bureau of Statistics of China, 2011). Their social networks are weak and their social activities are mostly confined to the identity of the ethnic groups in their community (Li Qiang, 1999). In view of these personal and social factors of disadvantage, the change in the status quo of migrant workers has to focus on the improvement of their personal qualities, awareness of citizenship rights, and social identity. The important issues for the improvement of migrant workers' personal qualities are to enhance their level of education, social capital, and competitiveness in the labor market by organizing non-formal education, such as job related skills and vocational training programs, and encouraging self-enhancement through continuing education (Li Peilin and Li Wei, 2007; Geng Li and Kao Zhongjian, 2009; Zhang Yu and Yang Caiyun, 2010). The enhancement of their 'rights consciousness' requires providing them with civic education and information on human rights and labor rights, which may change their traditional perspective toward citizen rights and authorities, as well as help them acquire some legal knowledge and foster the spirit of the rule of law.

Recognizing civil society's supporting role and services to migrant workers

Due to their low education and rural backgrounds, migrant workers' personal and social capital is relatively weak. They need the help and support of civil society – NGOS (e.g., social organizations, non-enterprise units run by NGOs, and foundations) to enhance their abilities, so as to overcome personal and institutional barriers in understanding and safeguarding their rights and interests. Civil society organizations possess the social or professional status, knowledge, resources, and skills to offer training, support and assistance. Thus the government should support them in conducting educational and training programs and to further encourage them to join together to provide services for migrant workers who lack expertise, power and resources. This can empower migrant workers to be aware of their own situation, their surrounding environment and the laws related to labor rights, and acquire the specific knowledge, skills and bargaining power to deal with employers, officials, government departments and other professional institutions within the system (Zhang Yunhao, 2005). In effect, the government has promulgated a Legal Aid Ordinance, which stipulates that the state supports and encourages social organizations and other institutions to use their resources to provide legal aid to those citizens with economic difficulties. This confirms that various NGOs can offer migrant workers legal aid and financial assistance to fight for their legitimate rights. Unfortunately, in China, many NGOs are non-registered organizations, and those that are registered are generally industrial or commercial organizations. NGOs lack the recognition and support from both official and semi-official social organizations to affiliate in order to meet the required conditions for registering as social organizations. As a result, they can only engage in industrial and commercial activities which are incompatible with the nature of social services. This limits their ability to support migrant workers, has actually weakened their contributions and hindered the development of civil society (Xu Ying and Ngan Pun Ngai, 2011). To remedy this unsatisfactory situation, the government has to change its skeptical attitude towards the social and political functions of NGOs by amending the existing Registration of Social Organizations Ordinances, with the aim to facilitate the official registration of various NGOs as social organizations, which would enhance their ability to help migrant workers to fight for their rights and benefits.

Reforming the social security system

The migrant workers' residency in the cities is regarded as temporary and their citizenship status is not recognized. Therefore, their social needs (e.g., housing, education, health) are not taken into account in policy planning (Li Si-ming and Siu Yat-ming, 1994). Moreover, their jobs lack security because they are employed in private enterprises under free market employment conditions. Their work status is short-term and their employment is always considered temporary. Moreover, due to differences in official residence status, migrant workers and urban workers are often treated differently in terms of working benefits. Migrant workers are not entitled to enjoy the city's social security benefits, including old-age insurance, unemployment insurance and medical insurance. The grave unequal treatment of migrant workers and urban residents has created a bad feeling of discrimination that has been accompanied by growing social disharmony (Li Qiang and Tang Zhuang, 2002, Wang Xiaozhang, 2009). Hence migrant workers never see themselves as full members of the city where they work and live. Many of them view the city as a temporary and transitional step and a place solely to earn a living. This phenomenon affects their sense of belonging to, or social identification with the city.

In line with this, there is increasing pressure on the central government to protect the social security benefits of migrant workers, and to change their unfavorable conditions by means of national policies concerning the social security system. Currently, the central government urges local governments and other relevant departments to ensure the implementation of the social security system for migrant workers and to protect their legitimate benefits. However, the disparities in social security between migrant workers and urban residents are closely tied to the official residence status, and the improvement of the migrant workers' social security benefits will have to rely on the revision of the current household registration system (Xie Guihua, 2007), as outlined above.

Conclusion

The miracle of contemporary China's economic success, founded on the contribution of migrant workers flooding into cities, is undeniable. However, the analysis and discussion in this chapter reveal that the issue of migrant workers is of critical importance. They are treated unfairly in many aspects such as citizenship rights, social policies and access to welfare benefits. Given the continuous opening up of the country, the blooming of the market economy, the rapidly growing private and foreign enterprises, the trend of globalization and technological development, and the rising consciousness among migrant workers about their rights, the demand for a greater protection of citizen rights, benefits, and interests are anticipated. Both the central and local governments need to understand these new social developments and formulate relevant policies and services to cater to the novel needs and problems of migrant workers. Tackling the current problems of migrant workers has to rely on substantial measures that are addressed by social policies and legal support, with the aim to promote a positive social recognition of the integration of migrant workers into society. From the above analysis, it is clear that many significant problems must be given particular attention as they have directly contributed to social discrimination, social discontent, and the violation of human rights: the exploitation of workers, the ineffective protection of labour rights and their subsequent violation, the unfair household registry system and the identification of migrants as 'second class citizens', the trans-generational and discriminatory 'non-local peasants' identity tag, and the lack of channels for political participation.

Effective measures that can alleviate migrant workers' grievances and disparities, as well as bring about social integration and national unity, should be considered for policy and practice intervention. The plausible integration strategies include the protection of migrant workers' labor rights through improved rules, regulations, policies and procedures; the safeguarding of migrants' political rights through the elimination of the dichotomous urban-rural social structure; the recognition of civil society's ability to provide support services to migrants; the improvement of their personal qualities and rights consciousness; and the elimination of disparities between migrant workers and urban residents in the social security system. These social integration strategies may improve the current vulnerability of migrant workers, satisfy their personal needs, strengthen their sense of belonging to the place where they live and work, promote mutual acceptance and respect between migrant workers and urban residents, and provide migrants with the chance to participate actively in domestic political, social and community affairs. Finally, increased social harmony and political stability may result from the resolution of the severe conflicts between migrant workers and urban residents.

Bibliography

Cai He and Wang Jin (2007) A study of the migrant workers' permanent migration, *Sociological Studies*, 6, pp. 86-11013. (in Chinese)

Cai He, Li Chaohai and Feng Jianhua (2009) Migrant workers' conflict behaviors against benefit damages: A survey of enterprises in Pearl River Delta, *Sociological Studies*, 1, pp. 139-161. (in Chinese)

Chan, C. K. R. (1991) Challenges to urban areas: The floating population, in Kuan Hsin-chi and Maurice Brosseau (eds), *China Review 1991*, Hong Kong: The Chinese University Press, pp. 12.1-12.21.

Chen Yingfang (2005) Migrant workers: Institutional arrangements and identity. *Sociological Studies*, 3, pp. 119-132. (in Chinese)

Geng Li and Kao Zhongjian (2009) The protection of youth rights and interests under empowerment theory, *Social Sciences Journal of Colleges of Shanxi, 21(3)*, pp. 56-58. (in Chinese)

Li Peilin and Li Wei (2007) Migrant workers' economic status and social attitude in the transition of China, *Sociological Studies*, 3, pp. 1-17. (in Chinese)

Li Qiang (1999. Occupational mobility of the urban migrant workers in Mainland China, *Sociological Studies*, 3, pp. 93-101. (in Chinese)

Li Qiang and Tang Zhuang (2002) Informal employment of urban migrant workers in the city, *Sociological Studies*, 6, pp. 13-25. (in Chinese)

Li Si-ming and Siu Yat-ming (1994) Population mobility, in Yeung, Y. M. and Chu, K. Y. (eds), *Guangdong: Survey of A Province Undergoing Rapid Change*, Hong Kong, The Chinese University Press, pp. 373-400.

Liu Jingming (2001) Flowing to non-agricultural occupations: A study of migrant workers' life history, *Sociological Studies*, 6, pp. 1-18. (in Chinese)

National Bureau of Statistics of China (2011) China Development Report 2011, *China Statistics Press*, pp. 99-105.

National Bureau of Statistics of China (2010) China Social Statistical Yearbook 2010, *China Statistics Press*, pp. 311.

National Bureau of Statistics of China (2009) China Labor Statistical Yearbook, 2009, *China Statistics Press*, pp. 469-470.

National Bureau of Statistics of China (2006) Communique on major data of 1% national population sample survey in 2005, available from http://www.stats.gov.cn/eNgliSH/newsandcomingevents/t20060322_402312182.htm

Pun Ngai (2010) Unfinished proletarianization: Self, anger, and class action among the second generation of peasant-workers in present-day China, *Modern China, 36(5)*, pp. 493-519.

Solinger, J. D. (1999) *Contesting citizenship in urban China: Peasant migrants, the state, and the logic of the market*, Berkeley: University of California Press.

Tan Shen (2003) Rural workforce migration: A summary of some studies. *Social Sciences in China, 24(4)*, pp. 84-101. (in Chinese)

Wang Chunguang (2001) The relationship between social identity and rural-urban integration among the new generation of rural floating population, *Sociological Studies, 3*, pp. 63-76. (in Chinese)

Wang Xiaozhang (2009) From survival to recognition: migrant worker's problems from the perspective of citizenship rights, *Sociological Studies, 1*, pp. 121-138. (in Chinese)

Xie Guihua (2007) Migrant workers and urban labor market, *Sociological Studies, 5*, pp. 84-110. (in Chinese)

Xu Qingwen, Guan Xinping and Yao Fangfang (2011) Welfare program participation among rural-to-urban migrant workers in China, *International Journal of Social Welfare, 20(1)*, pp. 10-21.

Xu Ying and Ngan-pun Ngai (2011) Moral resources and political capital: Theorizing the relationship between voluntary service organizations and the development of civil society in China, *Nonprofit and Voluntary Sector Quarterly, 40(2)*, pp. 247-269.

Zhang Jintao, Li Xiaoming, Fang Xiaoyi and Xiong Qing (2009) Discrimination experience and quality of life among rural-urban migrants in China: The mediation effect of expectation – reality discrepancy, *Quality of Life Research, 18(3)*, pp. 291-300.

Zhang Sheng Li and Sung Liang (2008) The current situation of political participation of migrant workers and its challenge to social stability, *China Youth Studies, 7*, pp. 14-18. (in Chinese)

Zhang Yu and Yang Caiyun (2010) An analysis of the effects of social capital on employment quality of migrant workers: Based on Shanghai survey data, *Journal of East China University of Science and Technology, 5*, pp. 9-20. (in Chinese)

Zhang Yunhao (2005) Empowerment: Case analysis of migrant worker's claiming wages and its implications, *Youth Research, 9*, pp. 11-16. (in Chinese)

Zheng Guanghuai (2005) Disabled migrant workers: The group cannot be empowered. *Sociological Studies, 3*, pp. 99-118. (in Chinese)

Zhou Lingang and Zhu Changhua (2009) An analysis of the 'private settlement' mechanism of injured migrant workers: The theory of empowerment perspective. *Gansu Sociological Studies, 1*, pp. 20-23. (in Chinese)

III. Re-examining young people's lives today: emerging perspectives for policy

1. Changing time experience, changing biographies and new youth values

By Carmen Leccardi

If over the course of the 20th century the image of the future as a field open to possibility became more and more evanescent, it is above all the new century – whose beginning coincided symbolically with the terrorist attack in New York on 11th September, 2001 – that has rendered increasingly evident the interconnection between the two processes of social acceleration on the one hand, and the crisis of the future (and of the modern temporal experience) on the other. It is not just that there is in fact a spread in the sensation of living in an epoch of uncontrollable risks (Beck, 2007) and of correspondingly great uncertainties, such as conceptualizing the future as undesirable in itself, but the growth in the speed of the rhythms of life together with the acceleration in the processes of economic, social and technological transformation also profoundly influences our very experience of time (Rosa, 2003). We refer to the contraction in temporal horizons and to the dominion of the 'short term' which affect the level of actions; to the out-and-out hegemony of the deadline, elaborated as a principle of action; to the discrediting of perspectives founded on the idea of 'once and for all' (i.e. irreversibility); and to the spread of a culture of the provisory. Together, these factors impact negatively not only on the ways in which we work, interact, and construct our actions in the present but also on our ways of looking at the future.

The consequence of living in a 'high speed society' (Rosa and Scheurman, 2009) is that the future is 'burned up': it folds back into the present, it is absorbed within it and is consumed before it can really be conceived. The present in its turn becomes "all there is" (Harvey, 1990, p. 240). Within the temporal frameworks redefined by the compression of time-space it appears as the only dimension available for the definition of choices, a fully-fledged existential horizon which includes and substitutes the future (and the past). The acceleration of social life and its various times renders these two dimensions ever more evanescent as reference points for action. To put it more precisely: although the evocation of the future continues to constitute a routine both for social systems and for subjects, it is in fact the present that is now associated with the principle of potential governability and controllability that modernity – through its normative ideal of progress – associated with the future.

Contemporary time therefore seems to erase not only temporal continuity but also the notion of the life-plan as developed in the modern era. In order to explain this process and its impact on the biographical constructs of young people today we must dwell further on the relationship between biographical time and planning (see Anderson *et al.*, 2005, Brannen and Nielsen, 2002, 2007; Machado Pais, 2003; Woodman, 2011). We must then consider the essential features of the transition to adulthood today; and finally we must resume the theme of the changing experience of time, connecting it with young people's new values. The new semantics of the future will help us in understanding them.

Biographical time and the life-plan

The analytical point of departure here is *biographical time*, understood as the unitary temporal dimension that emerges from the processes by which people consider the past, live the present, and look to the future. Biographical time and identity are closely bound up with each other – nor could it be otherwise. Personal identity, just like time-of-life, is the outcome of the dialectical relationship between permanence and change, between continuity and discontinuity, among past, present and future. Because it takes shape on the variegated terrain delimited on the one hand by the person's need for autonomy, and on the other by his/her need for recognition, passing through a delicate mixture of identification and dis-identification, the raw material of personal identity is by definition time, both existential and social (Luckmann, 1993).

If we adopt this perspective, biographical time must necessarily be put in relation with the social-temporal norms that determine and define the various life-stages from infancy to old age, set them in relation to each other, condition the transitions among them, and above all construct their meanings. The duration of these phases, the order in which they occur, their degree of constrictiveness, and so on, may vary according to the historical moment. Suffice it to consider, for example, how representations of the ages of life have changed since the Second World War. Though more diversified and certainly less cogent, the temporal norms which regulate life-courses still condition biographical construction – as they do every other aspect of social life (Zerubavel, 1981). They play an ambivalent role: on the one hand, they prevent individuals from exercising complete control over their personal time because they force them to comply with temporal orders external to that time; on the other, and in parallel, they provide important support to development of the life-plan by allowing, in general, subjective options to be transformed into socially legitimated life trajectories.

It should be stressed in this regard that the possibility itself of conceiving a dialectical relationship between time-of-life and social time is considered a historical product of modernity. In fact, it was modernity that furnished a representation of time consonant with a conception of the time-of-life as (auto)biography (Leitner, 1982): an abstract and empty dimension within a temporal flow depicted as linear, directed, and irreversible.

But a paradox arises. The 'subjectification' of time embodied by the concept of biography is one of the outcomes of modernity's 'exteriorization' and objectification of time whereby the latter is considered a 'thing' separate from its perceiver, a dimension which flows autonomously, overwhelms human beings, and is articulated by the unstoppable movement of the instruments used to measure it (Adam, 1995). This is a power feared more emotionally than space (Jaques, 1982) – with which, however, it is inextricably bound up – mainly because it, by definition, postulates death.

As said, a particularly sensitive analytical tool with which to analyse biographical time and its change consists of the *life-plan*, which results from an overlap between planning and biography. To adopt the perspective of social phenomenology, the life-plan can be considered emblematic of both biographical time – "an individual's biography is apprehended as [...] a plan" (Berger, Berger and Kellner, 1973, p. 71) – and of personal identity.[1] In this view, where long-term planning exists, there arises both a biography in the proper sense and a full-fledged sense of personal identity. Accordingly, biography and identity have an irrepressible need for the medium-to-long term future (and before that, a linkage among past, present and future).

---

1   The interest of Berger, Berger and Kellner (1973) in the life-plan stems directly from the attention traditionally paid by phenomenological sociology to planned action. Schutz (1971), who resumed Husserl's interest in the anticipatory character of action, analysed it in relation to action considered as 'planned behaviour', and studied its temporal structure.

This positive relationship among life-plan, biographical time, and identity, however, encounters difficulties when the future is foreshortened – as happens in the acceleration society – and mastery over time becomes more problematic, also because of the unpredictability of courses of action in the age of generalized risks. Put otherwise, when the accidental, the possible, the fortuitous can no longer be controlled by means of planning (as a form of insurance against the future) because of the exponential growth of those phenomena, then planning capacity in the traditional sense of the life-project is compromised. Yet even if the life-project is understood simply in terms of an intention, design, scheme or programme (Boutinet, 2003, p. 23), and even if one separates the noun 'project' from its qualifier 'life' and considers medium/short-term planning, the contemporary era requires that this key dimension of self-construction be re-thought.

The ungovernability of the future which largely accounts for present-day uncertainty, therefore, not only renders long-term plans potentially obsolete and predictions impracticable; it also alters the temporal structure of identities, creating fertile ground for redefinition of their postulates, and primarily among these the connection between identity and life-plan.

On discussing these matters, Hartmut Rosa has emphasised the close connection between the acceleration society and "biographical detemporalization". He writes:

> life is no longer planned along a line that stretches from the past into the future; instead, decisions are taken 'from time to time' according to situational and contextual needs and desires [...]. Thus, a conception of the good life based on long-term commitments, duration, and stability is thwarted by the fast pace of social change. (Rosa, 2003, p. 19)

The severing of the connections among the different dimensions of biographical time – among memory of the past, choices in the present, and expectations regarding the future – reverberates at the individual and social levels. At the individual level, it creates space for people to search out new forms of anchorage to the present for their expression of the self; at the social level, it uncouples life trajectories from the institutions as guarantors of individual and collective continuity. As a result, inner autonomy and social independence – the achievement of increasing degrees of independence made possible by a positive relationship with credible and non-fragmented social institutions – tend to split apart. The conclusion of the juvenile life-stage increasingly depends on wholly subjective factors which redefine the priorities and horizons of life rather than on completion of the canonical 'life-stages' marked out by institutional time-frames such as education, work, and couple formation.

The institutional system as such – that is, independently of the concrete relationships which individuals establish with it – is increasingly averse to the future. As a consequence, young people tend not to receive support from the institutions in regard to their entry into adulthood. In other words, key social institutions like the school, work, or the family no longer guarantee the success of that transition. Whatever the level of individual commitment may be, the outcome is uncertain. Young people must individually negotiate the manner and timing of their entry into adulthood.

The inability of the social institutions to ensure that entry into adulthood follows a predictable pattern, notwithstanding a positive relationship of young people with their times, is today entirely evident. Its impacts on biographical time – the existential discontinuities that it produces to radically redefine the modes and forms of biographical narrative – appear to be profound. *Anticipation*, a crucial part of the construction of action, is prevented. Hence, whilst in the "tradition of modernity",

> (s)tretches of time used to acquire their meaning from the anticipation of further sections of the time-continuum still to follow, they are now expected to derive their sense, so to speak, inside – to justify themselves without reference, or with only perfunctory reference, to the future. Time-spans are plotted beside each other, rather than in a logical progression; there is no preordained logic in their successions; they may easily, without violating any hard and fast rule, change places – sectors of time-continuum are in principle interchangeable. Each moment must present its own legitimation and offer the fullest satisfaction possible (Bauman, 1999, p. 78)

The fragmentation of the experience of time distinctive of our era, and which young people experience through the progressive separation between times-of-life and institutional times (less at the level of everyday routine than at that of overall meaning), therefore means that people 'navigate by sight' rather than following pre-established routes.

It is essential, however, not to restrict the discussion to the loss, or the reduction, of possibilities for action associated with contemporary processes of time redefinition. In fact, these processes also have a positive, visible side which should be carefully analysed. Values undergo modification while people devise their strategies for coping with these transformations and, as far as possible, controlling them. The result of these important processes whereby the relationship with social time is restructured do not necessarily consist only in absolutization of the immediate present. Perhaps with the exception of a minority of young people, identities are not exclusively declined in the present. Young people seem more to be frequently engaged in a search for new relations between personal creation – which is anyway associated with the future – and the specific conditions of uncertainty that today define them.

Before dwelling on this positive redefinition of the relationship with the future, however, it is advisable to consider more closely the form assumed by these conditions of uncertainty for young people 'in transit' to adulthood.

The uncertain transition to adulthood

The uncertainties of the transition to adulthood today seem to be due to a set of conditions. Firstly, the temporal duration of the transition has extended (young people become adults increasingly later in their lives), and it has fragmented. The various stages in this transition – conclusion of full-time education, exit from the parental home, stable entry into the world of work, and construction of an autonomous household – tend to 'de-synchronize' themselves: that is, they abandon the traditional temporal order. That order foresaw a practically perfect overlap among three crucial stages in the transition: exit from the parental home, entry in the world of work, and couple formation (Galland, 2001). Secondly, not only do young people undertake these transitions at an older age, but they frequently interrupt or delay them. In certain respects, as Cavalli and Galland (1993) put it, young people do not seem in a "hurry to grow."[2]

The tendency for a prolonged transition to adulthood is therefore accompanied by its destandardization (Walther and Stauber, 2002) and its fragmentation into discontinuous phases with no discernible connections between one and the next, as well as being reversible.[3] Salience is thus acquired by biographical patterns increasingly distant from linear life-trajectories (Côté, 2000; Wyn and White, 1997; White and Wyn, 2008). Within these biographical patterns, according to some authors (Beck and Beck-Gernsheim, 2002; du Bois-Reymond, 1998; Fuchs, 1983), arise bio-

---

2   'Senza fretta di crescere' ('In no hurry to grow up') is the title of the Italian version of the book Cavalli and Galland published in French in 1993.

3   This trend is apparent in all the European societies (Sgritta, 1999; Wallace and Kovatcheva, 1998), albeit with some specific characteristics in the countries of Northern, Central and Southern Europe. See on this Van de Velde (2008). See also Cavalli and Galland (1993).

graphical constructions marked by both strong individualization and the prominence of specifically risky features[4] due to the need to take decisions in a social context characterized by high degrees of uncertainty (as well as bureaucratic constraints).

This transition, amid the weakening of the consolidated trajectories of entry into adulthood, therefore tends to emphasize individual abilities to cope with the changes of course imposed by rapid shifts of circumstances, external and internal. We refer here not just to the continuous changes, big and small, that punctuate everyday life in an epoch, like our own, characterized by a rapid acceleration in the processes of transformation but also to the marked changeableness in 'internal landscapes', in the interior ways of considering and evaluating situations, that is especially accentuated in the life phase of youth. This particular emphasis on the individual capacity to control the world obviously conceals the differences among young people in the social and cultural resources available to them to deal with the world – differences in resources that determine *a priori* the likelihood of whether or not the confrontation with uncertainty will be successful (Roberts, 2003). In other words, the emphasis on the obligation to define the choices which ensure the success of the transition to adulthood subjectively does not off-set the weight of the inequalities with which young people have to cope (primarily of class and ethnicity, but also of gender and geographical area of residence: for example, as regards Italy, being young in the North or South still makes a difference; and the combination of individual differences reinforces it).

In general, a feature distinctive of our time is the emphasis on the *personal assumption of responsibility* for one's social circumstances (Martuccelli, 2001). This representation of individuality (and subjectivity) as a *deus ex machina* in regard to external difficulties appears particularly powerful among the young people of the new century, whose crucial years of political socialization have coincided with a historical period in which collective belongings have been singularly unfocused compared with those of the final decades of last century. This representation, moreover, appears symmetrical to the internalization of forms of social exclusion and marginalization regarded as 'natural' on the basis of a doctrine which holds that individuals are masters of their fates unaffected by social factors and inequalities.

The features of contemporary transition to adulthood should also be understood in terms of visions of the world produced by the disappear-

---

4   In this regard, Furlong and Cartmel (1997) used the expression "risk biography".

ance of collective referents able to link individual times and extra-individual times. This is the case, typically, with the loss of force of social institutions in our time, today less and less capable of offering themselves as models for action. And for this reason less and less capable of tying personal times and social times into a long-term perspective. The loss of the future as governable time also coincides, as we know, with the demise of politics as the ability to exercise collective control over change. Thorough understanding of the critical relation with the future now taking shape among young people, the cultures that they express (Nilan and Feixa, 2006), centred on the celebration of the present and the cult of immediacy, requires us to set them in relation to this demise of politics as openness to the future: an openness driven by the belief that it is possible to envisage a different, and better, future for all.

Young people, new values and the new semantics of the future

The young people of today therefore live their lives amid a social climate in which a person's right to choose who s/he wants to become is accompanied by the difficulty of identifying benchmarks for biographical construction which make it possible to evade uncertainty (Bynner, Chisholm and Furlong, 1997). Moreover, the imperative of choice for young people is not flanked by their conviction that personal decisions will be effectively able to condition future biographical outcomes, owing to both the accelerated pace of change and the evanescence of institutions as models for action.

Hence, the future is related above all with indeterminateness. However, two aspects of this latter feature should be distinguished: on the one hand, unpredictability – what Grosz (1999, p. 17) aptly calls the "anarchization of the future"; on the other, the virtuality which by definition characterizes the future (what is in potency, not in act). Given the parallel growth of both these aspects, apparently crucial is the capacity of every young man and woman to devise cognitive strategies able to guarantee their autonomy despite the growth of contingency: for example, by developing the capacity to maintain a direction or a trajectory notwithstanding the impossibility of anticipating the final destination.

A recent survey conducted on young French and Spanish people, which found a similar form of biographical behaviour, aptly termed this an "indetermination strategy" (Lasen, 2001, p. 90). This expression is intended to highlight the growing capacity of young people with greater reflexive resources to interpret the uncertainty of the future as a proliferation of virtual possibilities, and the unpredictability associated with it as additional potentiality instead of a limit on action. In other words, faced with a future increasingly less connectable to the present, a proportion of young people – perhaps not the majority, but certainly the most culturally innovative of them – develop responses able to neutralize fear of the future. Thus, a number of young people, young men and young women to an equal extent, display a willingness to embrace unpredictability, while also anticipating sudden changes of direction and responses constructed in real time as and when occasions arise. The training in the rapid responses required by the acceleration society is fruitfully 'exploited' in this case: rapidity enables young people to 'seize the moment', to begin experimentation with positive impacts on life-time as a whole.

This view appears consistent with the above-mentioned emphasis on the individual's responsibility for his/her future: biographical continuity springs primarily from the individual's capacity to define and redefine a set of choices of sufficient openness to allow revision of the priorities for action in light of the changes that occur. For young people, developing this capacity enables them to conquer new spaces of freedom and experimentation.

In sum, to understand new youth values in relation to the changing time experience it is necessary to focus on the predominance among young people of a particular cultural vision of action and strategies of action. This requires them to conceive themselves as autonomous actors, to assume constant responsibility for themselves, to impute the results of their actions only to themselves. A new figure emerges from this scenario: that of the hyper-activist individual able to construct his/her own biography, willing to explore and re-explore the present so greatly emphasised by the acceleration society. The "unplanned biographies" that young people seemingly pursue today appear congenial to the increasing frequency of this representation. At the same time, they suggest the desire and the determination not to be overwhelmed by events, to keep uncertainty at bay, to gain mastery over one's own time.

Time in one's grasp

For the above reasons, the more stereotypical notions of youth life-times must be abandoned. For example, those notions that unduly emphasise the pure and simple erasure of the past, or those that identify the present as the only domain in which, by definition, the search for gratification takes place, and in which the spontaneity of desires is paramount. These tendencies exist, as has been repeatedly emphasised, but they should not be generalized.

For example, young people appear aware of the fundamental changes taking place in their social age. They endeavour to enter this new scenario by negotiating, if necessary, forms of the active management of the contradictions that they face. Even when the time of their lives provokes worries – this is visibly the case of those who live in fear that they have wasted their time or will do so – one once again finds response strategies which indubitably signal a desire to regain control over time.

As said, the relation with time replicates this pattern. Young people reflect critically (individually and together) on the best ways to maintain firm control over their lives despite the uncertain and fast-moving social time in which they are embedded. They adopt a plurality of 'damage-control' strategies so that they can maintain their bearings amid the precarization of the future (Leccardi, 2005; Woodman, 2011).

In an age characterized by strong deregulation of time and by an equally intense process of individualization, it is increasingly widely believed that every individual has time 'in his/her grasp': that biographical success or failure, the capacity to stay on course in a baffling landscape which hampers forward projection in time, depends essentially on the individual's own decisions. From this also derives the widespread anxiety about failure to identify the shortest and most direct route, the fear of losing one's way in pointless explorations, the fear of falling behind.

Besides differences in the extents of time horizons, in abilities to cope with contemporary uncertainties, and in relations with the future, one is especially struck by the growth of what one may call an affirmative 'state of mind' towards time among young people. This centres on rejection of every form of submissiveness, the determination not to be overwhelmed by the speed of events, to control change by equipping oneself to act promptly, not to waste time by 'letting things happen', not to be cowed by widespread insecurity.

Not all young people appear able to turn this state of mind into suitable biographical responses. External social conditions and internal conditions may separately or jointly thwart these responses. Nonetheless, one may state that the desire not to succumb either to the acceleration of time and change, or to the objective slowness (and fragmentariness) of the transition to adulthood, is today the most distinctive feature of young people's relationship with time.

To conclude, new relations between present and future (and among past, present and future) are arising, ones suited to the short time-frame in which we are embedded and to an acceleration of social life – punctuated by the marked deceleration, for young people, of entry into adulthood. But which is the relation between these changes in temporal experience and values? If we consider values as a criterion of evaluation – a general principle through which we approve or disapprove certain modes of action and ways of thinking – which are the new values associated with this *Zeitgeist*? Values related to the positive evaluation of speed and flexibility (as well as to non-stop activities, for example in consumption) gain ground; flexibility in action, ability to seize opportunities – in short, being 'fast' in life – are all aspects of these new cultural horizons. Thus, short term undertakings seem to be preferred to long term commitments; quick reactions in facing changes to long decision-making processes. This affects biographies as well as the definition of the criteria to make use of in their construction.

Concluding remarks

Young people in the new century find themselves having to define their existential choices within a social landscape that is strongly characterized by the acceleration of change. As a consequence, openness to the new and to the 'everyday-ization' of the processes of transformation constitutes an unquestioned given in their biographical construction – thanks also, as is well-known, to the growing weight that the new technologies of communication have assumed in collective living. However, this reality – as has been underlined repeatedly in this paper – is not simply a fact that youth submit to. Rather, 'the new youth' (Leccardi and Ruspini, 2006) shows that in general it possesses sufficient capacities to be able to govern the dynamics of the 'high-speed society' in which they find themselves living.

It is possible to argue that the very training for velocity imposed by the historical time in which young people today become adults pushes in the direction of a definition of a new suite of values, at the centre of which stand autonomy, self-determination, experimentation and creativity

but also openness towards the other (Barni and Ranieri, 2010). The biographical constructions of the 21st century, less and less founded on the
idea of the 'life project' transmitted by early modernity, place these values at their very centre. Many young people rely on these to confront the
loss of the long-term future without retreating from the expression of
their own subjectivity. In this way they seek to transform the social pressure towards acceleration into a form of personal empowerment.[5]

But what are the youth policies, we might ask ourselves by way of
conclusion, which could most effectively work in harmony with this suite
of values and with the new ways of living biographical time that correspond to them? Without doubt, we could favor all those policies that are
capable of developing and promoting the support of young people's
autonomy and their expression of personal creativity, and that for this
reason are capable of facilitating their integration into the social world.

Within this framework an element of great strategic importance which
policies cannot forget to take into consideration is the contemporary obso-
lescence of the principle of deferred gratification: a principle, as we know,
that up to a few decades ago constituted a fully-fledged point of reference
in processes of socialisation. In a highly presentified environment like our
own, in which the relationship with the future – and here the global economic crisis is an accomplice – appears to be objectively problematic, it is
necessary to construct forms of support in favour of the integration and socialisation of young people that are attuned to transformed collective temporal orientations. In concrete terms this means support for the capacity of
individual young people (and their associations, where they exist) to come
to grips in an active manner with a transition to adulthood that is as slow as
the social climate in which it unfolds is 'fast' (and uncertain). It requires
maintaining an acute awareness, for example, of the centrality in young
people's biographical construction of the dimension of the extended present
– that temporal area that borders on the present without simply identifying
itself with the here-and-now – and of the short-term future.

More generally, it is possible to argue that the very support for active
citizenship and the participation of young people, one of the cornerstones of
youth policies, can achieve greater effect in the moment in which it takes
on board the contraction in biographical temporal horizons. This means, for
example, recognising and valorising those cultural practices and forms of
sociality among the young that are founded on reciprocal recognition, on

---

5   For a recent reflection on – and classification of – youth policies in Europe see Wal-
     lace and Bendit (2009).

dialogue and exchange in the present and for the present. Practices that guarantee forms of gratification that are not deferred but that at the same time appear oriented towards the reconstruction of public space: unleashing in this way a range of positive processes capable of recuperating a non-contracted temporality, one that is not exclusively entrenched in the present.

Bibliography

Adam, B. (1995) *Timewatch: The Social Analysis of Time*, Cambridge, Polity.

Anderson, M., Bechhofer, F., McCrone, D., Jamieson, L., Li, Y. and Stewart, R. (2005) Timespans and Plans among Young Adults, *Sociology, 39(1)*, pp. 139-55.

Barni D. and Ranieri, S. (2010) I valori e la loro trasmissione tra le generazioni: un'analisi psicosociale, *Ricercazione, 2(2)*, pp. 253-268.

Bauman, Z. (1999) *In Search of Politics*, Cambridge, Polity Press.

Beck, U. (2007) *Weltrisikogesellschaft. Auf der Suche nach der verlorenen Sicherheit*, Frankfurt a. Main, Suhrkamp.

Beck, U. and Beck Gernsheim, E. (2003) *Individualization: Institutionalized Individualism and its Social and Political Consequences*, London, Sage.

Berger, P. L., Berger, B. and Kellner, H. (1973) *The Homeless Mind: Modernization and Consciousness*, New York, Random House.

Bynner, J., Chisholm, L. and Furlong, A. (eds) (1997) *Youth, Citizenship and Social Change in a European Context*, Aldershot, Ashgate.

Boutinet, J.-P. (2003) *Anthropologie du projet*, Paris, PUF.

Brannen, J. and Nielsen, A. (2002) Young People's Time Perspectives: From Youth to Adulthood, *Sociology, 36(3)*, pp. 513-37.

Brannen, J. and Nielsen, A. (2007) Young People, Time Horizons and Planning: A Response to Anderson et al, *Sociology, 41(1)*, pp. 153-60.

Cavalli, A. and Galland, O. (sous la direction de) (1993) *L'allongement de la jeunesse*, Arles, Actes Sud.

Côté, J. (2000) *Arrested Adulthood: The Changing Nature of Maturity and Identity*, New York and London, New York University Press.

du Bois-Reymond, M. (1998) "I Don't Want to Commit Myself Yet": Young People's Life Concepts, *Journal of Youth Studies, 1*, pp. 63-79.

Fuchs, W. (1983) Jugendliche Statuspassage oder individualisierte Jugendbiographie?, *Soziale Welt, 34*, pp. 128-41.

Furlong, A. and Cartmel, F. (1997) *Young People and Social Change: Individualization and Risk in Late Modernity*, Buckingham, Open University Press.

Galland, O. (2001) *Sociologie de la jeunesse*, Paris, Armand Colin.

Grosz, E. (ed) (1999) Thinking the New: Of Futures yet Unthought, in Id., *Becomings. Explorations in Time, Memory, and Futures*, Ithaca-London, Cornell University, pp. 15-28.

Harvey, D. (1990) *The Condition of Postmodernity: An Enquiry into the Origins of Cultural Change*, Oxford, Blackwell.

Jaques, E. (1982) *The Form of Time*, New York, Crane Russak.

Lasen, A. (2001) *Le temps des jeunes. Rythmes, durée et virtualités*, Paris, L'Harmattan.

Leccardi, C. (2005) Facing Uncertainty. Temporality and Biographies in the New Century', *Young – Nordic Journal of Youth Research, 13(2)*, pp. 123-46.

Leccardi, C. and Ruspini, E. (eds) (2006) *A New Youth? Young People, Generations and Family Life*, Aldershot, Ashgate.

Leitner, H. (1982) *Lebenslauf und Identität. Die kulturelle Konstruktion von Zeit in der Biographie*, Frankfurt a. M., Suhrkamp.

Luckmann, T. (1993) Remarks on Personal Identity: Inner, Social and Historical Time, in Jacobson-Wigging, A. (ed), *Identity: Personal and Socio-Cultural. A Symposium*, Uppsala, Almqvist & Wiksell, pp. 67-91.

Machado Pais, J. (2003) The Multiple Faces of the Future in the Labyrinth of Life, *Journal of Youth Studies, (6)2*, pp. 115-26.

Martuccelli, D. (2001) *Dominations ordinaires. Explorations de la condition moderne*, Paris, Balland.

Nilan, P. and Feixa, C. (2006) *Global Youth? Hybrid Identities, Plural Worlds*, London-New York, Routledge.

Nowotny, H. (1996) *Time: The Modern and Postmodern Experience*, Cambridge, Polity Press.

Roberts, K. (2003) *Problems and Priorities for the Sociology of Youth*, in Bennett, A., Cieslik, M. and Miles, S. (eds), *Researching Youth*, Basingstoke, Palgrave Macmillan, pp. 13-28.

Rosa, H. (2003) Social Acceleration. Ethical and Political Consequences of a Desynchronized High-Speed-Society, *Constellations, 10*, pp. 3-33.

Rosa, H. and Scheurman, E. (eds) (2009) *High Speed Society. Social Acceleration, Power, and Modernity*, Pennsylvania, The Pennsylvania University Press.

Schutz, A. (1971) *Collected Papers*, The Hague, Martinus Nijhoff.

Sgritta, G. (1999) *Too Slow: The Difficult Process of Becoming an Adult in Italy*, paper presented at the Jacobs Foundation Conference 'The Transition to Adulthood: Explaining National Differences', Marbach Castle, 28-30 October.

Van de Velde, C. (2009) *Devenir adulte. Sociologie comparée de la jeunesse en Europe*, Paris, PUF.

Wallace, C. and Kovatcheva, S. (1998) *Youth in Society: The Construction and Deconstruction of Youth in East and West Europe*, Basingstoke, Macmillan.

Wallace, C. and Bendit, R. (2009) Youth Policies in Europe: towards a classification of different tendencies in youth policies in the European Union', *Journal of Social Policy, 10(3)*, pp. 441-458.

Walther, A. and Stauber, B. (eds) (2002) *Misleading Trajectories: Integration Policies for Young Adults in Europe?*, Opladen, Leske + Budrich.

White, R. and Wyn, J. (2008) *Youth & Society: Exploring the Social Dynamics of Youth Experience*, Oxford, Oxford University Press.

Woodman, D. (2011) Young People and the Future: Multiple Temporal Orientations Shaped in Interaction with Significant Others, *Young – Nordic Journal of Youth Research, 19(2)*, pp. 111-28.

Wyn, J. and White, R. (1997) *Rethinking Youth*, London, Sage.

Zerubavel, E. (1981) *Hidden Rhythms: Schedules and Calendars in Social Life*, Chicago, University of Chicago Press.

2. Participation among young people in Germany: forms, determinants and trends

By Wolfgang Gaiser and Martina Gille

1. The relevance of the participation of young people in the present day

Participation, self-determination and co-determination are elementary human rights, forming the foundation of democratic societies. Given this, participation is demanded by young people in particular and proclaimed by all representatives, from the political to the practical fields. At the political level, this extends from the UN Convention on the Rights of the Child, the EU Youth Strategy and the German Child and Youth Services Act (Kinder- und Jugendhilfegesetz, KJHG) to the local level of communities which – according to current assessments – need to establish structures of participation to ensure their future viability (cf. Roth, 2011).

However, for *governmental organizations* the objective of fostering participation is fraught with ambivalence: on the one hand, they wish to include all or, at least, as many young people as possible in the desired forms of participation (voting), while on the other hand they channel and regulate certain forms of articulation by young people, enforcing the boundaries of what is 'feasible' (e.g. during the student strikes) and a narrow definition of what is legal (e.g. at protests and demonstrations). At the same time, *youth organizations* strive to be a central place of education for democracy. They regard themselves as organizations and lobbyists of, and for, young people, thus paradigmatically advocating the principle of participation. However, they simultaneously need to position themselves vis-à-vis the corresponding adult organizations and frequently lose out in financial and ideological issues. In most instances, *young people* are more or less aware of the conflict between the opportunity of co-determination on the one hand and monopolization on the other. One question regards what preconditions and reinforcement processes are actually influencing participation. Researching into and informing on this issue is the task of *science*.

Whenever the participation of young people is addressed, the global changes in our economic system and their consequences for the next generation play a central role. The young generation not only has to face the personal challenges of growing up that are typical of adolescence. Young people today also have to master considerable problems caused by structural changes in the *labour economy*. They are at risk of becoming the losers of globalization, according to the conclusions of an international study: "The first central finding is that in a globalizing world, youth are increasingly vulnerable to uncertainty across all countries" (Mills *et al.*, 2005, p. 423).

The study emphasizes that young people with low qualifications are particularly vulnerable to precarious, unstable perspectives in their biographies. The problem is that exclusion from stable employment and solid social security is frequently connected with weak civic integration. Given this, we must examine where and how specific opportunities for deprived young people to participate in civic structures and at local level can be developed and offered.

2. Empirical results

The following analysis attempts to provide a diagnosis of the social and political participation of young people in Germany based on empirical and sociological aspects. The diagnosis considers both structural factors, including education, gender, migration background and differences between the former West and former East German states, and subjective factors such as interest in politics and perceived self-efficacy (cf. in detail: Gille, de Rijke and Gaiser, 2011; Gaiser and Gille, 2012). As a first step, the analysis addresses membership and activities in traditional organizations, clubs and associations. It then examines young people's activities in less formal groups that can be classified as belonging to the New Social Movement (NSM) or the category of NGOs. Subsequently, the article discusses the various forms of political articulation (e.g. participation in political parties, protests and demonstrations, etc.).

The analyses outlined below are based on the data of the 2009 DJI Survey *Growing up in Germany: Living Conditions* (AID: A, Aufwachsen in Deutschland: Alltagswelten). This article focuses on youth aged from18 to 29. For this age group, the data in the three waves of the DJI Youth Survey of 1992, 1997 and 2003 enable an analysis of the evolving forms of participation of young people since 1992 and allow tendencies to be identified.

2.1 Social participation: membership and activities in clubs and associations

Membership and active involvement in organizations, clubs and associations are not only important preconditions for the functioning of democratic systems. They also offer young people the opportunity to develop important competencies and are furthermore an expression of personal participation, networking and social integration. Membership is a frequent precondition for other forms of civic engagement.

Examination of the participation of young people in a wide range of clubs, associations or organizations shows that sports clubs head the list by a very wide margin, with 37% of young people saying that they are active in a sports club (cf. Table 1). 10% of young people are members of cultural associations such as choirs, music societies or theatre groups, 8% in parochial/religious groups, another 8% in the voluntary fire brigade and the Federal Agency for Technical Relief, 7% in a trade union or a professional association. Local tradition, citizens' associations or gun clubs and political organizations only account for a share of 5% or 4% respectively, i.e. they are only significant for a small number of adolescents and young adults. Civic initiatives are almost negligible in this age group. The 'Other memberships' category surveys all activities within formal organizations, and the relatively high share of 11% proves that young people engage in a host of clubs and associations apart from those explicitly addressed in the survey.

Even if some clubs or associations reach only a small percentage of the young population, overall almost two-thirds of young people are integrated into the large variety of clubs and associations as members: 60% of the 18 to 29 year olds are members of at least one club or association (cf. Table 1).

In some cases the level of engagement is considerable. Activities on a weekly basis were reported by 86% of respondents active in sports clubs, 74% of those in choirs and music societies and roughly 53% of those in parochial groups and the fire brigade.

Regarding the differences in participation between young women and young men, the results confirm the known gender-specific profiles: overall, fewer girls and young women are members of clubs or associations than their male counterparts: 53% versus 66% of young men. This applies in particular to sports, local tradition and gun clubs and the voluntary fire brigade, which count far fewer girls and young women among their members. By contrast, female respondents engaged in 'parochial/religious groups' and in cultural clubs and associations such as 'choirs, music societies and theatre groups etc.' outnumber male respondents.

Table 1: Memberships in traditional organizations and associations, 18-29 years, 2009 (in %)

Sports club	37
Choir/music society, theatre group	10
Parochial/religious group	8
Voluntary fire brigade, German Federal Agency for Technical Relief	8
Trade union/professional association	7
Local tradition/citizens' association/gun club	5
Political organization/party	4
Civic initiative	1
Other club/association	11
Membership in at least one organization	60
Active in at least one organization	63

Activities in clubs and associations: Question: 'Please tell me whether you are active in one or several of the following clubs or associations.'
Membership of clubs and associations: Follow-up question for respondents who said that they were active in one of the clubs or associations: 'Are you a member of this club/association?'
Source: AID:A – 2009 DJY Survey (weighted), 18- to 29 year olds; N=6,454.

With respect to the factor of age, the results demonstrate that the overall percentage of membership ('Membership of at least one group') decreases with age (cf. Table 2). A more differentiated approach, i.e. analysis of membership of individual clubs and organizations, reveals that in organizations in which membership is associated with integration into the world of employment (trade unions, professional associations) the rate of participation rises with age (more pronounced among young men). By contrast, engagement in sports clubs and primarily youth-related associations decreases with age. The other clubs and associations largely retain their members across all age groups.

The level of education as an indicator of cultural capital critically influences the extent to which young people engage in clubs or associations. The rate of participation increases with the level of education. This impact of education is particularly pronounced in sports clubs and cultural clubs and associations. By contrast, 18 to 29 year olds with intermediate secondary qualifications at maximum are overrepresented in trade unions, professional associations, local tradition, citizens' associations and gun clubs and in the voluntary fire brigade.

Table 2: Factors influencing membership of clubs and associations (in %*)

	Membership of at least 1 group
Total:	60
Gender	
Female	53
Male	66
Age	
18-20	66
21-23	59
24-26	58
27-29	55
Education	
No educational qualifications/General secondary qualifications	51
Intermediate secondary qualifications	56
University of applied sciences/university entrance qualifications (Abitur)	62
West/East	
West German states and Berlin	61
East German states	50
Migration background	
Native Germans	62
2nd-generation migrants	52
1st-generation migrants	44
Interest in politics	
Low	50
Moderate	60
High	66
Self-efficacy	
Low	54
Moderate	61
High	63

* The figures in the above table represent those who are members of at least one club or association.
Migration background: Native Germans: respondent and both parents born in Germany.; 2nd-generation migrants: respondent born in Germany, at least one parent born outside Germany; 1st-generation migrant: respondent and at least 1 parent born outside Germany
Interest in politics: Scale: 1=none, 2=a little, 3=moderate, 4=great, 5=very great.
Low: scores 1 and 2, Medium 3, High 4 and 5.
Self-efficacy: Summary indicator derived from the scores of three items: A. I enjoy assuming responsibility; B. Actively taking decisions instead of relying on fate has been beneficial for me; C. When I encounter problems or opposition I generally find ways of asserting myself. Scale: 1=does not apply, 6=applies fully. Trichotomizing of scale: 1-4.67=low, 5-5.34=moderate, 5.65-6=high.

Source: AID:A – DJI-Survey 2009 (weighted), 18- to 29-year-olds; N=6,454.

In the east German states, the percentages of young people integrated into clubs and associations are still significantly smaller than in the west German states. While 61% of 18 to 29 year olds are members of at least one club or association in the west German states, the same can only be said for 50% of young people in the same age group in east German states.

Participation of young migrants, in particular 1st generation migrants with personal migration experience, in clubs and associations is significantly lower than that of young native Germans.

However, structural factors are not the only aspects influencing social participation by young people. Young people's subjective personal orientations, including their interest in politics and their perceived self-efficacy, also play a role. Interest in politics as a motivational factor increases social participation. Similarly, personal experience of effective actions may increase participation in clubs. However, the opposite direction of effect is also plausible, i.e. young people's engagement in clubs and associations increases their interest in matters of public concern and strengthens their perceived self-efficacy. In addition, private networks and engagement in clubs and associations are not competing activities; instead, the extent and amount of time spent by young people on engagement in clubs and associations and their circle of friends actually reinforce each other.

Overall, the survey shows that an array of factors facilitates young people's integration into clubs and associations. However, the survey also reveals the problem that intermediary organizations are more likely to reach young people who are in a more privileged situation regarding their scope of available resources.

2.2 Activities in groups of the New Social Movement

AID:A also surveyed young people's participation in informal groups which are dedicated to specific social, political and ecological issues and frequently act using means of public protest. Based on their contents, action orientation and flexible forms of participation, these groups are very popular, particularly among young people (cf. Gaiser and de Rijke, 2006, p. 235). They develop their own forms of organization, deliberately dissociating themselves from the more hierarchically and formally organized large organizations, such as political parties, church or trade unions.

The AID:A survey questioned young people concerning their participation in five of these groups. Young people's participation as expressed in their active involvement or attendance of events amounts to 9% in neighbourhood or other regional initiatives, 5% in environmental protection groups and 4% in human rights groups. 2 to 3% of 18 to 29 year olds are engaged in the context of peace initiatives or anti-globalization groups. The rate of activity for the summary indicator 'Activity/participation in at least one group' amounts to 16%. When the same individuals are asked at two different points in time about a wider range of NGOs/NSM, participation adds up to around one-third of young people (cf. Gaiser, Gille and de Rijke, 2010)

Participation in the groups of the New Social Movement is equally distributed among young women and young men. Their structures, which are less formal and more strongly oriented to basic ideals, seem to create better access opportunities for girls and young women than traditional, clubs, associations and organizations. Involvement in this form of participation slightly decreases with age. Participation in these informal groups is also distributed equally among young migrants and young native Germans. However, young people with a lower level of education (maximum general secondary education) are less active in this form of participation than young people with intermediate secondary or university entrance level qualifications. Political interest is a factor strongly influencing the somewhat politically motivated participation in groups of the New Social Movement.

Perceived self-efficacy, orientation to social values and the readiness to help others or assume responsibility for others are also concomitant with a higher level of engagement in informal groups.

2.3 Political participation

Political participation generally refers to "activities by citizens in which the latter engage voluntarily, either alone or jointly with others, to influence political decisions" (Kaase, 2002, p. 350, trans. by author). Elementary forms of participation within a representative democracy include voting in elections and active involvement in political parties. In the 1970s, western democracies witnessed an expansion of the repertoire of participation. At present, some people even believe that the character of democracy has changed from a representative democracy to a "monitory democracy" (Keane, 2009). In this context, activities and groups taking a critical stance towards conventional politics play an additional legitimizing role in the political process.

In the following, this article discusses a broad spectrum of political attitudes and behaviours, from young people's willingness to act, i.e. their ideas of expressing their political attitudes, to their concrete behaviour, i.e. how they actually became involved in political life.

While some forms of participation demand more regular activities (e.g. active involvement in a political party), others express themselves through selective actions. The latter refer to political actions and expressions of opinion which require only a limited amount of time.

Table 3: Political participation: willingness and activities (in %)

	Would consider	Already engaged in
Voting in elections	94	87
Taking part in a petition	87	75
Participating in a legal demonstration	65	43
Participating in discussions at public gatherings	53	34
Boycotting or "buycotting" (not buying certain goods for political, ethical or environmental reasons	51	37
Participating in an online protest	50	25
Participating in a civic initiative	39	5
Being actively involved in a party	22	4
Participating in an illegal demonstration	20	7

Question: 'If you want to exert political influence or make your viewpoint known on a subject that is important to you, which options would you consider and which options would be out of the question?' Respondents were then asked with respect to all options that they would consider: 'Which of these activities have you already engaged or participated in?'. The table shows the percentages of all respondents for 'Would consider' and 'Already engaged in'.
Source: AID:A – DJI-Survey 2009 (weighted), 18 to 29 year olds; N=6,454.

Regarding *willingness to act*, voting in elections heads the list of forms of participation by a wide margin (cf. Table 3). Almost all young people obviously regard voting as the most important and natural form of democratic participation and political influence (94%). Participation in petitions ranks second among all forms of participation considered by respondents (87%), followed by willingness to participate in legal demonstrations (65%) and in discussions at public gatherings (53%). Half of 18 to 29 year olds would also be willing to boycott or 'buycott' certain goods for political, ethical or environmental reasons. The same percentage could imagine participating in an online protest. Almost two-fifths (39%) would be willing to consider more politically motivated participation in a civic initiative. By comparison, fewer young people are willing to become actively involved in a political party (22%). Compared to most other forms of participation, the percentage of young people who (in telephone interviews conducted on behalf of the DJI) said that they were willing to participate in political actions that may be on the fringe of legality is relatively small: 20% of young people could imagine participating in an illegal demonstration.

Comparison of *willingness to act* with *actual actions* reveals considerable discrepancies for all items except 'voting in elections' and 'participating in petitions'. These discrepancies can be explained by a lack of current occasions and structures of political opportunity that would enable concrete political actions. However, they also show that there is high willingness among young people to pursue active engagement, which may be leveraged in a targeted manner by politics and practice.

Analyses investigating how and to what extent potential factors such as interest in politics, educational qualifications, migration background, gender and region influence the realization of various forms of participation by young people point out possible *obstacles* or *reinforcing factors* in this context. The result reveals that the group of young people who are interested in politics tend more often to be engaged in various forms of participation than young people who are not interested in politics. High educational resources also increase the probability of engaging in a wide range of political activities. By contrast, migration experience proves to be more of a hindrance. This applies not only to voting in elections; the percentage of young people from a migration background is smaller across all forms of political activities. The difference is particularly pronounced among young first-generation migrants who have personal migration experience.

Gender-specific behavioural profiles demonstrate the differences in access opportunities open to young women and men: active involvement in political parties, participating in discussions at public gatherings and online protest campaigns are more male domains. Interestingly, a higher percentage of young women than young men participate in petitions and political boycott or 'buycott' action.

2.4 Development trends

The data included in AID:A and the three waves of the DJI youth survey allow a description of the development trends in the social and political involvement of young people between 1992 and 2009.

Among adolescents and young adults, interest in politics – an important precondition of political participation – significantly increased between 2003 and 2009.

While only 22% of respondents considered themselves to have a *very strong* or *strong* interest in politics in 2003, this percentage increased to as much as 34% in 2009 (cf. Figure 1). The rising interest in politics is also reflected in the higher level of activities. Constitutional political participation, for example, i.e. voting in elections or active involvement in a political party, rose significantly. However, the increase in the importance of protest-focused activities, such as participating in demonstrations, petitions or civic initiatives, was even more pronounced. While only 50% of the 18 to 29 year olds exercised at least one form of protest-oriented participation in 1992, this percentage had soared to 83% by 2009. While the percentage of young people engaged in the New Social Movement is not very high, it is actually increasing in certain areas. In summary, analysis over time revealed the participation profile of young people for the various forms of participation to be stable or even rising.

Figure 1: Development trends: Political interest, participation and activities among 18 to 29 year olds, 1992–2009 (in %)

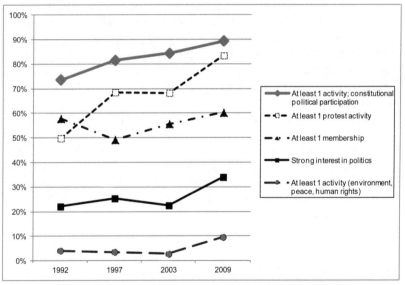

Constitutional political participation (at least 1 activity): Already voted in elections or actively involved in a political party.
Protest actions (at least 1 activity): Participated in (legal or illegal) demonstrations or petitions or in a boycott.
Regarding the indicator 'Membership of at least 1 group': the DJI Youth Survey first asked the interviewees about their membership in various clubs/associations and then followed up by asking only the 'members' whether they played an active role. In AID:A, by contrast, these steps were reversed, i.e. young people were first asked whether they actively participated in a club, organization or association and only 'active' respondents were then asked about their membership. Given these different approaches, this analysis over time refers to membership.

Interest in politics: Summary of respondents who indicated very strong or strong interest in politics (5-point scale: very strong/strong/moderate/little/no interest at all).
At minimum 1 activity (environment, peace, human rights): activity/participation in environmental protection, peace initiatives, human-right groups or civic initiatives.
Source: DJI Youth Surveys 1992, 1997, 2003 and AID:A – 2009 DJI Survey (weighted); 18 to 29 year old Germans; N=22,449.

3. Conclusion and outlook

Trends in the development of social and political participation over the last two decades give no cause for concern that young people may increasingly withdraw from social institutions and structures of co-determination. Engagement in clubs and associations, for example, is as significant as ever. Political participation in form of selective actions continues to be of central importance in this age group. Here, we can even identify a continuous increase in this form of participation and, in particular, protest-oriented actions.

With respect to young people's participation in the New Social Movement (NSM, NGOs), there are also no signs that this form of participation may decrease in importance.

Young people do not regard the various forms of participation as competing with each other or as mutually exclusive in terms of time, form or contents. Instead, the different forms of participation reinforce each other: participation experiences, motivation and competencies gained from activities in clubs and associations, for example, are simply transferred to other areas and vice versa.

The development of various forms of participation among young people does not give any reason for pessimistic scenarios of the future, conjuring up young people who increasingly turn their back on society and politics. However, the fact that young people's participation still depends significantly on structural aspects of life such as cultural resources, gender, migration background and region indicates that the opportunities of participation are not fairly and equally distributed among all young people. Since a more pronounced interest in matters of public concern and positive perception of self-efficacy are concomitants of engagement experiences, exclusion of young people from these opportunities of co-determination and active participation means that these young people will be unable to benefit from the opportunities to learn and gain competencies offered by these practical participation experiences.

Examining the summarized results of empirical sociology regarding young people's participation, from the perspective of social area, forms and networks, we can see specific local synergies between participation in associations and informal and selective engagement. Furthermore, contrary to the allegation that the Internet would step up young people's withdrawal into the private sphere, the Internet has evolved into the main channel of networking, activation, spontaneous political articulation and appropriation of the public domain. On-site, in reality, young people meet to shape their environment, for example by means of guerrilla gardening (i.e. the transformation of concrete roadsides into herbaceous borders), or saving trees, participating in flash mobs or artistic and political actions, including 'ad-busting', or simply creating a party zone free from entrance fees and bouncers (outdoor clubbing). The public domain is regarded as a space belonging to all. Community is established. Boundaries are scorned. This applies across age, gender, origin and nationality. Communities that work together to cross boundaries have a special appeal. Internationality and community, tradition and modern age must be linked. Even highly organized global events such as World Youth Day, an event established by the Catholic church, serve as an example in this respect. 'Back to the roots' and informally orchestrated cultural traditions parallel to enthusiasm for global presence are constantly evident, also in successful productions, events and 'encounters' aimed explicitly at regional and transnational integration, such as the recent 41st *Festival Interceltique de Lorient*, which gathered contributors ranging from the USA, Mexico, Chile and Vietnam to Australia (cf. www.festival-interceltique.com)

But what does this mean for more in-depth and fundamental questions of effective participation, the boosting of opportunities of activation through scientific findings, the enabling of participation by politics and the practical support of young people who want to realize their interest in a future worth living by contributing actively towards shaping their local and global environment? Concepts such as glocalization, social area analysis, local control, activating social planning, defence of place, and so on, offer a host of perspectives for the localized reflection of global development needs and local actions. Problems generated at global level should thus be countered by opportunities for thinking and acting at local levels which, through networking all players without the use of hierarchies, open up new opportunities for co-determination and for shaping our environment.

Bibliography

Dalton, Russell J. (2007) *The Good Citizen: How a Younger Generation is Reshaping American Politics*, Washington, CQ Press.

Gaiser, W., Gille, M., de Rijke, J. (2010) Bürgerschaftliches Engagement und Verantwortungsübernahme bei 18- bis 33-Jährigen: Ergebnisse des DJI-Survey 2007, in: Betz, T., Gaiser, W. and Pluto, L. (eds) *Partizipation von Kindern und Jugendlichen. Forschungsergebnisse, Bewertungen, Handlungsmöglichkeiten* (pp. 57-75), Schwalbach, Wochenschau Verlag.

Gaiser, W. and de Rijke, J. (2006) Gesellschaftliche und politische Beteiligung, in: Gille, M., Sardei-Biermann, S., Gaiser, W. and de Rijke, J. (eds) *Jugendliche und junge Erwachsene in Deutschland. Lebensverhältnisse, Werte und gesellschaftliche Beteiligung 12- bis 29-Jähriger* (pp. 213-275), DJI-Jugendsurvey 3, Wiesbaden, VS Verlag für Sozialwissenschaften.

Gaiser, W., Krüger, W. and de Rijke, J. (2009) Demokratielernen durch Bildung und Partizipation, *Aus Politik und Zeitgeschichte, 45*, pp. 39-46.

Gaiser, W. and Gille, M. (2011) Soziale und politische Partizipation. Trends, Differenzierungen, Herausforderungen, in Bien, W. and Rauschenbach, T. (eds) *Aufwachsen in Deutschland. AID:A. Der neue DJI-Survey* (pp. 136-159), München und Basel, Beltz Juventa.

Gille, M., de Rijke, J. and Gaiser, W. (2011) *Zivilgesellschaftliche Beteiligung in der Altersphase von 12 bis 32 Jahren. Entwicklung, Bedingungsfaktoren, Kontexte. Empirische Analysen auf Basis des DJI-Survey* AID:A – Aufwachsen in Deutschland, 14(4) ZfE, pp. 551-579.

Kaase, M. (2002) Politische Beteiligung. in Greiffenhagen, M. and Greiffenhagen, S. (eds) *Handwörterbuch zur politischen Kultur in der Bundesrepublik Deutschland* (pp. 349-363), Wiesbaden, Westdeutscher Verlag.

Keane, J. (2009) *The Life and Death of Democracy*, London and New York, Pocket Books.

Mills, M., Blossfeld, H.-P. and Klijzing, E. (2005) Becoming an adult in uncertain times: a 14-country comparison of the losers of globalization, in Blossfeld, H.-P., Klijzing, E., Mills, M. and Kurz, K. (eds) *Globalization, Uncertainty and Youth in Society* (pp. 423-441), London and New York.

Putnam, R. D. (2000) *Bowling Alone: the collapse and revival of American community*, New York et al., Simon & Schuster.

Roth, R. (2011) *Wieso ist Partizipation notwendig für die Zukunftsfähigkeit der Kommunen?* BBE-Newsletter5/20, available at: http://www.b-b-e.de/fileadmin/inhalte/aktuelles/2011/05/nl5_roth.pdf (accessed June 15 2011).

3. Participation: a new place for youth in society and policy

By Dina Krauskopf

Globalization has broken the uniformity of culture. Given this context, policies need to consider young people in terms of the diversity of actors and populations involved. Latin American society has brewed strong antagonistic tensions between adults and youth. On the one hand, adults are reluctant to accept the leading role and decision-making powers that young people show, while on the other, youths express their mistrust towards institutions where scarcely any youth-inclusive proposals are seen. In a more traditional conception of political culture in which a state model addressed wide-ranging functions within society, the prevailing perspective was to view youth as a generational stepping-stone towards a future adult stage. This stand-point has been replaced due to changes in the state apparatus, the speed of social change and its consequences on generational relations, improved life expectancy and the increasingly hybrid nature of identities.

A pre-requisite for social achievement and satisfactory interaction between adults and young people is the existence of an intergenerational dialogue and mutual acknowledgement. The current situation is no longer that of an informed adult generation *versus* a young generation devoid of any rights or knowledge and needing to be prepared for adulthood. The place of youth in society has changed and with it the traits required for participation.

Participation is a concept which cannot be univocal, devoid of history and isolated from other dimensions. In analyzing youth participation, it is important to at least take into consideration the following: 1) the relationship of young people to the quality of democracy, 2) the political system, 3) inclusion policies, 4) cultural diversity, 5) gender relations, 6) existing channels for proposing initiatives, 7) methods to institutionalize and legitimize participation, 8) methods to solve generational gaps, and 9) forms of association (Krauskopf, 2009a).

Obstacles to youth participation

The difficulty of incorporating current changes into the relationship between electoral processes and young people is largely responsible for interpretations that lead to the widely disseminated concept of maladjusted
youth, placing emphasis on the apathy or alienation that young people
feel towards politics. The ways in which youth participation is seen to
operate, as violent, rejected and self-affirmative, exacerbate the negative
perception held by society regarding youth. This suggests that there are
important obstacles to recognizing, empowering and promoting the influence of young people in societal projects. Promoting youth participation
in the design, management and monitoring of relevant government actions and the assessment of politics makes it possible to put a stop to the
mistrust that young people feel towards institutions. and thus to reduce
communication gaps among generations.

Youth surveys in Latin America report the resistance young people
feel towards participating in electoral processes. The logic behind party
policies tends towards co-option, to which young people are particularly
averse. Many perceive political parties and the political system as being
far removed from the demands of youth and, furthermore, they feel that
they lack any commitment to greater levels of equality. All told, a rejection of politics does not mean that democracy is rejected by youth. In several National Surveys on Youth in Latin America, young people mention
that democracy is preferable as a government system, although it requires
further tuning (ECLAC-IYO, 2008).

The speed at which traditional cognitive and social tools become obsolete, and the ease with which the young absorb new technologies, also contribute to triggering an adult crisis in intergenerational management (Krauskopf, 2003b). Interventions aimed at promoting youth participation ought to
take into account this generational approach. Currently, the young dele-
gitimize any adult intervention not based on clear communication which
may enable openness. This will influence the relations established among
young people and adults. Just as a gender approach laid bare the existence
of sexism, a modern focus on youth lays bare what can be called 'adultism',
with its specific problems in inter-generational relations, and this may create difficulties for young people's development and participation. Both
generational groups exhibit difficulties in hearing and understanding each
other and in paying attention to each other. Such a communicational blockage leads to the rise of parallel discourses and realities which, in turn, lead
to difficulties in undertaking joint construction of understandings. Inter-

generational bridges are urgently required as a pre-condition for dialogue, where the space available for the young as producers and participants – with their own codes and visions – is not merely ritualistic (*Ibid.*).

New information and communication technology invariably accentuates the generation gap and is addressed in radically different ways by young people and adults. The current situation is no longer one of a well-prepared adult population opposite a young one lacking in rights and knowledge that needs to be fully prepared for adult life. The truth is that, in times of change, nobody is completely prepared for the rest of their lives. Both groups require permanent preparation (Lutte, 1991). These are elements that require input from both generations in order to attain thorough understanding and progress. Changes in the position occupied by youth in intergenerational relations calls for the creation of opportunities that allow them to be protagonists in social development.

Youth participation today

Youth participation not only needs to be understood in terms of the relationship between youth and the adult world; forms of empowerment built by young people, and the transformation of the contents of youth participation must also be acknowledged. Because they regard participation in an autonomous manner, young people initiate action, develop projects and their own proposals, establish objectives and methods, and express themselves if necessary with their own codes while seeking support, assessment and hand-holding from adults only when they need it. (Krauskopf, 2003b).

Young people can play different roles in the various participation spaces available to them. These include consultative, deliberative, decision-making, and executive roles. They can also act as volunteers, promoters, and activists, building their own sphere of knowledge, and also as allies. Their participation assigns priority to the right to have different lifestyles, which is where many youth initiatives find themselves, and which provides greater pluralism and acts against any forms of censorship imposed on their life options.

Participation in volunteer associations is increasingly accepted among youth. Ethical motivations are mentioned, where gratification lays both in providing welfare to others and in being acknowledged in that role. It is about balancing-out personal efforts with mutual learning opportunities; developing gratifying intra- and inter-generational relationships, making visible the practical effects of their own efforts and presenting themselves in a more horizontal fashion within organizations. This ethical aspect – more than the ideological one – in social relations is therefore an issue that motivates participation, fitting in with mobilizations consisting particularly of young people organized in struggles against corruption, social injustice, impunity and discrimination against marginalized groups. "In ethics (what for?)and in aesthetics (how?) actions are a call to consistency and to a commitment that transmits goals and actions" (Gamboa and Pincheira, 2009, p. 148).

All of the above is set in new political understandings, where young people have internalized the idea that power relations have a role to play in the many spaces created, and which are not necessarily restricted to state institutions (Krauskopf, 2008). Everyday life is political and, thus, new forms of action and new areas of influence develop. Hopenhayn (2007) holds that the commonplace is also political and that young people participate by politicizing the cultural and culturizing the political. In this sense, the young take over public space to make themselves visible.

The disqualification of politics and politicians by youths is followed by a reappropriation of the idea of citizenship to which they transfer certain attributes pertaining to the political sphere, such as action, awareness-raising, rights, appreciating common areas, searching for solutions to problems (Novaes and Vital, 2006). This can be seen as a divorce between politics and political processes. As a consequence, contemporary youth seeks to participate in spheres removed from politics and state policy: support groups, social forums, community initiatives and collectives, local youth movements, youth volunteer groups, alliances between youth, ecologists and native Indian groups. In recent years, Latin America has seen a rising level of participation in these groups, particularly among young people aged 15 to 25 (ECLAC-IYO, 2008).

Young people have also expressed their civic role through the arts, sexual orientation, musical tastes, religious, political, and sports groups, and other common interests. Movements that address new issues, new subjects, and new types of awareness-raising, mobilization and organization among young people coexist with traditional social associations. For example, there are almost no traditional youth organizations (student unions, youth groups in political parties, Catholic and Protestant youth pastorals) that are not required to include an ecological item in their projects, programs and agendas (Novaes and Vital, 2006).

There are various forms of organization and association. There are pyramidal organizations that emphasize traditional centralism and highly institutionalized participation, where a sense of belonging and socialization predominates over a citizen approach. New proposals oppose this bureaucratization and regulation, and prefer forms of participation which are scarcely institutional. Youth organizations are preferably horizontal, where flexible and linked networks have a strong role to play. Individual participation is valued and emphasis is placed on the horizontal nature of coordinating processes. Respect for diversity and individual skills becomes central in practices, while peer groups respect heterogeneity. Thus, organizations where individuals matters less than the mass cease to be of interest to new generations. In this perspective, networks of youths strive to function as facilitators and not as centralizing elements (Serna, 1998). Information and communication technologies (ICTs) play a decisive role in recreating these forms of participation and reference spaces, and in generating youth association guidelines through interactive networks. Thus, new technologies enable a new conception of the scale of information, the limits between things public and private, and the ways in which these spheres are appropriated. Decentralization and off-centre approaches coincide within the logic of youth groups that link together and join forces to promote collective action in the economic, civic and cultural domain (Lash, 2005).

Youth and participation in policies

At the heart of policies currently being built in Latin America is the acknowledgement of youth as an important force in the development of our societies. Given this approach, policy makers are currently looking upon youth no longer as targets for certain services, but also as individuals entitled to legal rights and as strategic players in development. It thus becomes necessary to include them for addressing both general issues and those in their own agenda.

It is a well known fact that acknowledging youth participation is a positive approach and that it is also an opportunity appreciated by young people. However, a potential 'denaturalization' of current youth participation spaces through the formalization of youth participation may generate a crisis in confidence because results are not always observable or evident. In this case, the mere extension of spaces for participation will not bring with it improvements in democratic quality. Enhanced democracy can be achieved by synchronizing a clear interaction with policy development.

According to Isabel Licha (2006), public policies on youth that fall within a citizen approach aim at strengthening the collective action of the youth movement, strengthening citizen action that may reaffirm a sense of belonging, equality and cultural identity of the Young, attaining spaces for participation, for dialogue and negotiation, the development of solidarity approaches, and the building of a shared vision and practice. Thus public policies on youth must be geared towards promoting participation of young people in the social, economic and political life of their country. This approach contradicts old paradigms that see young people as incomplete human beings, who are not yet capable of exercising citizenship.

A youth policy devoid of high levels of participation in all its phases runs the risk of being a set of actions or programs that may benefit the young, yet without any coherence, and be of questionable legitimacy in their eyes. Youth may also be completely unaware of its existence. As Tejeda points out: "In order to be credible, an integral youth policy ought to be sustained within an ample youth participation initiative that may serve as a support, providing updated information, and be seen as a permanent form of accompanying the young." (Tejeda, 2008: 18).

Worthy of note are the so-called Youth Laws in Latin America. The first one appeared in Colombia in 1997. Other countries picked-up on this initiative, passing their respective youth laws: the Dominican Republic in 2000; Ecuador and Nicaragua in 2001; Costa Rica and Venezuela in 2002; Honduras in 2006. Both Guatemala and El Salvador have youth laws that have not yet been enacted. These laws create youth institutions, describe a set of rights and establish procedures for the development of a national policy on youth, define a target population, and establish guidelines for structuring the institutional framework and the possibility of youth being consulted. Some youth laws have operational problems that appear to be fundamental, such as the absence of strong binding characteristics and the absence of budgets organized and coordinated on the basis of clearly defined policies. Nevertheless, they appear as important commitments by the state towards youth in their respective countries.

Important dimensions in youth participation

Youth participation should be viewed as an issue related to citizenship. This approach views young people as individuals with full rights and responsibilities. Promoting youth participation guarantees greater efficiency and representativeness and is a necessary condition for the exercise and consolidation of active citizenship. In this perspective, citizenship becomes the framework through which participation is enabled, within a rights perspective.

Young people's citizenship is not merely expressed through the right to vote, i.e. the traditional way in which citizenship is exercised. The exercise of citizenship should enable individuals to go from being mere passive recipients into dynamic agents of transformation within their societies. Young people have expressed their status as citizens through art, their culture or subculture, and in the various ways in which they organize and articulate themselves. An expression of the legitimization of this progress is seen in the Ibero-American Convention on Youth Rights (IYO, 2005), an international instrument that has been ratified by many countries in the region (see a discussion of the related Ibero-American Youth Plan in Chapter 5 in this volume).

Consolidating young people's citizenship is important for youth policies, as it allows young people to become full players who are integrated into and capable of acting in the public life of their societies, while also promoting their role as the leading players in their own development. The creation, implementation and evaluation of national youth policies and programs are not merely instruments to promote participation; they are also becoming a space for young people to exert their citizenship.

An aspect that has been much ignored to date is youth participation in the building of knowledge. The participation arena has failed to promote the influence of the cognitive capital present in youth, perhaps because the possession of knowledge has traditionally been attributed to older generations or because they are seen as equals in the working world and consequently as competitors in the job market. Young people possess a non-circulating cognitive capital, regarding which they themselves are often unaware, and it is not socially acknowledged. Conversely, what prevails in educational systems is a cultural capital which has lost its edge and which is transmitted down in ritualistic fashion, blocking the emerging forms on which youth build their knowledge base. Hence, it becomes important to create spaces so that youth may participate in the creation of knowledge from their own kick-off points.

However, it is commonplace to find that the areas where youth participation is actually promoted do not consider the production of knowledge as a form of participation in its own right. Young people are fully capable of being agents and promoters of knowledge within their societies and communities and of having the opportunity to study and influence various societal proposals through their own vision and skill set.

Experience (Krauskopf, 2009b) has shown that democratic, self-built and freely available knowledge is increasingly an important practice and source of reference for many young people. The production of knowledge by young people about youth may promote greater self-understanding and, furthermore, it generates linkages among young people on the very subjects of the knowledge they produce, its effects on political processes and the empowerment to enable transformations.

We thus understand that youth participation may be encouraged in various ways which are enhanced when linkages among them are built. The following figure (Figure 1) illustrates participation as a triangle where three dimensions interact: i.e. young people as agents of change and intervention using their own capabilities, young people as producers of knowledge on youth, and young people as agents of influence on their surroundings in the further development and strengthening of democracy.

Figure1: Interactive axis in youth participation

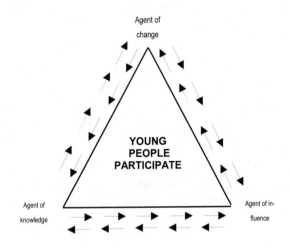

Final Comments

Societies are experiencing rapid processes that place young people in new circumstances and determine different subjectivities and practices. A large portion of the classical sequence of age and stages of development cease to be irreversible. Globalization and increased life expectancy in modern times have modified the goal of a fixed and predetermined life project, thereby adding new ways for young people to join society and its movements. This shows great potential for innovation and flexibility and in this light being young becomes a reference point for actions and goals.

The speed of social change and its consequences in generational relations, the individualization of life courses and the complex nature of identities, as well as the incorporation of clear rights and citizenship perspectives lead to new strategies for dealing with the different situations affecting young people. Youth has a central role to play in helping to enrich the spaces for public action and democratic development. Consequently, the need arises both at the state and society levels for having not only relevant sectoral policies, but also policies for social actors.

Young people give greater relevance to immediate actions and tangible results regarding collective and individual action. They are pragmatic in their own way, and combine the motivating aspects of their actions with creativity in the resources they are capable of mobilizing with greater reflection on participatory processes. The flexibility of networking as well as the reaffirmation of autonomy and identity become almost commonplace landmarks in the participation of young people, who prefer linkages devoid of hierarchy and the values of diversity and uniqueness. In their own way, they build consistency into means and ends, as well as object to the lack of consistency evident in conventional politics. The classic social asymmetries, both material and symbolic, are struggled against through innovative ways of using communication and knowledge.

Youth policies need participation to ensure permanent enrichment, improvements and renewal processes that keep them up-to-date and prevent loss of validity. By including the political participation of youth in public spaces and in the formulation of local policies, and by promoting the participation of young people in the design, implementation, and monitoring of actions as well as the evaluation of policies, it is possible to reverse young people's distrust in institutions and reduce intergenerational gaps, which are found in communication and in the exercise of civic rights. Social participation scenarios that involve decision-making instances regarding personal, peer and local growth alternatives are required for the further democratic strengthening of society. Such a contribution represents not only a tool for the promotion of participation but also a space for the integration of citizens in public affairs.

Bibliography

CEPAL-OIJ (ECLAC- IYO) (2008) *Juventud y Cohesión Social en Iberoamerica. Un modelo para armar*, Santiago de Chile,CEPAL.

Gamboa A. y Pincheira, I. (2009) *Organizaciones juveniles en Santiago de Chile*, Santiago de Chile, Editorial LOM.

Hopenhayn, M. (2007) *Juventud y Política: un binomio para armar*, paper delivered at the Congreso Latinoamericano y Caribeño de Ciencias Sociales de FLACSO – 50 años, Quito, Ecuador.

Krauskopf, D. (2009a) Youth Participation in Latin America – Policies and Developments, *European Journal on Child and Youth Policy, 14* (December), pp. 94-99.

Krauskopf, D. (2009b) *Proyecto Colectivo Latinoamericano de Jóvenes*, Santiago (Chile), FLACSO-Kellog Foundation.

Krauskopf, D. (2003a) Proyectos, Incertidumbre y Futuro en el Período Juvenil, *Archivos Argentinos de Pediatría, 101(6),* pp. 495-500.

Krauskopf, D. (2003b) *Participación social y desarrollo en la adolescencia*, San José, Fondo de población de las naciones unidas – Costa Rica.

Lash, S. (2005) *Crítica de la Información*, Buenos Aires, Amorrortu editores.

Licha, I. (2006) *Desafíos teóricos y prácticos de las políticas públicas para la construcción de ciudadanía juvenil en América Latina*, http://www.joveneslac.org/portal/000/opiniones/politicas-publicas-de-juventud.pdf (accessed June 15, 2012).

Lutte, G. (1991) *Liberar la Adolescencia. La Psicología de los Jóvenes de Hoy*, Barcelona, Herder.

Novaes, R. and Vital, C. (2006) Today's Youth: (re) inventions in social participation,in W.K. Kellog Foundation, *Partnering with youth to build the future*, Sao Paulo, Petrópolis.

Organización Iberoamericana de Juventud (OIJ) (2005). *Convención Iberoamericana de los Derechos de los Jóvenes* (Ibero-American Convention on Youth Rights), http://www.laconvencion.org/index.php?secciones/convencion (accessed June 15, 2012).

Serna, L. (1998) Globalización y participación juvenil en Jóvenes, *Revista de Estudios de Juventud 5(4).* México, Centro de Investigación y Estudios sobre la Juventud, Instituto Mexicano de la Juventud.

Tejeda, E. (2008) Policy Memo Nacional, en *Jóvenes en el Saber*, República Dominicana, FLACSO- República Dominicana-Colectivo Latinoamericano de Jóvenes.

4. Gender and transitions from school to work: Evidence of youth inequality in Argentina and consequences for youth policy[1]

By Ana Miranda

Transitions are processes establishing the entrance and exit of roles related to different moments of the cycle of life (Ferraris, 2009). Regarding youth, 'transitions' refer to the movement by means of which people acquire 'adult' roles. Going through the stages of life is an inevitable fact and is present in every historical period, but characteristics and rites change within different historical contexts (Davila, Ghiardo and Medrano, 2008). With respect to the Argentine case, it is important to mention, for example, the existence of binding military service until early nineties[2], which modified educational continuity and the labor market inclusion of many generations of young people.

Today, the 'limits' of transitions have become quite indefinite. What age defines the beginning of adolescence or youth? What age defines its completion? What age or under what circumstances does a person become adult? In this sense, even though it is generally accepted that youth is delimited at its beginning by physical puberty and in the end by labor market integration and the setting up of an autonomous living environment, there is also some discussion on the diversification of the biographical trackings and the vanishing of the 'normalized adult' figure as point of arrival. Therefore, the affirmation regarding a more diversified

---

1   This work was carried out with the collaboration of Santiago Marti Garro in producing statistics and tables.
2   The Military Service was binding in Argentina from 1900 to 1994. The ages of recruits and the length of time they spent attending such service fluctuated. At the time the Military Service was suspended, 18-year old men were recruited by a variable raffle system. Reasons for interrupting military service were related to abusive episodes reported by soldiers. Such circumstances were made known to the public due to the assassination of an 18-year old conscript by two soldiers encouraged by an officer.

and varied youth condition where limits are vanishing is frequent (Casal, 2000; Miranda, 2007; Jacinto, 2010).

The diversification of youth transitions, the individuation of selections regarding aspects of the life cycle, as well as the urgency of new situations of vulnerability are processes which have been widely discussed and documented by many of the experts which are part of the International Network of Youth Researchers (Bendit and Hahn-Bleibtreu, 2008). Within this context, the purpose of this chapter is to contribute to the empirical history regarding the inequality of transitions between education and work among young people in Argentina. Throughout the chapter, the analysis focuses on the educational and labor situation of young people from different socio-economic groups, with the aim to show that inequality in the access to education has a strong relationship with job and income opportunities, i.e. the conditions of life that young people face; also with regards to their future adulthood. Moreover, such opportunities produce social situations which add yet more complexity to the biographical diversity currently existing among young people. This implies hybridizations and accelerations which impact the conditions of youth within wide population groups.

Secondary statistical data is used throughout the analysis. The data stems from the National Institute of Statistics and Census *(Instituto Nacional de Estadísticas y Censos – INDEC)* and is produced for the main urban agglomerations of the country. Information is divided into different age groups which are then considered according to stages or roles pertaining to youth. First, aspects related to young people in the theoretical age to be high-school students are detailed. Second, the situation of those of the age to be 'students' in higher education and/or 'young workers' is analyzed. Finally, the link between access to educational diplomas and labor inclusion among 'young adults' is adressed.

Education-to-work transitions: Features of the Latin American case

Studies on youth transitions propose to analyze the different phenomena involved in two key aspects of the cycle of life: the transition from education to employment and the movement towards independence from the family home. They attempt to inform about trends of reproduction and social change (Merkler, 1991). In this sense, they state that the result of transitions is to obtain a place within the occupational structure and a cor-related general social status. This perspective assumes that in Western capitalist societies employment is still considered the main means of clas-sification, stratification and social distinction, and that social recognition and self-steem are still strongly related to the characteristics of occupa-tional inclusion (Morch, Morch *et al.*, 2002). And that settling in one's own home and, in many situations, marriage are also deemed landmarks related to adulthood and the acquisition of 'adult' status.

The interest of these studies with respect to transitions is linked to the possibility of studying the social changes and trends of the social struc-ture through the life stories of specific individuals (Cachon, 2000). Based on this interest, many studies bring up queries suchs as: what is the role of individual strategies? What is the strength of structural limitations dur-ing transitions? (Jacinto, Wolf, Bessega and Longo, 2005). Is it feasible to propose social involvement that eases or promotes trajectories of greater mobility? (Bendit, Hahn and Miranda, 2008), what is the impor-tance of educational inequality and the weight of labor market structures in the access to opportunities of young people during their transitions? (Filmus, Miranda and Otero, 2004).

During the last decades, research on youth transitions was widely dis-cussed among academics and specialists of youth policies, particularly in the European countries (Walther, 2006; Biggart, Furlong and Cartmel, 2008; Wyn, 2008). However, during recent years such research was the object of different approaches. On the one hand, from a policy design point of view, there has been discussion about the emphasis that the no-tion of youth transitions places on the question of 'passages' and move-ments, and the implications of such a perspective for policies. It has been pointed out that such policies do not take into account the different mo-ments that young people experience and their relationships within proc-esses leading to vulnerability. A classic example of this refers to how schools give great importance to the passages between educational cycles without considering the inequality that young people face within educa-tional levels (Wyn, 2008).

On the other hand, from the analytical point of view, there have been questions regarding the role given to marriage and paternity/maternity as marking the completion of the transition processes. Indeed, many studies are based upon the assumption that youth transitions are defined in rela-tion to productive and reproductive independence, or the establishment of one's own family home. This assumption does not consider the situation of those people who decide to live alone and/or form new couples or enter maternity/paternity, and/or continue living in their parents' home. In this sense, critical studies question whether people who choose to live alone represent 'transitionless' biographies to adulthood (Molgat and Vezina, 2008). In large cities in particular, living alone seems to be an increasingly relevant option for young adults. And finally, what about those people who continue live in their parents' home: can it truly be affirmed that they never reach an adult status?

Within the context of this discussion, the analysis of youth transitions in Latin America acquires greater complexity because of the specificities pertaining to peripheral capitalist societies. Among such specificities are wide inequality of opportunities and access to social activities which structure the transitions towards adulthood. Such inequality is highly visible not only in the differences among countries, but also within the each country that is part of the region.

It is important to note that inequality in Latin America has been analyzed in classical works. The co-existence of population groups under conditions of poverty, many of which do not participate in formal employment, with populations of great wealth and high levels of consumption, gave rise to the creation of concepts such as *structural heterogeneity and dependent capitalism*, among other concepts that attempt to define the major social questions of a territory marked by such differences (Prebisch, 1949; Cardoso and Faletto, 1990).

In this perspective, the analytical approach to the transitions to adulthood must take into consideration patterns of early high school leaving, child labor, informal self-employment, early maternity/paternity and the co-existence of various family groups under the same roof. On this last subject, one of the most significant problems of the region is related to the difficulties in accessing a home of one's own. This has a strong impact on the independence processes of young people and is the reason why many young people continue to live with their parents even after they have formed a couple and had children.

These situations produce even more complexity and diversification in the youth condition. Some of these can be considered as accelerations, for example the birth of a child during the theoretical age of basic schooling. Others are forms of hybridization, such as paternity/maternity combined with schooling and the consumption of products targeted to youth populations such as concerts, going out at night, etc. Yet others are connected with social processes which produce greater concern, such as absolute inactivity and youth exclusion, which sometimes point to a breach in the nature of the social contract and relationships which are characteristic of capitalism at the beginning of the 21st century (Jacinto, Wolf, Bessega and Longo, 2005).

All of these situations co-exist with those of wealthier groups of young people who live in more advantaged environments and have access to resources. These groups, called 'globalized young people' are those in which the transition to adulthood is developed in a more standardized and planned manner; the transition from their family home to their own house is facilitated through access to economic and financial resourses (CEPAL-OIJ 2004).

In order to demonstrate the gap in opportunities and access to resources among young people in Argentina, the following analysis deals with a combination of educational and labor variables, and concludes with a typology that attempts to sum up the complexity of the youth condition in the Southern Cone of the Latin American region.

The social situation of young people in Argentina

The Republic of Argentina is located in the Southern region of the American continent and is part of a set of countries of intermediary economic level. Within its boundaries, the main problems of Latin America are structural heterogeneity and inequality of living conditions. However, certain features of the nations of the so called 'Southern Cone' are distinctive; among them, an advanced demographic transition (less population) as well as a greater extension of formal education, above all among young people. For example, Argentina, along with Chile and Uruguay, show general rates of enrollment in higher education that are superior to 50% (CEPAL, 2010)3.

The importance of education is evidenced not only in the level of involvement of young people in the different stages of the educational system, but also in the treatment that public opinion and state policies give to this system. In Argentina, as of 2006, education is compulsory up to the second level of teaching; it includes 13 educational years between the ages of 5 and 18. Notwithstanding the foregoing, in 2010 only 6 out of 10 young people had graduated from high-school.

---

3   Except for Cuba, which has historical rates close to 100% and Venezuela, which substantially increased schooling during the last five-year period. For further details, please see the CEPAL 2010 report.

High school completion is related to the economic capital of young people's families, and thus sets a context for wide inequality in schooling. In this respect, time exclusively devoted to studies and training is one of the most distinguishing features. In fact, among young people living in households with lower economic resources, school and non-school activities often begin to co-exist at very young ages, a situation which competes with their involvement in their studies. Among such activities, frequent intervention in household duties, babysitting of younger brothers/sisters and work within and outside the family group can be mentioned.

Table 1: Education and labor activities of young people aged 15 to 18 years who have not completed high school studies, by socio-economic level of households
Total in urban agglomerations (2007-2010)

	MEN			WOMEN		
	LOW*	MEDIUM	HIGH	LOW	MEDIUM	HIGH
Just studying	76.3%	85.8%	95.3%	83.9%	89.7%	98.0%
Neither studying nor working	13.5%	5.6%	3.0%	13.0%	6.7%	1.9%
Just working	10.3%	8.6%	1.7%	3.1%	3.6%	0.1%

* Low, medium and high refer to the socioeconomic level of young people's households.
Source: Table produced by author based on EPH-INDEC data.

Table 1 shows the education and employment activities of young people who are of age to be attending high school. The highest rates of activity relate to those who devote time only to study because, as previously mentioned, education is one of the main activities of young people aged 15 to 18 years. Notwithstanding the foregoing, the table also shows a gap in the school involvement of young people according to their gender and the economic capital of their families of origin.

It must also be noted that educational attendance is the main activity of 100% of young people belonging to wealthy families. These young people tend to complete their high-school studies, to pursue higher education and to finally prepare for a prestigious career in terms of occupation and higher income. At the other side of the social structure, among those who belong to families with low economic resources, the proportion who devote time exclusively to studies is lower than 80%. In this last case, labor and domestic activities with their respective gender features co-exist and sometimes compete with each other.

In general, labor participation is higher among young men. Among young women, inactivity or household duties are the most common situation, many of them having married at an early age. According to data from same source, 3 out of 10 of the young women who do not study or work are married or live with a partner out of wedlock; in most cases they live in the same house as their parents due to the general difficulties of accessing housing on their own, especially for young people in the younger age groups.

For both men and women, the identity and consumption characteristics of the youth period co-exist with the assumption of roles socially related to adulthood. The experience of this hybrid condition, in which different statuses and roles dictate very different ways to 'live' youth are combined, is very interesting in itself because some years ago it was thought that those experiencing such circumstances did not obtain the 'social moratorium' pertaining to the youth condition. However, the conditions of today's youth experience, and the products and cultural consumption related to this stage of life, produce scenarios very different to those previously recognized during the 20th century.

Furthermore, young people's situations change drastically once the high school stage is completed. Generally speaking, the current practice for young people is to look for work once they reach the age of 18, which is the age at which they theoretically finish high-school. At that moment, young people enter the labor market, and sometimes combine this with studies at a higher level. Indeed, one of the features of Argentina today is related to wider participation in higher education, which can be detected in the reported activities of young people between 19 and 24 years of age.

Table 2: Education and labor activities of young people aged 19 to 24 years, by socioeconomic level of households
Total in urban agglomerations (2007-2010)

	MEN			WOMEN		
	LOW*	MEDIUM	HIGH	LOW	MEDIUM	HIGH
Just studying	18.7%	22.1%	22.0%	24.1%	32.0%	31.1%
Studying and working	10.7%	20.1%	38.4%	11.9%	22.3%	38.7%
Neither studying nor working	22.8%	10.3%	2.5%	43.2%	17.0%	4.3%
Just working	47.8%	47.5%	37.0%	20.8%	28.7%	25.9%

*   Low, medium and high refer to the socioeconomic level of young people's households.

Source: Table produced by author based on EPH-INDEC data.

Table 2 again shows in detail the educational and labor activities of young people. In this case, such activities refer to the group that has theoretically reached the age of being enrolled in higher education. The data show a set of trends, among which, the following should be highlighted: a) the previously mentioned involvement of young people in higher education, which is clear from the first two rows of the table; b) the significant influence of family income on educational participation (but also the income of young people themselves because some have remunerated occupations); c) the importance of work among men; and d) the significant inactivity of women in low income households.

Some features related to the youth condition in Argentina may be underlined by focusing on the first two trends. Among them, the social gap regarding access to education and the greater educational involvement of women should be highlighted. For example, among young people who are only studying and who are studying and working, women in high income households have an educational participation rate that is double that of men from low income households (69.8% and 29.4% respectively).

Another feature related to Argentinean society, is the large percentage of young people combining education and work. Contrary to what could be supposed, this combination is more often found among groups with higher incomes and seems to have become one of the main ways making transitions after high-school. There are various factors which explain this situation, among them the access to part-time employment through social networks that enable and promote the continuity of studies in higher education.

In stark contrast to these situations, the absolute inactivity of women living in low-income homes stands out here again. The explanation of this trend comes through the comparison of numbers: more than 4 out of 10 women from low income households do not get involved in education or employment. This means that they participate in public activities only through their family, as mothers, wives or daughters. When focusing the attention on young men, the situation of young people acquires yet more nuances: their inactivity is of lesser importance, but their access to job opportunities is also differentiated because men who are from higher income households have greater job opportunities.

On the basis of these trends, it can be affirmed that different opportunity schemes are configured for women and men from various social sectors. The opportunity schemes and the decisions which accompany them configure a certain polarization of transitions once the higher education stage is completed. Among those young people who have been granted higher education degrees, access to good quality employment has widened. However, among women who dropped out of education early, inactivity often becomes a permanent condition. This situation tends to perpetuate their conditions of labor market vulnerability, as well as the difficulties they face in gaining autonomy and their own income.

Table 3: Activity, employment and unemployment rates according to educational level* of young people aged 25 to 29 years

Total in urban agglomerations (2007-2010)						
	MEN			WOMEN		
	LOW	MEDIUM	HIGH	LOW	MEDIUM	HIGH
Activity rate	93.1	89.6	96.7	47.4	66.7	90.2
Employment rate	84.4	81.9	91.3	39.7	57.6	83.6
Unemployment rate	9.4	8.6	5.7	16.2	13.6	7.3

* Low: Up to incomplete high-school; Medium: Complete high-school; High: Complete university studies

Source: Table produced by author based on EPH-INDEC data

Final comments: Inequality variations in the education-employment transition in contemporary Argentina

Youth is an active stage of labor market integration and family formation, which is related to a set of social structures and activities that are constantly changing over time (Casal, 2000). Among the distinguishing transition features of youth in Western societies there are: transitions to education, labor market inclusion, housing opportunities and access to youth cultural goods (Balardini and Miranda, 2000). During this stage, two key transitions are developed: the transition from education to employment and the transition leading to independence from the family of origin.

At the beginning of this chapter, two general themes related to current youth transitions were discussed. Among those who have contributed to this volume, and who have been among the leading youth researchers over the last two decades, many have recently argued that the theoretical developments in the study of youth transitions should account for individuation, biographization and the diversification of transitions towards adulthood. Also, many of them have discussed new critical observations about the place that the notion of youth transitions gives to all the various moments of passage and about the role of marriage and/or the acquisition of one's own home as markers of the completion of the youth period.

Situated within this interesting discussion, this chapter aimed to analyze the transitions between education and employment in Argentina, a country at an intermediate level of development in Southern Cone of the Latin American continent. The situation in Argentina is quite particular because at the beginning of 2000 it experienced an economic crisis of great significance, during which more than 50% of the population found itself living in conditions of poverty. Such a crisis was the corollary of a great recession which started in 1998 as the result of the application of neoliberal reforms within the context of an unfavorable international situation.

Today, more than a decade later, the social situation has improved significantly, arising from a general change in economic strategy and an international context that is much more favorable to the export of goods produced within the country. However, a set of structural problems – which deepened during the crisis – continue at present and are a source of concern and analysis. Among these problems are trends towards inequality of opportunity and access to education and employment for young people from different social groups and backgrounds.

For the purpose of drawing out more clearly how inequality of opportunity operates among men and women from different social groups, data from a combination of educational and labor variables among different age groups was analyzed. On the basis of this analysis, a typology was produced to illustrate the transitions between education and employment of young people (Figure 1).

This typology differentiates six transition tracks. The first two refer to structural poverty situations and account for cases of poor school performance and premature school drop-out. They concern boys and girls who, between the age of 10 and 14, start experiencing different disadvantages that affect educational performance and then prematurely drop-out of school; they then become involved in child labor networks, at early ages take on activities related to household maintenance (especially among women), and then move on to work in the informal labor market.

The third track refers to those who leave school later, between 15 and 18 years old. In these cases, as explained earlier, labor market inclusion through self-employment in the informal sector or early maternity are scenarios of hybridization and acceleration through the taking on of roles which are socially linked to adulthood.

Figure 1: Typology of education – employment transitions
Educational levels reached – situation at the labor market

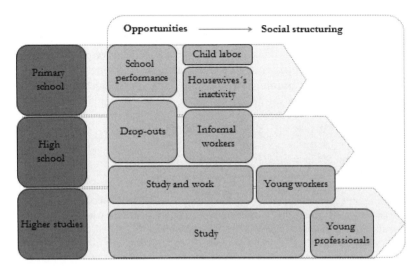

The fourth track refers to situations where compulsory education is completed (high school studies), resulting in an immediate inclusion in the labor market. In most of these cases, occupational inclusion is produced by means of the so called 'new youth jobs' in the services sector. These occcupations are, in general, linked to precarious working conditions and low salaries which generate plenty of instability and worker turnover; these transitions to work follow a pattern of successive approximations in the search for a formal job.

The fifth and sixth tracks lead into university careers and include either a combination of work and study, or the exclusive devotion to study. According to the data, these tracks guarantee greater access to employment and create conditions of greater equality among men and women. Based on this evidence, it could be said that education becomes a virtuous cycle of accumulation allowing subsequent access to resources which then enable the possibility of acquiring one's own home.

These transition tracks form different ways to live out the youth condition. In the first tracks, where taking on labor and family activities occurs at an early age, the time and resources that are necessary for training and experimentation are scarce. Therefore, only consumer goods offered by the market propose ways of identifying as a 'youth'. In the last tracks, family resources guarantee the time needed for experimentation and training – related to trips or more extensive education periods – which allows identity to be developed in a more extensive process of approximation to adulthood.

In light of what has been previously discussed, and due to the valuing of transition tracks that allow time for the equal personal development of young men and women, there appears to be a need to develop public policies which favour the right to live youth as a space for active searching, experimentation and training, irrespective of the economic capital of the family of origin.

Bibliography

Balardini S. and Miranda A. (2000) Juventud, transiciones y permanencias, in Vasilachis de Gialdino, I. (ed) *Pobres, Pobreza y Exclusión Social* (pp. 76-99), Buenos Aires, CEIL – CONICET.

Bendit, R. and Hahn-Bleibtreu, M. (eds.) (2008) *Youth Transitions: processes of social inclusion and patterns of vulnerability in a globalised world*, Opladen and Farmington Hills (MI), Barbara Budrich Publishers.

Bendit, R., Hahn-Bleibtreu, M. and Miranda, A. (eds.) (2008) *Los jóvenes y el futuro: procesos de inclusión social y patrones de vulnerabilidad en un mundo globalizado*, Buenos Aires, Prometeo.

Biggart, A., Furlong, A. and Cartmel F. (2008) Biografías de elección y linealidad transicional, nueva conceptualización de las transiciones de la juventud moderna, in Bendit, R. Hahn-Bleibtreu, M. and Miranda, A. (eds) *Los jóvenes y el futuro: procesos de inclusión social y patrones de vulnerabilidad en un mundo globalizado* (pp. 49-71), Buenos Aires, Prometeo.

Cachon L. (2000) *Los jóvenes en el mercado de trabajo en España, Juventudes y empleos: perspectivas comparadas*, Madrid, INJUVE.

Cardoso F. H. and Faletto E. (1990) *Dependencia y desarrollo en América Latina*, Mexico, Siglo XXI.

Casal J. (2000) *Capitalismo informacional, trayectorias sociales de los jóvenes y políticas de juventud. Juventudes y Empleos: perspectivas comparadas*, Madrid, INJUVE.

CEPAL-OIJ (2004) *La Juventud en Iberoamérica: tendencias y urgencias*, Santiago de Chile, CEPAL-OIJ.

CEPAL (2010) *Anuario Estadístico de América Latina y el Caribe*, Santiago de Chile, CEPAL.

Davila, O., Ghiardo, F. and Medrano, C. (2008) *Los desheredados: trayectorias de vida y nuevas condiciones juveniles*, Valparaiso, CIDPA.

Filmus, D., Miranda, A. and Otero, A. (2004) La construcción de trayectorias laborales entre los egresados de la escuela secundaria, in Jacinto C. (ed) *¿Educar para que trabajo?: discutiendo rumbos en América Latina* (pp. 201-222), Buenos Aires, La Crujìa editions-redEtis.

Jacinto, C., Wolf, M., Bessega, C. and Longo, M. E. (2005) *Jóvenes, precariedades y sentidos del trabajo, 7th National Congress of Studies on Work*, Buenos Aires, ASET.

Jacinto, C. (2010) *Introducción: La construcción social de las trayectorias laborales de jóvenes*, Buenos Aires, Teseo IDES.

Merkler, V. (1991) *Juventud, educación y trabajo en la Argentina: estudio de la situación laboral de los jóvenes de la Gran Ciudad*, Buenos Aires, FLACSO.

Miranda A. (2007) *La nueva condición joven: educación, desigualdad y empleo*, Buenos Aires, Fundación Octubre.

Molgat, M. and Vézina, M. (2008) Transitionless biographies? Youth and representations of living alone, *Young – Nordic Journal of Youth Research, 16*, pp. 349-371.

Morch, M., Morch, S. et al. (2002) Sistemas educativos en sociedades segmentadas: 'Trayectorias Fallidas' en Dinamarca, Alemania oriental y España, *Revista de Estudios de Juventud, 56*, pp. 31-54.

Prebisch, R. (1949) *El desarrollo económico de la América Latina y sus principales problemas*, Buenos Aires, Consejo Económico y Social – Naciones Unidas.

Walther, A. (2006) Regimes of youth transitions: choice, flexibility and security in young people's experiences across different European contexts, *Young – Nordic Journal of Youth Research*, 14, pp. 119-139.

Wyn, J. (2008) Nuevos patrones de la transición de la juventud en la educación en Australia, en Bendit, R. Hahn-Bleibtreu, M and Miranda, A. (eds) *Los jóvenes y el futuro: procesos de inclusión social y patrones de vulnerabilidad en un mundo globalizado* (p. 33-48), Buenos Aires, Prometeo.

5. Youth Unemployment: Causes and consequences and the role of evidence-based youth policies

By Stefan Humpl and Eva Proinger

Key facts on youth unemployment

Young people have been particularly affected by rising levels of unemployment associated with the recent recession in 2008 and 2009. In the European Union, about 100 million young people are aged between 15 and 30, comprising around one fifth of the EU population. Many of these people are in a disadvantaged position in the labour market and they face a number of challenges in making the transition from education and training to employment. In all employment systems in the world the integration of young people into the labour market is an important task. Statistics (e.g. on all EU countries) show a higher rate of youth unemployment compared to the overall unemployment rate. Even minor economic crises make the youth unemployment rates grow faster. In the light of the global economic depression (2008, 2009), youth unemployment (in the age group 15 to 24) was rapidly growing all over the world: it increased more than twice as fast as the unemployment rate of people aged over 25. Based on recent OECD economic data, the youth unemployment rate in the OECD area in May 2012 was approximately 16%[1] unchanged from the previous year. By comparison, the total unemployment rate for the OECD area also remained unaltered over the last year and was near 8% in May 2012.[2]

---

1   OECD (2012): Employment Outlook 2012.
2   OECD Statistics. Available at http://www.oecd.org/statistics

Chart 1: Youth unemployment rate (YUR) compared to overall unemployment rate (UR), 2011, by states

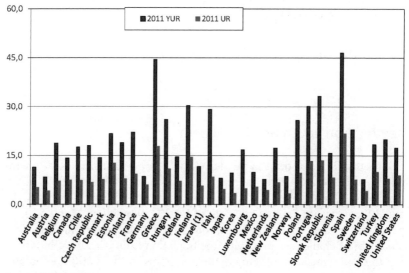

Source: OECD, 2012

As mentioned above, youth unemployment is at risk of growing rapidly during an economic crisis. Young employees and workers are often the first ones to lose their jobs, or are those whose temporary contracts are not renewed. Furthermore, early unemployment can cause long term consequences for future employment and wage potentials.[3] Another result of the economic crisis is the high increase of youth participation in higher education, creating risks of rising unemployment rates even for young people with higher education. Accordingly, youth unemployment is a specific issue with specific solutions necessary.

Main causes of youth unemployment

If we try to subsume globally the problems that cause youth unemployment, we can define them at the interfaces and transitions between 1.

---

3   European Employment Observatory Review (2011): Youth employment measures. http://www.eu-employment-observatory.net/resources/reviews/EEOReview-YEM2010.pdf (20.6.2011)

school education and the labour market, and 2. school education and other forms of education. The transition from (school) education to the labour market is particularly problematic for socially excluded groups. In general, the high youth unemployment in many countries can be attributed to a variety of factors, which can be summarized as having three main causes: a) institutional, b) educational and c) individual. In the following sections these causes will be discussed separately.

a) Institutional causes refer to the fact that qualifications from school often do not fit the demands of employers. There are also transitional problems from initial education to working life, which generally stem from the 'low trust' employers have in the competences of young people. In addition, the educational counselling provided, together with the information on jobs and careers offered by schools and the educational environment are mostly inadequate. Further reasons for high youth unemployment are the 'new forms of labor', resulting in the increasing use of temporary contracts, while social safeguarding for young people in the labour market is diminishing. New forms of employment and working conditions include, for example, non-standard arrangements such as part-time, temporary and fixed-term employment, temporary agency work, self-employment and teleworking. In particular, the new forms of labour promise individual and flexible working conditions for young people entering the labour market, but most of the jobs offered consist of part-time employment requiring employees to work 'whenever needed' and to be 'paid for performance'. Insecure working contracts as well as lack of safeguarding and insurance sometimes lead to a precarious situation for many employees, resulting in the high economic risk of day-to-day jobs.

At the European level, more than 50% of low-educated young people aged 15-24 have temporary contracts. This percentage decreases with the level of education and is less than 40% among young people with tertiary education. However, between the age of 25 and 29, approximately 25% are on temporary contracts, independent of the level of education. About 25% of young people aged 15-24 are employed part-time mainly because they are in education. The majority of young people in temporary contracts did not choose this type of work. According to a survey commissioned by Eurostat in 2007[4], the number of young people who have a temporary job because they could not find a permanent one differs greatly from country to country. In the European Union, 27 countries

---

4   Eurostat (2007): Labour Force Survey.

have on average 38% of young people with temporary contracts. The highest rates were shown in Spain and Portugal with 72-73% followed by Romania (70%), Cyprus and Slovakia (66%).

However, the general increase in the incidence of temporary jobs does not have to be regarded only negatively in terms of the career prospects for young people. Depending on the type of jobs held by young people during the transition process, and also on the skills and qualifications of the person, the extent to which these jobs serve as so-called 'traps' or conversely 'stepping-stones' to a permanent contract, differs. Based on the EU Survey on Income and Living Conditions (2005-06)[5], among the nine European countries where data was available, the probability for youth of getting a permanent job one year after being in a temporary job is higher than after being unemployed. This probability is generally higher for youth with tertiary education than for those with lower levels of education.

This leads to the second of the above-mentioned main causes for youth unemployment:

b) Educational problems: As general (not personal) variables, educational problems include the relatively high proportion of young people leaving school without a basic education qualification, as well as the fact that skills acquired in initial education are not always well adapted to labour market requirements. A poor preparation for the labour market in (school) education and other educational problems of young people, like early school leaving (dropping out) or not achieving a higher level of education, clearly intensify the risk of youth unemployment. In addition, many countries face several problems concerning an educational system with no recognised qualifications and no valued diploma on different levels. In general, there are some essential aspects of the educational career that affect position in the labor market: the level of education, the field of education or specialization and the certification or diploma achieved.

Unemployment rates decrease with the level of education in nearly all European countries. Among the EU Member States, people with lower secondary education are nearly three times more at risk of unemployment than people with higher education. However, graduates from higher or tertiary education are seen as 'more demanding' in terms of expected wages or working conditions, which contributes to the difficulty of finding a decent job. Within the European countries, Greece, Italy, Portugal

---

5   EU-SILC (2005-06).

and Turkey showed the highest unemployment rates among young people aged 25-29 with tertiary education.[6] This may also disclose the inadequacy of some tertiary education programmes to meet the need of the national labour markets. It should be noted that unemployment rates vary significantly across European countries among the population of the same age and educational attainment level. Nevertheless, adolescents entering the labor market without any certificate or diploma have the greatest problems in finding a job.

Chart 2: Former and future qualification level in the EU-workforce (EU 27)*

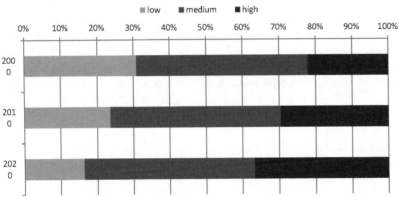

* The qualification level indicates the highest level of education or training successfully completed: low qualification: at most lower secondary (ISCED 0-2); medium qualification: upper secondary (ISCED 3-4); high qualification: tertiary (ISCED 5-6).

Source: Cedefop, 2012

Chart 2 shows the former and future qualification level within the workforce of the EU. This indicates that in the future (2020), more than 35% of the workforce will be highly qualified. Compared to the year 2000, the amount of low qualified workers will decrease by almost half until the year 2020 (from about 31% to 17%).

c) Individual (personal) variables, such as sex, ethnic origin and social problems like integrational problems, drugs, crime and early motherhood, are considered important factors for youth unemployment, even if they vary highly in different economic and social circumstances. Additionally,

---

6   Eurostat (2009): Youth in Europe.

pupils and young people often have different expectations and perceptions of careers and the labour market compared to the real world of employment, which can cause problems in choosing a suitable profession or deciding whether to continue education or not. These different views about occupations are influenced by dominating gender role models in society. Stereotyping is frequently found in vocational guidance and counseling on the part of school staff or employment services. In many countries, young women are encouraged to train in relatively low-skilled and poorly paid 'feminine' occupations with little prospect of upward mobility.[7] These occupations are often related to household work, such as food preparation and garment manufacturing, while young men are more encouraged to go for modern technology-based training and employment. Segregation also exists at higher levels of education, where women are often driven into the traditional caring occupations of teaching and nursing. An important employment' challenge is to tackle occupational segregation of traditionally accepted 'male' and 'female' jobs and to break the barriers in opening up professions to both sexes. Until now, often because of a lack of adequate role models, women are only slowly entering job markets traditionally dominated by men.

In Austria for example, around 40% of young people at the age of 15 begin apprentice training in one of about 230 legally recognised apprenticeship trades. Approximately 50% of all young women that choose this route want to join one of only three occupations: Saleswoman, Office Clerk or Hairdresser. There are several jobs and educational pathways with nearly no young women. In almost the same manner, 30% of the young men that choose an apprenticeship want to join one of only five occupations: Car mechanic, Electricity installation technician, Machinery engineer, Salesman or Cook. These preferred careers are an expression of gender role model stereotypes, but also result from the media presentation of different images of occupations which are often wrong.

In accordance with the inappropriate funding of career guidance and counselling in many countries, a higher investment in this service relevant to decision-making is necessary. With decent and objective information on different educational and job opportunities, this investment would pay off through less drop-out and unemployment rates due to information gaps at specific stages in the future.

There is also a need to look at the images of jobs. Guidance must reach not only youth, but also peer groups (parents, friends). The transi-

---

7   ILO (2008): *Youth employment: Breaking gender barriers for young women and men.*

tion between education and employment in most countries takes place at between the ages of 18 and 24. However, in some countries, the decision to undertake a certain job is made at the age of 15 or 16 for large groups (for example, in Austria). The apprenticeship systems are seen on the one hand as very positive in terms of easing the transition between education and employment. On the other hand, a 'wrong' job decision is crucial to the career. Besides the problem of guidance, there are also different expectations about wages and salaries, so that many young people prioritize earning money at the time (which is possible, e.g. in the service and tourism sector), instead of thinking of a long term career development. The hope of making a lot of money refers to another aspect of the 'mismatch' between students' expectations and labour market needs. Especially in countries where payment is driven by seniority this aspect causes severe problems, because young people are looking for jobs with good payment opportunities – these are often short-term, seasonal, demanding and offer nearly no career opportunities. Tourism jobs in particular are often acceptable only for short periods and do not last a lifetime. After a few years a young person will have to change jobs, possibly in totally different fields. As long as this goes hand in hand with educational pathways, it is not a problem. However, it is demanding for people with low education. Furthermore, the possibility that these jobs are driving young people out of education is high. Proper career development requires a higher level of education, which has been given up for 'quick money', resulting in many leaving school too early. One out of seven young persons aged 18 to 24 in the EU leaves the education system with no more than lower secondary education and participates in no further form of education and training. A further problem in the educational system can be estimated by the lack of personnel in technology and natural sciences in most European countries, compared to the increase of students in human and social sciences.

Chart 3 shows the percentage of early school leavers in European countries: it tends to show a north-south divide on this issue. Some of the southern countries record more than 25% as early school leavers (Spain, Malta and Portugal) while other countries (predominately northern states) register much lower numbers. In eight Member States of the EU (Austria, the Czech Republic, Lithuania, Luxembourg, Poland, Sweden, Slovenia and Slovakia) there is a percentage of less than 10% as early school leavers.

Chart 3: 'Early School Leavers'* (as a percentage of the total population aged 18-24 within the EU 27 Member States, 2010)

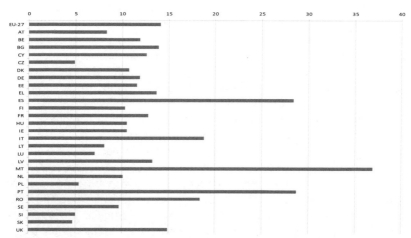

* Early leavers from education and training refers to persons aged 18-24 with at most lower secondary education and not in further education or training.

Source: Eurostat, Statistics on education and training, online: http://epp.eurostat.ec.europa.eu/ portal/page/portal/education/data/main_tables (accessed June 26 2012).

Classical factors for youth unemployment are often mentioned in employment research, such as low education and high drop-out rates in education. However, social problems have a major influence on the development of adolescents and the risk of unemployment. Social problems, like crime or drug abuse, as well as integrational problems, as, for instance, in the case of indigenous groups and ethnic minorities as well as problems related to migration, cause unemployment. Even in countries with statistically good integration of youth into the labour market, major unemployment problems within these specific groups persist. Early motherhood is also a factor for unemployment in many societies. Most of these factors do not arise in isolation, therefore several of the mentioned factors for youth unemployment are often combined.

Unequal access to opportunities deepens the differences in young people's life prospects. The problems experienced by the groups already mentioned can – amongst other things – be translated into decreased access to necessary services, poor health, lack of decent housing or homelessness, financial exclusion, reduced participation in the community and further exclusion from the labour market. Accordingly, access to education and training and specific opportunities for entering employment are needed among other facilities for directing life in 'decent pathways' in terms of housing, health care, and basic services such as transport and finance.

Conclusions and ways out of the problem

The prospects of young people vary widely, according to their socio-economic background and other variables. Some youth groups are more exposed to social exclusion and poverty than others. The main factors that lead to this situation are: dropping out of school early, low educational achievements, migrant background, mental health problems, difficult socioeconomic background, disabilities, and exposure to violence and substance abuse.[8] For young people, the transition from education to employment is an important step towards independence, but this process may vary significantly between and within countries. The path to independence can be straightforward (from formal education directly into full-time work) or more fragmented (combining schooling with part-time work or alternating inactivity, work and/or unemployment).

In many countries we can identify three major groups of youth in the transition process from education to employment. There are the 'high performers' who are achieving higher education and have nearly no problem with integration into the labour market. Another group of youth are the 'poorly integrated (or new entrants)': they are facing barriers to finding stable employment through the lack of basic skills, like literacy or mathematical skills, or due to social exclusion of whole groups. The third group is the 'youth left behind': they cumulate multiple disadvantages and are facing multidimensional problems in education and social exclusion. The recent and severe economic crisis deepened employment integration problems for youth in many countries. Many young people decided to stay within the educational system for longer, especially from the group of high performers,' to avoid problems in integration into employment and 'precarisation' at the beginning of working life. Therefore we are facing growing numbers of student enrolment in universities in many countries, but on the other hand also growing numbers of integrational problems in employment even for 'high performers'. Both the 'poorly inte-

---

8   European Commission (2009): *EU Youth Report*. p 37.

grated' and the 'left behind' definitely could not improve their situation on the labour market.

At the European level, one third of young people are neither in employment, education or training (the so-called NEET[9] group): they are not only unemployed, some of them are inactive in education and employment, due to family reasons. According to the EU Youth Report 2009, more than one third of young people aged 15-24 are NEET in the European Union. Between the age of 25 and 29 20% are still NEET. Most of the adolescents explain their situation by saying that they were unable to find a job; others stated they chose to be unemployed and some are simply 'not interested' or 'don't need to work'.[10] Unemployed young people and especially those who are long term unemployed are at risk of social exclusion. Generally, those people have a socially unacceptable income, which does not finance a life that meets social standards. At the European level, 26% of the unemployed aged 15-24 and 35% of the unemployed aged 25-29 were unemployed for 12 months or more.[11]

The consequences of youth unemployment resemble the causes, because early unemployment determines persistant unemployment to some extent. Youth unemployment leads to low self-confidence and low self-empowerment. Young people who are unemployed are at the risk of losing their place in society, and turn instead to seclusion, drug abuse and sometimes criminality. Other consequences are the loss of perspectives through having no chance for a straight-forward career development, and the loss of qualifications through not using them on the labour market. These negative effects of unemployment create a vicious circle. To tackle this 'doom loop' it is necessary to:

• help with integration into society: placing arrangements for activation;
• help with all transition processes: through guidance, job orientation, self-empowerment, etc.;
• tackle systemic preconditions: school systems with no alternatives to 'drop out' have to be modified.

Over the past years, several countries have implemented additional measures to reduce youth unemployment. Some examples are mentioned in the following section according to the type of measurement.

---

9   The term NEET was first used 1999 in the UK for people in the age group of 16 to 24 who are neither in employment, education or training.
10 Lázaro Morales, C. (2010): *Youth Generation or Degeneration?*
11 European Commission (2009): *EU Youth Report.*

Examples of help through activation

The OECD has recommended different strategies for tackling youth unemployment. For example in the Slovak Republic[12] and in Spain[13], the
OECD proposes further reforms to ensure that unemployed youth register
with the public employment service (PES) even if they do not get a grant.
Further, youth on social assistance should be obliged to register with the
PES. It is crucial for the PES to devote enough time and resources to
screen young jobseekers at an early stage and make proposals adapted to
individual needs. Those with low or inadequate qualifications should, as
soon as possible, be offered an opportunity to receive more education in
second-chance schools, combined with the possibility to acquire work
experiences in a company.

In Belgium[14], the Federal authorities enacted at the end of 2005 the
Pact on solidarity between generations. This pact includes the extension
of the existing measures for young people, with greater emphasis on
young people with very few skills, unskilled young people of foreign origin and unskilled young people with disabilities. The strategy comprises
help in activation that ensures that youth leave education with recognised
qualifications and a valued diploma. Furthermore, the education system
has to offer differentiated paths enabling young people to obtain a diploma valued by society and by companies. In order to achieve this, it is
important to prevent school failure. Young people who drop out should
be able to have another opportunity to benefit from education later in life.
Additionnaly, 'mutual obligations' should be redesigned to better match
the needs of school drop-outs or new graduates. Every young job-seeker
should sign an action plan that is monitored by the Public Employment
Service (PES). Additionally, the PES ought to provide jobs or training for
young people who have been unemployed for more than one year. In order to remove the remaining barriers to the recruitment of young people,
like the relatively high wages for job entrants in Belgium, the adjustment
of labour costs and productivity should be considered.

Another example for activation and integration into society pertains to
an action plan in France.[15] It is a fact that young people who deviate from
the linear educational path have more difficulties obtaining an initial di-

---

12 OECD (2007): *Jobs for Youth*: Slovak Republic 2007.
13 OECD (2007): *Jobs for Youth*: Spain 2007.
14 OECD (2009): *Jobs for Youth:* Belgique 2009.
15 OECD (2009): Jobs for *Youth*: France 2009.

ploma that protects them from unemployment, and when entering the labour market face multiple barriers. Therefore, a second-chance system of training for young people who have left the school system without basic skills, a qualification and/or a diploma has to be created. Offering every individual a 'second chance at a qualification' also includes strengthening access to diplomas and to all professional certifications aside from continuing vocational training, in particular by the validation of job experience.

Examples of help in the transition process

In Belgium, one of the main goals of the strategy for helping young people in the transition process is to better promote the combination of work and study. It is important to make the transition from school to work less abrupt by extending apprenticeship systems into all skill levels as well as improve apprenticeship contracts in order to fit to its target population. Furthermore, the number of apprenticeships should be increased while available partnerships between training centres, the PES and companies should be subsidised.

In France, policies that would provide the possibility for young people to develop basic skills in order to enter the labour market and advance their careers are being considered. For example, more small enterprises could benefit from funds for vocational training, particularly those training budgets targeted at young workers with low job skills. France could also develop an exploratory phase during which vocational experience can be built up before definitively leaving school. In many OECD countries, the experience of combining work and study shows that this facilitates labour-market entry (as long as the work does not exceed about 15 to 20 hours per week). To encourage students to gain work experience, young people (for example, full-time students who work year-round), could benefit from a subsidy.

In the Netherlands[16] as well as in Spain, in order to improve the transition process for young people, there is a demand for the development of more youth-friendly 'one-stop shops'. These facilities provide a single point of contact in order to help young people take the required steps for the transistion process, by providing convenient and efficient services

---

16   OECD (2008): *Jobs for Youth/Des Emplois pour les Jeunes*: The Netherlands 2008.

such as guidance on labour market opportunities, job-search training, information on labour rights and help with access to housing and healthcare. In order to allow for disengaged young people to be in reach of activation strategies, support should exist at the local level and be 'unbundled' from the right to financial benefits. For instance, guidance on labour market opportunities, help with finding adequate training, and job-search training should be provided as well as information on labour rights and on special contract types available for the hiring of young people.

For the Slovak Republic, the OECD recommends improving the links between the education system and the labour market to ensure that adolescents leave education with adequate skills. To achieve this, the education authorities should work closely with the social partners in defining the content of curricula. Additionaly, the collaboration between companies and vocational schools should be strengthened, for example through involving companies in the definition of curricula.

Examples of improving school and employment systems

In order to tackle systemic preconditions, Belgium is seeking a better link between flexibility and security. A better balance between the permanent contracts of those in work and the temporary contracts which many young people have needs to be found, without increasing labour market duality, by moving towards a single contract. Also, subsidies for on-the-job training should be reserved for the least-skilled unemployed. Coupling the recruitment of a job-seeker with a subsidy for individual on-the-job vocational training can only be a sucessful strategy if candidates are not chosen due to their former work experience.

In France, educational counselling for pupils is viewed rather negatively, therefore disciplines are chosen largely by default. Because general and technological studies are considered more valuable than vocational courses, the weakest pupils are often driven into vocational courses with the least demand, which often offer only poor preparation for employment. Middle and high school students and apprentices should be better informed about the manifold vocational specialties and gateways that exist, in order to better coordinate educational and vocational guidance. Developing the use of internships in study programmes in France is an obligation to put pupils and students into contact with the world of business. In order to professionalise initial education, the use of compulsory on-the-job internships is now growing. However, it is often hard to find a company offering internships for young people from immigrant or disadvantaged backgrounds. To counter this 'doom loop', an internship programme was launched, which aims to provide access to compulsory internships regardless of origin or social background.

In the Netherlands, some measures are envisaged to further improve opportunities for youth to acquire the skills needed in the labour market. Tertiary educational attainment is relatively low in the Netherlands by international comparison. In order to reduce drop-out rates and meet the target of 50% of a cohort at tertiary level by the year 2020, it is necessary to keep focussing on core topics (mathematics, sciences and reading) within vocational secondary education. To increase the average educational attainment at the tertiary level, the offer of short-cycle tertiary degrees are further developed and to provide advanced scientific and technical skills some short-cycle tertiary degrees are specifically created.

In the Slovak Republic, vocational secondary schools are not well adapted to the rapidly changing labour market requirements. The links between tertiary education and the labour market are also weak. The OECD recommends putting dual apprenticeship systems in place, where teaching in school alternates with learning at the workplace. It is important that the programme leads to qualifications that are recognised and valued in the labour market in order to encourage young people to take up apprenticeships. Additionaly, tertiary vocational education should be promoted and co-financed by companies requesting specific skills.

The reform plan of university education in Spain is implementing a measure to evaluate teaching and research quality at university on a regular basis. Consideration is also given to making public funding partly related to the outcomes of these evaluations. Furthermore, the use of internships at graduate level is broadened and employers are involved in their design.

Action in a European Perspective

In Europe several common actions aim to improve possibilities for youth (and society as a whole) in education and employment through providing more transparency and comparability:

- EQF – European Qualification Framework, as a 'translation tool' between qualification systems in Europe.
- ECVET – European Credit System for Vocational Education and Training, as a transparency tool for learning outcomes in VET.
- ECTS – European Credit Transfer System, as a transparency tool for learning outcomes in Higher Education.

Education and training can also help to reduce barriers to mobility by recognising skills and competences acquired abroad, and making people, especially young people, more familiar with training and work in other countries. The lack of mutual recognition of qualifications and competences is interfering with mobility within the EU. The European Qualifications Framework together with other transnational placements, are essential tools for achieving a true 'European' labour market. Furthermore, the implementation of transparency and comparability systems at European level is also giving incentives to developing national approaches. The conjunction of separate education and training systems into a national system contributes not only to the development of each learner but also to the social and economic development of the nation at large.

Bibliography

Cedefop (2012) *Skills Forecast,*Online data available at http:www.cedefop.europa.eu/ (accessed August 1, 2012). Luxembourg, Publications Office of the European Union.

European Employment Observatory Review (2011) *Youth employment measures,* Luxembourg, Publications Office of the European Union.

European Survey on Income and Living Conditions (EU-SILC) (2005-2006) *OECD Social: Employment and Migration Papers, No. 106,* Paris, OECD Publishing, available at: http://www.oecd.org/dataoecd/10/8/44986030.pdf (accessed July 26, 2012)

European Commission (2009) *EU Youth Report,* Brussels, OPOCE.

Eurostat (2007) *Labour Force Survey (LFS),* Luxembourg, Publications Office of the European Union.

Eurostat (2009) *Youth in Europe: A statistical portrait,* Luxembourg, Publications Office of the European Union.

International Labour Office (ILO) (2008) *Youth employment. Breaking gender barriers for young women and men,* Geneva, International Labour Organization, http://www.ilo.org/gender/Events/WCMS_097919/lang--en/index.htm (accessed June 26, 2012).

Lázaro Morales, C. (2010) Youth Generation or Degeneration? *Kairos Future's Newsletter Watching and Global Watching, 3/2010,* http://www.kairosfuture.com/en/publications/youth-generation-or-de-generation?pub=youth-generation-or-de-generation (accessed June 26 2012).

OECD (2012) *OECD Employment Outlook 2012*, Paris. OECD Publishing, http://dx. doi.ort/10.1787/empl_outlook-2012-en (accessed August 2, 2012).

OECD (2009) *Jobs for Youth: Belgium*, Paris, OECD Publishing.

OECD (2009) *Jobs for Youth: France*, Paris, OECD Publishing.

OECD (2008) *Jobs for Youth: the Netherlands*, Paris: OECD Publishing.

OECD (2007) *Jobs for Youth: Slovak Republic*, Paris, OECD Publishing.

OECD (2007) *Jobs for Youth: Spain*, Paris, OECD Publishing.

6. Suicide and ethics: reflections on the reality of young people in Latin America and the Caribbean

By Vânia Reis

In the last two decades, there has been an increase in the reasons that may lead a person to commit suicide. These range from the most complex to the most futile of situations, notably among youth.

Although the issue of suicide among young people is growing to greater prominence, the problem is still underestimated. The lack of more precise data, the incipient interest of governmental authorities and the difficulties in analyzing and understanding suicide are some of the significant aspects that make the phenomenon very private and difficult to confront.

In the Latin-American and Caribbean context, we can observe a progressive growth in suicide rates among young people. In spite of the greater precariousness of social conditions in some countries, such growth cannot be understood as a mere reaction to such conditions.

The constructed approach here seeks to focus on aspects of the ethical dimension that circumscribe youth realities, establishing an invitation to reflect upon the phenomenon beyond social and psychological conditions. From the ethical and moral point of view, there are two challenges: the first one is to understand the ethical and moral dimension itself and its developments in the context of the phenomenon of suicide; the second one is to incorporate it into preventive actions and follow-up actions with family and friends after the consummated act.

The issues currently presented, which center on the ethical questions themselves, have as referential data the statistics on suicide of young people in ten countries of Latin-America and the Caribbean: Argentina, Brazil, Chile, Costa Rica, Cuba, the Dominican Republic, Ecuador, El Salvador, Guatemala and Mexico.

It is presupposed that suicide leads the way to the core questions of life. In taking an individual to the limit, it exposes human frailties and ignorance about what life is and about what comes after death.

Observing the statistics: a starting point

Analyzing the statistical data provided by the World Health Organization (WHO, 2011a) in the years 1995 and 2005 (or the closest years available), there was a great increase in suicide rates in the age groups 15 to 24 and 25 to 34, particularly among men of both age groups, in three of the ten countries studied: Argentina, Chile and Ecuador. In Argentina, among men from 15 to 24 years old, the rate (per 100,000 inhabitants) increased from 8.9 to 19.1 within the ten years, while in the age group 25 to 34, the rate increased from 9.1 to 15.0. In Ecuador, in the age group 15 to 24, among young men, the rate rose from 9.6 to 16.2, and in Chile, the rate increased especially among young women from 25 to 34 years old, rising from 1.6 to 4.1.

Only in Cuba, Costa Rica and El Salvador the numbers showed a significant decrease in this ten-year interval. The rate reduction in Cuba is remarkable, especially among young women: among those aged 15 to 24, the rate dropped from 17.9 to 4.6; for 25 to 34 year olds, the rate fell from 14.8 to 4.0.

In the other countries the rates increased, some more slowly, others less dramatically than in the cases presented above. In Mexico, attention was drawn to the increase in suicide among men aged between 15 and 24 years old, from 7.6 to 10.3.

To gain a global perspective of the Latin American region, the estimates presented by the WHO (2011b), referring to the year 2008 in the Region of the Americas, ranked it third in suicides among individuals between 15 and 29 years old, with 6.69% of total suicides in this age group for the entire world – technically the same total rate of the African Region, which is 6.78%. The highest rates are from the South East Asia Region, with 11.36% of the world total. This is also the region with the highest rates of suicide in general, totaling 27.81% of the whole world. The Region of the Americas has 15.84% of all suicides in general in the world. The lowest rate in the youth group mentioned above is found in Europe, with 2.38%.

The data presented above refers only to the subcategory 'Self-inflicted injuries', which is a part of the larger category 'Intentional injuries'. The other subcategories are: 'Violence', 'War and civil conflicts' and 'Other intentional injuries'. Another category used by the WHO is 'Unintentional injuries', which has six subcategories: 'Road traffic accidents', 'Poisonings', 'Falls', 'Fires', 'Drownings' and 'Other unintentional injuries'. From this, it can be deduced that the situation is graver and more alarming than what the systematized evidence about suicides suggests. Many cases that are included in the category 'Unintentional injuries' are in fact suicide cases, but this is almost impossible to prove.

For the main causes of youth suicide, specialists point to a varied list, in which we find highlighted: loneliness, family problems, intra-familiar violence, emotional problems, physical or psychological violence of peers, failure in school, depression, grave or incurable diseases, mental problems, economic difficulties, alcohol and illegal drug usage, uncertain future and discrimination against homosexual orientation.

The greatest tendency for suicide is among homosexual youth, who present twice as much risk as other groups, due to problems of prejudice, fear of family and friends' reactions, or a problem of self-identity that may lead them to isolation (Pérez, Borrás, Zubieta, 2008). It is estimated that this last proportion is even bigger, taking into account that many homosexuals commit suicide without ever revealing their sexual orientation.

These are factors that may originate suicide tendencies. However, at the bottom of it all lie other aspects that are even more relevant, such as low self-esteem and difficulties in dealing with sufferings.

When it is said that depression, alcohol and illegal drugs, and loneliness are motivators, it is important to remember that they do not constitute causes per se, because they are the product of previous problematic situations. That is to say, other problems lead the individual to depression, drugs or even to loneliness.

Stories of suicide in the family or among acquaintances are also an important risk factor. A study conducted by the Mexican Institute of Social Security has attested that after such events, in about 30 to 40% of the families involved, there is another family member who also tries to commit suicide. Such attestation contributes largely to preventive measures, including special care for family and friends of youngsters who have committed suicide.

Research conducted by Dagenais (2011) suggests the hypothesis that suicide has the identity as a target, although in a differentiated angle, for it does not portray the person in their singularity, but in a "transpersonal identity". In his analysis, young people may assume, in their journey to adulthood, an attitude of rejection or fear of becoming adults. Such situations may usher them on to suicide. For that reason, he considers the suicide of young people to be a pathology of the contemporary transition to adulthood. He suggests the use of Durkheim's categories of anomic suicide and fatalistic suicide as a basis for analysis; for he believes it is a case of refusal and disruption of social norms and rules. Dagenais considers that, in a general way, the suicide of young people appears as a rebuff against the proposed existence presented to them.

It is necessary to incorporate in this reflection two more categories of suicide also proposed by Durkheim: the egoistical suicide and the hybrid category[1]. Durkheim has established his whole typology using as a basic criterion the motives of suicide. Therefore, it seems to be undeniable that, in some cases, the egocentric dimension of the adopted action stands out, and private interests outweigh the interests of groups of coexistence, especially in suicides of young people. Secondly, the egoistical suicide is the most common in contexts of greater individualism, which is the case in the societies presently studied.

Finally, it is Durkheim himself that adds hybrid types to his classification, among which is found the *ego-anomic*, which associates the egoistical type with the anomic, in a mixture that favors the analysis of cases that present unequivocal characteristics of both types, to the point of it not being possible to establish prevalence.

Suicide has been an underestimated problem for various reasons:

a) It is surrounded by many different taboos and prejudices. It is relatively usual that families facing a consummated fact try to hide the signs of the suicide. Various motives contribute to such behavior, like religious orientations (mainly the Christian faith, which is predominant in the Latin-American region); and the attitude of trying to preserve family privacy by omitting to mention individual or family problems that might have led to such an end.

As an example of this, according to the Pan-American Health Organization (PAHO) in Guatemala, family oppression and lack of opportunities contribute greatly to the suicide rate among young people. Nevertheless, relatives usually hide the circumstances or even the suicide itself due to prejudices, which leaves health authorities to identify it only by the

---

1 The suicide typology established by Durkheim in his classic work "Suicide" contains three basic types: the "egoistical suicide", resulting from the supremacy of individual interests over social ones, that is to say stemming "from an unmeasured individuation" (Durkheim, 2000, p. 259); the "altruistic suicide" which, if it is not committed, leads to dishonor, and therefore is not the result of an *a priori* wish to end one's own life; and the "anomic suicide", which is a consequence of fragilities in the regulation of social life and a fairly common type in moments of social or economic crisis. A fourth type is briefly mentioned by Durkheim, the "fatalistic suicide" which, unlike anomic suicide, derives from excessive social regulation. Hybrid types of suicide are those that are characterized by two basic types. They can be ego-anomic, anomic-altruistic or ego-altruistic.

method used, such as the those consummated by hanging and some kinds of poison, which seem evidently to be cases of suicide.

b) The manifestations of suicidal tendencies are very subtle, which result in great difficulty in finding out and confirming if a certain act was motivated or not by a desire for suicide.

Considering the peculiarities surrounding youth reality, especially concerning risk behaviors, doubts in the analysis of certain facts are very frequent. However, this is not about fallibility in determining the facts, nor is it desired to indicate that everybody who adopts these behaviors is willing to take their own lives, but it must be understood that these behaviors may favor the genesis of suicidal tendencies.

Moreover, these behaviors confuse and make it difficult to analyze those suicide cases that present themselves disguised by a supposed 'accidental' feature. Such is the case of car accidents, fights, intoxications and poisonings, radical sports, certain games with friends etc., which are behaviors that may reveal a self-destructive disposition.

c) Because of the reasons listed above, the obstacles in notification of cases, the social prejudices and the difficulty in implementing preventive measures contribute largely to the under-appreciation of the problem from the social as well as governmental point of view.

But as precarious as notifications may be, the data is still terrifying. The Cuban assessor from PAHO, Pérez Barrero (2007), has reported that in Argentina three million minors have already thought about or tried to commit suicide and eleven million children and youths have received treatment for depression. In Chile, according to the same assessor, the mortality rate among street children is eleven times higher than among other children, and almost half of the deaths are by suicide.

In general, the principal means used have been hanging, firing weapons and poisoning by ingestion of medicines. The first is used more often by men, whose tendency is to look for quicker and more violent methods. The last is used more often by women, who resort to 'softer' means, which is the reason why they can sometimes receive help and be saved.

The Problem: life without value

Suicide has always been a nebulous subject, for it entails life questions which centuries of philosophy, science and religion are still insufficient to answer. If the purpose of suicide is intended to free a person from suffering by ending their own life, what expectations, beyond that of supposed relief, do they have about what is to come? Or yet, what is the suffering and how do we learn to deal with it? The theme of suicide makes us face core questions about life. It brings a quest right to our door: to comprehend the meaning of life and, consequently, the meaning of death. What is life to someone who wants to get rid of it? What does a person expect of death when they seek to go beyond the dimension of life?

Albert Camus begins *The Myth of Sisyphus* by declaring that suicide is the only serious philosophical problem, because it makes us analyze whether life is worth living, which he considers to be the core question of philosophy. Voluntary death has always been marked by the anxiety and awkwardness it leaves in the social environment where it occurs. Such repercussion expresses the bonds and the developments between the suicide act and the values and beliefs of a particular age. Ignorance of the sense and meaning of the act of suicide has produced uncountable taboos throughout the history of humanity, particularly in the West. The advent of instrumental reason and modern science was not enough to overcome mythological knowledge and religious dogmas rooted for so many centuries.

Interpretations of suicide have been varied (Minois, 1998). It has meant failure, heroism, strategies to save one's soul, demonic disturbance, and mental illness, among many other things. Depending on the interpretation, social reactions have ranged from glorification of the act, to condemnation and indignation in the face of failure to observe basic duties towards oneself and society and, from a certain point of view, God. From this last perspective, in the past, once the person was dead, their family would suffer especially if they were of plebeian origin. Besides losing their possessions, the whole family was discriminated against sometimes over the course of consecutive generations.

Notwithstanding the absence of plausible explanations, religious dogmas and popular beliefs were sufficient to create ostensive social rituals and behaviors against suicides and their families.

Summing up, it is possible to affirm that the development of such moral conducts and codes reflects certain ideas in modern times, which justifies partially the old origins of many families' denials of a suicide among their own. The prejudices that surround this situation, in addition to the invasion to which the family may have to submit in the search for possible causes of the event, constitute thorough and compelling reasons for such a denial. Furthermore, the suicide per se, when it is evidence of disenchantment or disillusionment with life, indicates the existence of a tension in a determined context.

The Enlightenment promoted the necessary conditions for the development of individualism when capitalism emerged, accompanied by the desire to ensure the supremacy of reason over the then-prevalent dogmatism, and favoring the construction of opportune values and behaviors to the breaking or enfeeblement of social bonds. In that context, the progressive detachment from philosophy as the basic source of reflection on essential life questions consolidated a new social era, designed by pragmatism and immediacy; a time of ruptures with the previous lifestyle.

It is not by chance that suicide rates increased in the period of the beginning of capitalism (Minois, 1998). Since Durkheim, it has been known that suicide is an expression of the rupture of social bonds. It reveals problems and questions about life in a determined social, economic, political, cultural, and religious context, in a multidimensional movement that involves the individual and the collective, the objective and the subjective, the biological, the psychological and the social.

Nowadays, when we live what Lipovetsky (2005) calls "the twilight of duty" and "the painless ethics", it is possible to say that the laxity of the rules of social interaction has brought along complex ambiguities and ambivalences. The end of "duty", understood as sacrifice and discipline, carries along with it the beginning of free choice, the opening of life to uncountable possibilities of becoming. The expression "painless ethics" conveys an action without sacrifices, guided by new and ephemeral social values directed to the here and now. Even with the emphasis on the individual, the demand for an ethic is still valid, but only if it incurs neither inconveniences nor burdens. As the author states, this is a "minimalist ethic", directed at ensuring only what is strictly necessary and individually acceptable to social interaction. It is a narcissistic and hedonist ethic, based on immediate and ephemeral pleasure. It must be remarked that these processes reveal the weakening of social bonds, and create social contexts that are favorable to suicide.

The new is always seen as better than the old. Pragmatism and immediacy are converted into values. Under the individualistic optic and in the face of so many social, ethnic, religious, political, sexual and emotional differences, tolerance becomes of the utmost importance. Nonetheless, to tolerate difference has changed into a synonym of 'putting up with difference' or 'enduring the difference', in a strict sense, and it is not used in the sense of 'accepting the difference' or, as Cortella and La Taille (2009) say, in the sense of "sheltering". In reality, the term *to tolerate* is very limited for such purposes, because it is possible to endure something in different ways, including by contingency, without respecting the right of another person to be different. Conceptualized like this, tolerance brings along the legitimacy to impose boundaries to the respect of differences.

It is important to perceive that this is a fertile ground for the exercise of alterity, which is another concept poorly understood. Alterity incites us to see the other as one of us and not as a stranger, according to the analysis of Cortella and La Taille (2009). Being one of us, the other is part of the environment we live in, and as such they must be respected in their own way. This is another difficult aspect to be reflected upon, for it leads to two seemingly mutually-exclusive paths: the defense of particular ethics disregarding universal principles on the one hand, and a 'universalized particular ethic' on the other. This expression intends to highlight that there are no delineations of a universal ethic yet and, therefore, any attempt will still be the result of the imposition of some particular ethic. The history of religion is a particularly relevant example in that analysis.

Notwithstanding the fact that we do not have a universal ethic (yet), the lack of universal ethical parameters makes it truly impossible to build points of convergence that favor the constitution of values and behaviors that respect life. The real possibilities of building a universal ethic, in spite of not being the focus of the present text, touches this moment of reflection, for they present themselves as the only plausible way to establish parameters that transcend geographical, social, political, economic, cultural and religious limits and enable communication around essential principles and values. The universal ethic must be thought of as something that is to come and that could be under construction.

To think about moral values, virtues, and ethics, presupposes a clear and aware notion of what is to come. It is impossible to think about ethics and morals without habits, without the past, without the future, without time in the process. The ethical-moral dimension implies always a cultural substrate and a notion of what should be.

In circumstances of intolerance and non-acceptance, distinguished by the flagrant absence of ethical reflections that might be opportune to substantive changes in ways of thinking and acting, young people have been great victims of a lack of essential and consistent values to direct them.

They live in very heterogeneous groups, where different values, diverse ethical-moral attitudes and multiple behaviors are presented. An unstable and fragile ethical conscience is shaken at every difficulty or discontentment, which may lead the person to a general and permanent state of dissatisfaction with life and with the world, for it is the ethical dimension that articulates our rationality and our affection.

Our reactions to the notions of right and wrong, good and bad, virtuous and evil are also emotional and not only rational. The moral principles and their exercise lead to distinct emotional reactions, both in intensity and in type. If the moral conduct is based only on what is supposedly a pleasure, then it is certain an adverse situation may become unbearable, because it will be contrary to the desire (egoistic) and to the understanding (limited).

In the opposite situation, elevated principles and moral values, when lived and internalized, may constitute a dependable support in the face of adversities. The ethical fragility, in its turn, will reverberate in emotional and affective enfeeblement.

Tugendhat (2007) analyzes that in current times, when diverse and contradictory conceptions of morals coexist; the necessity of the justification of moral judgments is clear. After all, how can one be demanded to follow a determined moral orientation if one does not understand it, if one has not internalized it or, even worse, if one disagrees with it? For Tugendhat, it is necessary to the individual to recognize moral rules as their own rules, that is to say, that these rules were established by a collectivity which they feel a part of and which they respect. Without that condition, there are no reasons to follow them. This means that the emotional and affectional connection with social rules is inherent in living healthy social experiences fully.

In the same way, it is plausible to think that the difficult moments in life, if not analyzed under parameters that make them easier to be absorbed and overcome, be it through a pragmatic, a philosophical or a religious view, may constitute insurmountable situations, and fertile ground for radical solutions such as suicide.

It is evident under these guidelines that the ethical crisis of young people is not focused on themselves. It is a problem of society as a whole, although it is magnified in youth.

We are in the middle of a crisis of values. It is not a crisis of behavior, as it is frequently studied in the family or in schools, but a crisis of an individual idea of life. Cortella and La Taille (2009) observe that it is a mistake to focus on conduct, because it is not a case of looking for new strategies to make children and youth behave in a supposedly more adequate way; instead it is a question of problematizing the crisis of collective life values.

As part of the corollary of such a crisis, parents in some countries have reduced their expectations that their children will have a better future than their own, according to the data provided by ECLAC (2011) for years 2005 and 2006. This is the case of the Dominican Republic (where the rate of citizens who believe their children will have a better life than own fell from 65% in 2005 to 28.7% in 2006), Guatemala (from 60% to 40.5%), Costa Rica (from 50% to 39.4%), El Salvador (from 43% to 22.8%) and Chile (from 76% to 71.9%). In our view, parents' disenchantment with the possibilities of improvement in their children's living conditions is an indicator of hopelessness. Education no longer appears as an instrument of social mobility, while structural unemployment has driven many young people to illegal ways of occupying their time. According to Gil Calvo (2011), alongside youth trajectories predetermined by class origin, and others defined by accomplished academic merits, there are an uncountable number of young people who cannot achieve success in either of these ways; many others take on yet more uncertain paths, such as getting involved with gangs. Be that as it may, whatever the path, the possibilities of success are impossible to foresee for many young people.

In a social reality interspersed with so many uncertainties, and in the face of difficulties in social development and relationships with parents, and those created by young people themselves, problems in making choices and following a planned course are completely understandable. The future is not susceptible to reliable planning anymore.

Suicide has been studied in its micro and macro dimensions and separated in polarities that prioritize either society or the individual (Minayo, Cavalcante and Souza, 2006). Nonetheless, there have been significant changes in the established approaches, in which it is possible to observe the perception that this phenomenon requires interdisciplinary measures, due to its multifaceted and relational nature, for it deals with the comprehension not only of individual motivations and dramas, but also of the relationships between individual and society, as well as the social contexts themselves, which reveals the possibilities of the increase or decrease of suicide rates in a given moment.

Durkheim (1977) has elaborated a conceptual and categorical structure with incontestable validity in the study of the theme, and has also demonstrated the sociological aspect of the phenomenon, placing it in the relationship between the individual and society. However, the necessity to traverse dichotomies, polarities or unilateral approaches has propelled the pursuit for more integrative methods of analyzing the different aspects inherent in suicide processes.

Such demands of rigor and carefulness placed on the researcher are founded on the unmistakable fact that, when individuals take their own lives in the face of difficult moments, suicide shows that their life has lost all meaning. Behind every suicide there is a lost meaning of life.

But after all, what gives life meaning? That is an eminent philosophical question that can be supposedly answered by different or complementary views, which range from philosophical perspectives in a strict sense to common sense, passing through religious doctrines. But no matter how, having a meaning capable of offering some support and foundation to life, with all its adversities and challenges, is an essential condition to keeping oneself alive.

The meaning of life, however, does not definitively exist on the level of discourse. The reflection must be enriched by and integrated with individual and collective life experiences. And here lies another problem to be observed: the quality of the social experience to which young people are subjected is not simply about social experience as a mere passage through the facts, but as a perceived, aware, thought and felt experience.

In his classic essay *The Narrator*, Benjamin (1994a) proclaims the value of the transmission of knowledge acquired from experience, inherited from the past, recreated and created in the reflection with the present. In *Experience and Poverty*, the same author (1994b) analyzes the impoverishment to which modern societies are subjected, although remarkably it is the age of the supremacy of information. Received information is structured in a logic that confines the subject's possibilities of reflection, away from the narrative that makes them think and, presumably, makes them assimilate and recreate what they are being told. As Bondía (2002, p. 21-22) says, information is neither experience nor does it generate experience, in spite of "the contemporary emphasis on the information, on being informed, and the whole rhetoric aimed at making us informing and informed subjects."

It is on this ground, impoverished by the superficial and the ephemeral, that new values are being outlined. Sanabria (2001, p. 114) is emphatic that: "the crisis which Western Society is facing is global: political, economic, social, cultural, but, fundamentally, moral. The meaning of life has been lost (...) Disorientation is general."

In general terms, the capacity to transcend, the only way to encounter oneself and the world, has been lost. The inheritance from the classical Greeks or from the pre-Hispanic civilizations, culturally so rich and so full of meaning, such as the Mayas, Incas and Aztecs, seems to have volatilized.

This point of view enlightens the frequent mistake of imputing to youth certain moral transformations, for such transformations concern the whole social body, even though they assume specific and exponential nuances in youth groups. On the other hand, the lack of consistent, elevated and life-essential values, as well as the void in the meaning of life have a dramatic effect in young people's experiences, inasmuch as they are aggravated by their condition of vulnerability.

Instead of experiences with what is conventionally known as 'ethical pluralism', in reference to the rising diversity of values and behaviors, there is a big void: of values, of meanings, and of ethics.

The precariousness of material conditions of existence also offers its contribution to the aggravation of young people's situation in Latin America and the Caribbean. Emblematically, a Guatemalan youth from the municipality of Nebaj, department of Quiché, where 48 young people have committed suicide in six years, concludes that young people take their lives for reasons of hopelessness and lack of means to confront their problems:

> We begin to work because the death of our lives leaves a destroyed surrounding. Young people are not prepared to face their problems. The ones with more initiative choose the 'pandillas'[2] while the weak ones opt for suicide. Young people are going through a confusing time, just as the country is. The solution is to help the families, and the authorities must have the proper means to look after young people with problems and contribute with a sustainable development capable of creating opportunities. (Eduardo Cruz, a group leader in the Nahual Association)[3]

In Conclusion

The concerns expressed here originated from empirical indications must be elevated to other levels. The elaboration of public policies targeting the prevention of youth suicide and the support and care for family and friends of young people who have committed suicide constitutes the beginning of complex social intervention, which requires interdisciplinary

---

2   A kind of gang.
3   Testimony made available by Lorena Seijo, '¿Jóvenes sin esperanza?' on the PAHO official website: http://www.paho.org/spanish/DD/PIN/Numero18_box01.htm. Translation by the author from the original text in Spanish: "Empezamos a trabajar porque nuestra juventud se muere, y deja destrozado su entorno. Los jóvenes no están preparados para afrontar sus problemas; los que tienen más iniciativa eligen las pandillas y los débiles optan por el suicidio. Los jóvenes pasan por un momento confuso, como el país. La solución es ayudar a las familias y que las autoridades aporten los medios para atender a jóvenes con problemas y contribuir a un desarrollo sostenible que dé oportunidades."

work and, above all, the political will of authorities to intervene in such a problematic issue.

To discuss with young people themes like life and the meaning of life, the act of living, the dramas of the human existence, the essential moral values, can be a measure to support fruitful reflections, which may propitiate more consistent thoughts and actions. Issues of this nature must not be circumscribed to specific areas or domains, due to its centrality to human existence itself. Religions have provided a privileged space to reflect on these topics, but such a subject is transversal and any quotidian matter may become an access door to what is essential.

Boff (2003) teaches that ethics reveals itself when the other shows up in front of us. Some ethic is implemented in this relationship with the other, but what is the ethic that we want? Even without a clear awareness of the answer, it is comforting to know that as long as there is the other in front of us an ethical relation is established, which demonstrates and reaffirms permanently that the ethical dimension is constitutive of social life. Such certainty and conscience produce the hope that young people and adults will still be able to share noble moral principles, with the respect and value of life as the primary source of the ways of living.

Bibliography

Benjamin, W. (1994a) O Narrador, in *Magia e técnica, arte e política: ensaios sobre literatura e história da cultura*, São Paulo, Brasiliense, pp. 197-221.

Benjamin, W. (1994b) Experiência e pobreza, in *Magia e técnica, arte e política: ensaios sobre literatura e história da cultura*, São Paulo, Brasiliense, pp. 114-119.

Bondía, J.L. (2002) Notas sobre a experiência e o saber de experiência, *Revista Brasileira de Educação*, São Paulo, ANPED, pp. 20-28.

Boff, L. (2003) *Ética e moral: a busca dos fundamentos*, Rio de Janeiro, Vozes.

Cortella, M. S. and La Taille, Y. de (2009) *Nos labirintos da moral*, São Paulo: Papirus 7 Mares.

Dagenais, D. (2011) Le suicide des jeunes: une pathologie du devenir adulte contemporain, *Recherches sociographiques*, LII(1), Québec, Université Laval, pp. 71-104.

Durkheim, É. (1977) *O Suicídio: estudo de sociologia*, Lisboa, Editorial Presença/Martins Fontes.

Economic Commission For Latin American And The Caribbean (ECLAC) (2011) Base de datos y publicaciones estadísticas, available at: http://websie.eclac.cl/sisgen/ConsultaIntegrada.asp?idAplicacion=12&idTema=203&idioma (accessed June 15, 2011).

Gil Calvo, E. (2011) A roda da fortuna: viagem à temporalidade juvenil, in Pais, J. M., Bendit, R. and Ferreira, V. S. (eds) *Jovens e rumos*, Lisboa, ICS/Imprensa de Ciências Sociais, pp. 39-57.

Lipovetsky, G. (2005) *A sociedade pós-moralista: o crepúsculo do dever e a ética indolor dos novos tempos democráticos*, São Paulo, Manole.

Minayo, M. C. de S., Cavalcante, F. G. and de Souza, E. R. (2006) Methodological proposal for studying suicide as a complex phenomenon, *Cadernos de Saúde Pública, 22(8)*, pp. 1587-1596.

Minois, G. (1998) *História do suicídio: a sociedade ocidental perante a morte voluntária*, Lisboa, Teorema.

Pan American Health Organization (PAHO) (2010) *Health Information and Analysis Project*, available at: http://www.paho.org/English/SHA/coredata/tabulator/newTabulator.htm (accessed November 5, 2010).

Pérez, M., Borrás, J. J. and Zubieta, X. (2008) *El suicídio entre jóvenes homosexuales*, available at: http://www.soitu.es/soitu/2008/08/19/sexo/1219146036_880973. html (accessed May 20, 2009).

Pérez Barrero, S. (2007) *El suicidio de niños y jóvenes*, Portal Jurídico Peruano, available at: http://www.ciberjure.com.pe/index2.php?option=com_content&do_ pdf=1&id=1807 (accessed April 18, 2009).

Reis, V. (2008) Lo tradicional y lo nuevo en las experiencias juveniles, in *XV Congreso Internacional de Historia Oral*, Guadalajara, México: CD-Rom.

Sanabria, J. R. (2001) Ética y postmodernidad. Dikaiosyne, *Revista de Filosofía Práctica, 6,* Mérida/Venezuela, Universidad de Los Andes, pp. 93-121.

Tejeda, E. and Reis, V. (2008) *En búsqueda de visibilidad: la condición juvenil en América Latina y el Caribe*, Chile, Colectivo Latinoamericano de Jóvenes, W. K. Kellogg Foundation, FLACSO, Foundation Friedrich Ebert Stiftung.

Tugendhat, E. (2007) Reflexões sobre o que significa justificar juízos morais, in de Brite, A. N. (ed) *Ética: questões de fundamentação* (pp. 19-35), Brasília, Editora UnB.

World Health Organization (WHO) (2011a) *Global Health Observatory*, available at: http://www.who.int/gho/en/ (accessed June 15, 2011).

World Health Organization (WHO) (2011b) *Causes of Death 2008, Summary Tables* available at: http://www.who.int/healthinfo/global_burden_disease/estimates_regional/en/index.html (accessed June 15, 2011).

Conclusion

Researchers, research and the development of youth policy: some considerations about the nature of evidence

Marc Molgat, Eugénie Boudreau and Marina Hahn-Bleibtreu

We would like to conclude this book by addressing a few practical considerations about the role of researchers in the development of policies for young people. If the various contributions to this book do not dwell directly on these practical aspects, the reader can nonetheless gain insights as to their importance when considering the roles researchers play in youth policy. We will begin this short conclusion by first highlighting how the chapters, when taken as a whole, reveal a fundamental tension about how to approach youth from both research and policy perspectives. We will then outline, in parallel to this tension, how research 'evidence' may be integrated into the policy development process.

The contributors to this volume refer in various ways to two different perspectives on young people. On the one hand, young people can be seen as individuals who need to be helped along in the development of their personal skills and capacities in order to better prepare them to complete high school, to pursue higher education and training, to find and maintain employment, to build positive relationships, to construct their identities, etc. This approach, one could argue, essentially leads to policies, programmes and measures that are geared to fostering the *adaptation* of young people to society, to labour and housing market conditions, to discourses about the so-called 'knowledge-based economy', and to a host of social and psychological prescriptions concerning the prevention of risk behaviours in the fields of youth justice, health and education, to name but a few.

On the other hand, young people can be seen as social actors who have the ability to bring about social change, and to make transitions between institutional settings, families and relationships, but face various structural obstacles in doing so, ranging from gender inequality to constraining market structures, and from socioeconomic disparities to rigid and out-of-sync policies that affect youth. From this perspective, policies would need to consider how to *support* young people, not only by helping them individually to succeed but also by intervening in the obstacles they face, i.e. by changing and strengthening the institutions that they must deal with on a regular basis. This would lead to policies based more on rights, citizenship and integration than on adaptation to existing contexts and restrictive social and psychological norms.

These theoretical outlooks provide a very general framework for thinking about youth policy, and are amenable to many researchers' ways of approaching and analyzing policy. Although this is a useful step in bridging the worlds of research and policy, it does not deal with some of the more practical considerations about how policy is forged in relation to researchers' work. Of course, we all know that knowledge deriving from research in the social sciences plays a role in the development of policy. But as Anthony Giddens (1990) pointed out more than twenty years ago, social scientific knowledge in late modern societies is uncertain and continually subjected to revision, because the speed of social change can suddenly alter or invalidate previously accepted knowledge, analyses and hypotheses (or 'evidence' if one prefers to employ the term currently in vogue in policy making arenas). Paradoxically, in this specific context, the status of scientific knowledge is heightened, particularly from the point of view of institutions, in part because they can consider this knowledge as reliable, and in part because they can use this knowledge to constantly revise their practices. In this way, 'expert' knowledge – as opposed to experiential knowledge – acquires a particularly strong legitimacy for political decision-makers. It is in this setting that policy makers, including those involved in youth policies, express a need for hard facts in developing 'evidence-based policy'.

But what is evidence-based policy exactly, whether in the area of youth or in other policy dossiers? This question can be answered relatively simply: it concerns the use of research to define policy, above all at the level of directives and measures, by allowing policymakers to be informed and to discuss relevant matters before decisions are made and actions defined. Ideally, this enables policymakers to discuss not only with interested parties but also with experts, and to actively acquire a reliable base of information. The effects of policy-related and professional actions are then analysed so that new knowledge arises in a dynamic fashion, which can in turn be integrated into a continuous cycle of analysis, reflection and evaluation. But above all, it would seem important that this cycle remain open and accessible and that the generation of knowledge not be subject to any binding, predefined structures. Although these principles of openness and accessibility may protect the classic freedom of science and research, it also creates conditions that facilitate innovation in policy and practice. In effect, high quality youth policies cannot remain stagnant, no more than can any field of modern science afford to remain a closed cycle of reproduction of ideas.

As long as the principles of openness and accessibility are resolutely held, the challenge of evidence-based policy does not seem to lie so much in *what* may count as evidence as in *how* it does so. Siurala (2005), who has proposed an integrated approach to youth policy to the Council of Europe, sees evidence-based youth policy as the sign of a "realistic turn" in the area of youth, which considers not only political and moral objectives, but also "accurate information on the social situation of young people across the society and their changing expectations, attitudes and lifestyles" (p. 47). These are best and most reliably presented and analysed by research. Within such a model, although the state would continue to exercise a function of control on policy, it does not determine the substantive course of the generation and application of knowledge. The feedback from an open and plural network of research enables new determinations to be made in youth policy, leading to critical reflection and analysis concerning implementation. In order that such an innovative cycle be put into motion and kept running, the knowledge network must be robust and able to systematically monitor actions, as well as provide reliable empirical information on young people's lives.

This ideal of joining up policy and research is not for all researchers. Indeed, not all researchers may enter the youth policy-making realm, which occurs through having research contributions read or cited directly in the work leading up to policy development, or through direct involvement in policy-making within government departments or agencies. The ability to provide evidence, i.e. to have undertaken and published 'useful' empirical research, is a key to entering this realm, but by far it is not the only criteria of inclusion. In effect, based on our own experiences within policy-making processes, in various capacities, we know that apart from the fit between the concerns of policy and government departments and the researchers' areas of work, many other considerations are at play. There are at least three: 1) the quality of the research, which is often evaluated according to the reputation of researchers among their colleagues (informal contacts between civil servants and researchers seem essential in this respect); 2) the timeliness of research (the more recent, the better); and 3) the ability of researchers to speak out and to convince.

So, from this perspective, researchers face a tall order: they should ideally be well-spoken, have undertaken research very recently, been active in research networks, and received recognition from their peers.

Finally, we would be remiss if we did not refer to the other side of the 'magic triangle' of youth policy development. This triangle of course includes government actors and researchers, but should also incorporate the experiential knowledge of young people and of non-governmental organizations as a form of 'evidence' in the development of youth policy. Ideally, this knowledge would be linked to the expert knowledge produced by youth researchers in the development of youth policy. Examples of this may be found within European youth policy frameworks and strategic action plans, as we outlined in the introduction. Other societies have also included young people's voices and concerns in the construction of youth policies.

But in reality, through these processes, young people who are less organized and who do not benefit from greater levels of socioeconomic and cultural capital may encounter difficulties in having their own voices heard, either because others speak for them in an effort to represent their views (i.e. youth service organizations) or because they are simply not present at the policy development table. In some countries, such as Canada and the United States, it is in fact striking to observe that young people who are in the most marginalized and precarious situations are often not heard in these processes; instead, it is frequently the experts who speak about them, through research that is more often than not focused on the prevention of at-risk behaviours and the ways of making these young people adapt to society. This refers to the first approach we outlined at the beginning of this conclusion, but is not necessarily an accurate reflection of how these young people speak of their own experiences and needs.

From the point of view of young people themselves then, it seems that the role played by their experiential knowledge within the development of youth policies poses some fundamental questions about democracy, participation and power. In an era when governmental institutions want to develop 'evidence-based policy', does young people's knowledge not run the risk of being put aside or simply ignored because it is not stamped by the seal of science? As youth researchers engage with policy-makers in democratic societies, it seems essential for them to reflect about ways to integrate and validate the voices of marginalized youth in the processes that lead to the adoption of policies and interventions that affect them often first and foremost. Many of those contributing to this volume already do so and invite others to follow along such a path.

Bibliography

Giddens, A. (1990) *The Consequences of Modernity*, Stanford, Stanford University Press.

Siurala, L. (2005) *A European Framework for Youth Policy*, Strasbourg, Council of Europe.

Index

About the editors and authors

Marina Hahn-Bleibtreu (Academic market and opinion researcher, University of Vienna) is the former Director of the Austrian Institute for Youth Research (1992-2000) and was Political advisor to the Federal Minister for Social Security and Generations (2000-2002). Until 2011, she was the Deputy Head of Unit for youth policy in the Federal Ministry for Economy, Family and Youth, and responsible for the national implementation of European youth policy objectives and youth research. Since 2012, she has been Coordinator of national and international projects at FAA-Holding, Vienna.

Professor **Marc Molgat** works at the University of Ottawa, where he is also the director of the School of Social Work. His research focuses on transitions to adulthood from the perspective of life course theory. He has studied housing trajectories, relations between young people and their parents, the socio-economic integration patterns of high school dropouts, and youth migration. He has a strong interest in youth policies and how they reflect the socio-economic integration problems facing disadvantaged youth. He has edited the following books: *Vivre la citoyenneté* [Experiencing citizenship] (2000), *La migration des jeunes* [Youth migration] (2004) and *Habiter seul. Un nouveau mode de vie* [Living alone: a new way of life] (2009). He is currently directing a four-year comparative research project on the life course and forms of support of young people enrolled in technical/vocational education in the provinces of Ontario and Quebec, Canada (2011-2015).

René Bendit is a senior researcher at the German Youth Institute. He was member of the Youth Directory Network of Experts on Youth Research and Information at the Council of Europe. He is currently Lecturer at the

Ludwig Maximilian University, Munich and at the Autonomous University of Barcelona, and visiting Professor at the Latin American Faculty of Social Sciences (FLACSO), Buenos Aires. His areas of interest are empirical and theoretical research on youth transitions to adulthood, youth policies in Europe and Latin America, and educational and social integration of young migrants and ethnic minority groups in Europe. His publications include "Youth and Youth Policies in a Globalized World", in M. Tornare (ed) *Monographic City, Youth and Education* (2011), and *Youth Transitions: Processes of social inclusion and patterns of vulnerability in a globalised world* (2008).

Eugénie Boudreau is a Master's student at the School of Political Science at the University of Ottawa, in Canada. From her background in International Development and Globalization and her experiences studying at the Université de Polynésie française and at the Universidad de Lima in Peru, her research interests became directed towards socioeconomic alternatives to a 'development' framework, rural socioeconomic projects, community organization and indigenous/non-indigenous relations and solidarity.

Vincenzo Cicchelli is Associate Professor at Paris Descartes and Research Fellow at Gemass (Paris 4/CNRS). He is the Secretary General of the European sociological association (ESA), chair of the Research Network 'Global, transnational and cosmopolitan sociology' (ESA), and series editor at Brill Publisher (Leiden, Boston) for *Youth in a Globalizing World*. He is currently working on how young people engage with globalization, and on cosmopolitan socialization processes from an international comparative perspective. Among his recent publications are: *L'esprit cosmopolite. Jeunes en mobilité et cultures en Europe* (2012); with Gerôme Truc, *De la mondialisation au cosmopolitisme* (2011); with J. Hamel, O. Galland and C. Pugeault (eds), *La jeunesse n'est plus ce qu'elle était* (2010); and with A. Cavalli and O. Galland (eds), *Deux pays, deux jeunesses. La condition juvénile en France et en Italie* (2008)

Dr. **David Hansen** is Assistant Professor at the University of Kansas in the School of Education where he teaches and maintains an active research program as a graduate faculty member. He completed his doctorate (2001) and post-doctorate experience (2001 to 2007) at the University of Illinois at Urbana-Champaign. He is a developmental scientist with expertise on adolescent development in a variety of out-of-school settings. Dr. Hansen is particularly invested in understanding *how* adolescents from impoverished communities learn 'real-world' skills and competencies needed for adult life and engaged citizenship. His recent publications include "Differences in Developmental Experiences for Commonly Used Categories of Organized Youth Activities: It's Time for a 'Tune-up'"(with Skorupski and Arrington) (2010), *Journal of Applied Developmental Psychology, 31*(6); and "On Measuring Youth Work in the United States: The Role of Qualitative and Quantitative Methods" (with M. J. Crawford) (2011), *Youth and Policy, 107*, pp. 71-81.

Stefan Humpl studied Geography at the University of Vienna and worked for the Institute for Industrial Research until he co-founded 3s Unternehmensberatung GmbH (www.3s.co.at). Dr. Humpl is today managing director and partner of 3s Unternehmensberatung GmbH and chairman of the 3s research laboratory. His main topics of research are higher education development concerning labour market requirements. He is a consultant in curriculum design and the strategic development of educational institutions (vocational education and training (VET) as well as higher education (HE)) and public bodies concerned with VET and HE, but also quality improvement in education. 3s acts as a consulting enterprise for many Austrian and international projects for the support of educational policy (e.g. regional studies for qualification demand, development of the National Qualification Framework, development of the Continuous Vocational Training Survey). 3s also supports the Austrian Public Employment Service through information about job and qualification trends (www.ams.at/qualifikationsbarometer.html).

Wolfgang Gaiser, PhD, is a researcher in social and political participation, as well as in comparative and longitudinal youth studies. He was a Senior Researcher at the German Youth Institute in Munich until 2011. His recent publications include *Youth and Political Participation in Europe* (co-edited with Spannring and Ogris) (2008) and *Who counts on Europe? – An empirical analysis of the younger generation's attitudes in Germany*, published in a special edition of the *Revista de Estudios de Juventud* (2008).

Martina Gille is a sociologist and scientific associate at the German Youth Institute (DJI). Until 2009 she was head of the competence team Youth of the DJI-Survey 2009: AID:A (Aufwachsen in Deutschland: Alltagswelten). She has researched and published on a range of 'youth is-

sues' such as value orientations, gender role attitudes and social and political participation. Her research focus lies on quantitative empirical
youth research and on issues of social change. She edited the book *Jugend in Ost und West seit der Wiedervereinigung. Ergebnisse aus dem
replikativen Längsschnitt des DJI-Jugendsurvey* (2008), in which the results of the three waves of the DJI-Youth Survey (1992, 1997 and 2003)
are presented. Together with Wolfgang Gaiser she contributed to the
book *Soziale und politische Partizipation im Wandel*, (2012) in which the
historical trend data of young people in Germany relating to their living
conditions and their social and political participation are adjusted for the
time period 1992 to 2009.

Helena Helve, PhD, holds the Professorship of Youth Research for the
Master's Programme of Youth Work and Youth Research at Tampere
University in Finland. She has been a professor for the M.A. European
Youth Studies Curriculum Development Project (2009-2011). She is a
chair of the Executive Board of the Finnish University Consortium
YUNET on Youth Research studies coordinated by Helsinki University,
where she is an Adjunct Professor of Sociology and Comparative Religion. She has been Vice president of the European Association for the
Study of Religions (2000-2007), President of the International Sociological Association's Research committee 34 – Sociology of Youth (2002-
2006) and President of the Finnish Youth Research Society (1992-2005).
She has directed several international and national research projects.
Among her publications on youth research and youth work are the co-
edited books *Youth, Work Transition and Wellbeing* (Helve and Evans,
forthcoming, 2012,), *Youth and Social Capital* (Helve and Bynner, 2007)
and *Contemporary Youth Research: Local Expressions and Global Connections* (Helve and Holm, 2005).

Claudia Jacinto, PhD in Sociology in Latin American Studies (Université Paris III, France), is a researcher at the Instituto de Desarrollo
Economico y Social, IDES-CONICET in Argentina, where she coordi-
nates the 'Programa de Estudios en Juventud, Educación y Trabajo'
(PREJET). She is former RedEtis IIEP/UNESCO coordinator and coordi-
nates research into tertiary technical education in Latin America. Her
subjects of interest are youth, education and employment, vocational
training, program evaluation, poverty and inequality. Her recent
publications include: *La construcción social de las trayectorias laborales
de jóvenes. Políticas, instituciones, dispositivos y subjetividades* (ed)

(2010); "Learning from transition projects in Latin America," *Forum 21 European Journal on Child and Youth Policy* (2010); and with A. Fanelli:, "Equidad y educación superior en América Latina. El papel de las carreras universitarias y terciarias," *Revista Iberoamericana de Educación Superior* (2010).

Siyka Kovacheva, PhD, is Associate Professor in Sociology and Social Policy at the University of Plovdiv and Head of the New Europe Centre for Regional Studies in Bulgaria. Her research interests are in the field of youth transitions to employment and parenthood, civic participation, and changes in family life, including gender and intergenerational relations. Her recent publications include *Work-Life Balance: Young Working Parents between Opportunities and Constraints*, (2010) (in Bulgarian); *European Youth Studies: Integrating research, policy and practice* (2011) (co-edited with L. Chisholm and M. Merico), and *1989: Young people and social change after the fall of the Berlin Wall* (2011) (co-edited with C. Leccardi, C. Feixa, H. Reiter and T. Sekulic).

Dina Krauskopf is Chilean, holds an M.A. in Clinical Psychology, and is Professor Emeritus at the Universidad de Costa Rica and Professor in Adolescence in the Juvenile Graduate Studies program at the University of Chile and the University of Development, Chile. She has been a guest lecturer in Masters and Doctorate courses in the field of adolescence, youth and public policy in various countries. She has undertaken research and consultancy work on youth issues relating to fields such as health, violence, pregnancy, education, identity, social participation and human rights. Her national and regional work has brought her into close contact with United Nations agencies and various international organizations. She participated in the formulation of national youth policies in Nicaragua, Costa Rica, Panama and Guatemala. Some of her recent publications include *Youth Participation in Latin America – Policies and Developments* (2009); *Voluntary Service, Youth Development and Non-formal Education* (2008); and *Youth in Latin America and the Caribbean: Social Dimensions, Subjectivities and Life Strategies* (2006).

Carmen Leccardi is Professor of Cultural Sociology and Director of the PhD program in Applied Sociology and Methodology of Social Research at the Department of Sociology and Social Research, University of Milan-Bicocca, Italy. She has researched extensively in the field of youth cultures, cultural change, generations and gender, and time experience.

Co-editor (1999-2009) of the Sage journal Time & Society, now consulting editor of the same, she was vice-president for Europe of the International Sociological Association, Research Committee 'Sociology of Youth' (2006-2010). Her recent books include *1989. Young people and Social Change after the Fall of the Berlin Wall* (2011) (co-edited with C. Feixa, S. Kovacheva, H. Reiter, T. Sekulic); *Sociologie del tempo* [Sociologies of Time] (2009); *A New Youth? Young People, Generations and Family Life* (co-edited with E. Ruspini) (2006); *Sociologia della vita quotidiana* [Sociology of Everyday Life] (with P. Jedlowski) (2003); *Tra i generi* [In-between Genders] (2002).

Sunaina Maira is Professor of Asian American Studies at the University of California, Davis. Maira's teaching and research interests focus on youth, popular culture, South Asian, Muslim and Arab American communities, and U.S. empire. She is the author of *Desis in the House: Indian American Youth Culture in New York City* (2002) and co-editor of *Youthscapes: The Popular, the National, the Global* and *Contours of the Heart: South Asians Map North America* (with Rajini Srikanth), which won the American Book Award in 1997. Her latest book, *Missing: Youth, Citizenship, and Empire After 9/11* is on South Asian Muslim immigrant youth in the U.S. and issues of citizenship and empire after 9/11.

Veronica Millenaar is an Argentinean sociologist and a PhD candidate at the Universidad de Buenos Aires. She has a doctoral scholarship from CONICET and is a student researcher at the Instituto de Desarrollo Económico y Social, where she is a member of PREJET (Programa de Estudios sobre Juventud Educación y Trabajo) coordinated by Claudia Jacinto. Her areas of research are vocational training and training programmes, education and labour trajectories and gender. Some of her recent publications include: "Los nuevos saberes para la inserción laboral. Formación para el trabajo con jóvenes vulnerables en la Argentina", in *Revista mexicana de investigación educativa* (with C. Jacinto) (in press); "La incidencia de la formación para el trabajo en la construcción de trayectorias laborales de mujeres jóvenes" in C. Jacinto (ed) *La construcción social de las trayectorias laborales de jóvenes. Políticas, instituciones, dispositivos y subjetividades* (2010)

Ana Miranda, Ph D. Social Sciences, is the Academic Coordinator of the Youth Research Program at the Latin American School of Social Sciences (FLACSO) in Argentina. She is also Researcher for the National

Council for Scientific and Technological Research of Argentina (CONI-CET). Her areas of specialization are youth studies, economics of education, and social policies. Her main publications include "Job integration of young people in Argentina", in R. Bendit and M. Hahn-Bleibtreu (eds) *Youth transitions: processes of social inclusion and patterns of vulnerability in a globalised world* (2008); *La nueva condición joven: educación, desigualdad, empleo* (2007); and *Cada vez más necesaria, cada vez más insuficiente: la escuela media en épocas de globalización* (with D. Filmus, C. Kaplan and M. Moragues) (2001) (also translated into Portuguese).

Dr. **Ngan Pun Ngai** is Professor of the Department of Social Work at the Chinese University of Hong Kong, in Hong Kong Special Administrative Region, China. From 2006-2010 he was President of the International Sociological Association Research Committee 34: Sociology of Youth. He has previously worked as a frontline social worker, and later as Executive Secretary for the Hong Kong Federation of Youth Groups. His research and publications span a wide range in youth policy, youth services, and social work fields, covering China, Hong Kong and Macau such as: children and youth centers services, operation of youth work organizations, summer programs for young people, youth unemployment, youth policy formulation, youth participation and legislation, youth problems, youth support for aged parents, whole-person development strategies for young people, delinquent behavior, social work education, and social work services. Currently, he is Associate Director of the Editorial Board of the *Journal of Youth Research*, Guangzhou Youth Institute of Hong Kong Macau and Guangzhou, China, and member of the Editorial Advisory Board of numerous international academic journals such as *Youth Studies Ireland; YOUNG – Nordic Journal of Youth Research; Journal of Comparative Social Welfare;* Sociopedia.isa, and the journal *Social Modernity.*

Eva Proinger studied at the University of Vienna and holds a diploma degree in Educational Science. Her fields of specialization were media pedagogy and adult education with a focus on the use of video in school teaching. After graduation she worked in the field of special education and accessible adult education. Since 2010 she has been assisting in research and consulting projects at 3s, with a focus on vocational education and training, and the tertiary sector. Her fields of work include quantitative and qualitative analyses of labour market needs, and the analysis of demand and acceptance in study programs for universities and universities of applied sciences. Presently, she is working on a project to ensure future skills needs in the renewable energy sector and a Leonardo da Vinci/EQAVET project for further professionalization of Quality Managers by developing supportive training and certification models (VET-CERT).

Alejo Ramírez is the Secretary General of the Ibero-American Youth Organization (OIJ), an international multi-governmental organization created in 1992 to promote cooperation on youth between the 21 Iberoamerican countries. The OIJ is headquartered in Madrid and has a regional office in Buenos Aires. Ramirez was born in Temperley, Buenos Aires, Argentina, and is 38 years old. He is a professional journalist (Instituto Grafo-Técnico, 1998) and graduated in social communication (UCES, 2001) with a specialization in corporate communication. He also completed postgraduate studies in film semiotics (Escuela Superior de Periodismo, 1999) and on youth and employment (FLACSO, 2009). Between 2002 and 2003 was Associate Professor of Sociology at UCES.

Vânia Reis is Professor at the Federal University of Piauí (Brazil), in the Social Work Department, and collaborator in the Post-Graduate Program in Public Policies. She received her Ph.D. from the Pontifical Catholic University of São Paulo (PUC-SP), with internship in the Autonomous University of Barcelona. She is coordinator of the Research Group on Families and Generations (FAMGER). She has focused her studies and research in the fields of youth and family. She is currently developing research about suicide among young people and about poor families in Teresina. Her most recent publications deal with youth sexuality and affection, and youth conditions in Teresina, the Northeast of Brazil, Latin America and the Caribbean.

Susannah Taylor is a doctoral student in the School of Social Work at the University of Ottawa in Canada. She holds a B.A in Contemporary Studies and English, and a Master's in Social Work. Her research mainly concerns youth, their transitions to adulthood, youth related policy and homelessness. Susannah's Masters research (entitled '*Entre le sans toit et le chez-soi. Une enquête sur les parcours de vie et la signification du chez soi des jeunes de la rue à Ottawa*') explored the significance of both the street and the concept of home in the transitions of street involved youth. Susannah recently co-authored *The transitions of at-risk youth*

Find our JOURNALS on
www.budrich-journals.de

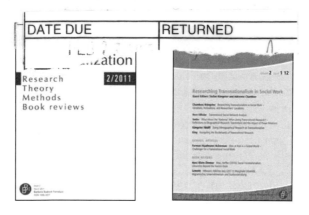

DATE DUE	RETURNED

INFORMATION

- **Download of single articles**

- **Print + Online Subscription**

- **Free Content:**
  TOCs, editorials, book reviews

Verlag Barbara Budrich •
Barbara Budrich Publishers
Stauffenbergstr. 7. D-51379 Leverkusen Opladen
Tel +49 (0)2171.344.594 • Fax +49 (0)2171.344.693 •
info@budrich-journals.de

www.budrich-journals.de

from adolescence to adulthood, a report for Human Resources and Skills Development Canada.

Dr **Howard Williamson** is Professor of European Youth Policy at the University of Glamorgan, in Wales, United Kingdom. Previously he worked at the universities of Oxford, Cardiff and Copenhagen. He has researched and published widely on a range of 'youth issues' such as learning, justice, substance misuse, exclusion and citizenship at European and national levels. Currently he co-ordinates the Council of Europe's international reviews of national youth policies. One of his more recent books is *The Milltown Boys Revisited* (2004), a follow-up study of a group of men he first wrote about when they were young offenders in the 1970s. He has also written a seminal text on youth policy in Europe: *Supporting Young People in Europe: principles, policy and practice* (2001), and, with various co-editors, has edited three volumes of the *History of Youth Work in Europe* (2009, 2010, 2012).

Professor **Johanna Wyn** is Director of the Youth Research Centre in the Melbourne Graduate School of Education at The University of Melbourne, Australia. Her work focuses on the interface between young people's learning and wellbeing in formal and informal educational settings, on young people's transitions and on the question of what kinds of knowledge and skills professionals who work with young people in these settings need in the 21st Century. Her recent books are: *Youth and Society: exploring the social dynamics of youth*, with Rob White (2004, 2007, and in 2011 a Canadian edition with Rob White and Patrizia Albanese); *Youth Health and Welfare (2009)*; *Touching the Future: Building Skills for Life and Work* (2009); *The Making of a Generation*, with Lesley Andres (2010) and *For we are young and... Young people in a time of uncertainty*, edited with Sally Beadle and Roger Holdsworth (2011).